OPERATOR 56

OPERATOR 56

A CALL, A KISS & A BODY COUNT

HEMBURY
BOOKS

LUCIA DOMENICA

Copyright © Lucia Domenica 2025
First published by Hembury Books in 2025
hemburybooks.com.au
info@hemburybooks.com
Paperback ISBN 9781923517035
Ebook ISBN 9781923517028

The moral right of the author has been asserted.
All rights reserved. No portion of this book may be reproduced in any form without permission from the author and publisher, except as permitted by Australian copyright law.

 A catalogue record for this book is available from the National Library of Australia

Dedication

For my mama — the original warrior woman

You didn't always hold me.
Instead, you forged me —
like steel wrapped in flames.
When the fire came,
I rose above the shame.

Now, I understand you and all you endured.
The love you gave, though quiet, always ensured
that our legacy of strength would carry on —
a story I now hold, and one I'll pass on.

With special thanks to the women who helped me speak loud and proud

A special, heartfelt thanks to my editor, **Carlie Slattery** @carlieunderthestairs - from Under the Stairs Editorial, whose sharp eye, steady guidance and brutal honesty (the kind I actually needed) helped this story land on its feet. You didn't just polish words—you helped me find my voice when you told me to lean into my spunky self.

To **Hazel Lam** @hazellam___ — your brilliant book cover design turned my story into something truly beautiful. Thank you for your creativity, your vision, and for actually listening to what I wanted — rare and magical! I'm so grateful.

To **Jessica Mudditt, the founder of Hembury Books,** @hembury_books. For steering me straight and making this book happen. Your guidance changed everything. Writers need you in their corner and the world needs you. **End of story.**

A special shout-out as well to **Meg English, Publishing Consultant at Hembury Books**, for keeping me on track and focused (no small feat!).

To **Alison Hill** @alisonhillwriter.com.au
A brilliant editor, whose expertise and knowledge helped see this book through to completion — ready to be revealed to the world.

To **Dana Da Silva** @writerdanadasilva
Author of *The Shift* and an amazing friend and fellow author whose own journey lit the path ahead. Your strength and truth showed me why pushing forward matters.

To **Sandy Bollard**, my ride-or-die cheerleader. In over twenty years of meltdowns, madness and mayhem, you never flinched. Your golden rule? *Screw them, and move on.* Still works every time.

Writers thrive with the right people around them. These seven amazing women brought the strength, support and heart that made telling my story not just doable, but unforgettable.

ACKNOWLEDGEMENTS

Be brave, be yourself, let courage be your banner—show the world what you're made of.

My gratitude goes to the remarkable individuals who have shaped my perspective and earned my respect.
To the women I worked with—true comrades in every sense.
To my girlfriends—your unwavering support, free of judgement, has meant the world to me.

To my daughters—my reason for pushing through when I thought I couldn't. Always remember, a mother's love is boundless, forgiving, and eternal. Even when you hated me, I never stopped loving you. I hope you'll remember me as a woman whose determination made a difference.

Bae, my unique forever friend—your encouragement fuelled my passion for every wild idea.

To my past lovers—the good, the bad and those with endless banter—
you taught me invaluable lessons.

To the men I met in the bordellos and on the other end of the phone—
you gave me the courage to find my own reality.
And to the men who failed me, a reluctant thanks—you made me
stronger, and for that, I'm grateful.

Let me be clear: this is not a platform for hatred against men, though
men have played big roles in my story. Some brought my worst
moments; others helped me heal and grow. Life isn't black and white,
and neither are these stories.

I hope my story helps other women discover the endless possibilities
within themselves.
So, buckle up and feel the words, not just read them. Life's a mix of
strength, laughter and survival.

This is my soundtrack to it all.

Contents

Prologue XV
Chapter 1: **Beautiful trauma** 1
Chapter 2: **Misfortune twists** 11
Chapter 3: **Triple murder - Hit me with your best shot** 22
Chapter 4: **Battlefield** 33
Chapter 5: **The Establishment's new recruit** 40
Chapter 6: **Maiden voyage** 47
Chapter 7: **One-armed bandit** 52
Chapter 8: **The hunk from the club** 57
Chapter 9: **Survival hacks** 61
Chapter 10: **The meet-ups** 64
Chapter 11: **Reckless rendezvous** 67
Chapter 12: **Thelma and Louise** 71
Chapter 13: **Liquorice Allsorts** 75
Chapter 14: **Valentino and the escort** 79
Chapter 15: **1300 Advice at your service** 84
Chapter 16: **Lace up your bootstraps** 87
Chapter 17: **The zookeeper and me** 90
Chapter 18: **The Viagra conference** 99
Chapter 19: **Josie and the Pussycats and other fun tales** 103
Chapter 20: **What's your colour?** 108
Chapter 21: **Psychic women** 112
Chapter 22: **Footgasm: The perfect fit** 116
Chapter 23: **The grease pit** 119
Chapter 24: **Connections** 126
Chapter 25: **The social circle** 130
Chapter 26: **Conversations with Murphy** 136
Chapter 27: **The golden stream man** 141
Chapter 28: **Operation schmuck: Tales from the client list** 145
Chapter 29: **An Englishman's fantasy** 156

Chapter 30: **A sense of wonder** 159
Chapter 31: **Bankroller, saviour, and friend: The PI** 162
Chapter 32: **Knock, knock, who's there?** 174
Chapter 33: **The noose around her neck** 178
Chapter 34: **Londoners and ingenious scams** 185
Chapter 35: **Every dog has its day** 190
Chapter 36: **Break free** 194
Chapter 37: **What's old is new again** 197
Chapter 38: **Hook, line, and sinker** 200
Chapter 39: **Bittersweet Bambi** 203
Chapter 40: **My not-so-glorious brothel debut** 208
Chapter 41: **Not on my watch** 214
Chapter 42: **Working hard for the money** 217
Chapter 43: **How to toughen up** 225
Chapter 44: **Unusual duty calls** 232
Chapter 45: **Lipstick olympics** 239
Chapter 46: **Bambi's return** 243
Chapter 47: **Brothel catastrophes and more** 248
Chapter 48: **The haunted bordello** 261
Chapter 49: **A legacy of dysfunction** 265
Chapter 50: **Moving on, not up** 269
Chapter 51: **Divorce, it sucks!** 274
Chapter 52: **Missing person case** 283
Chapter 53: **Karma's a bitch and then some** 288
Chapter 54: **Three's a crowd, four's chaos** 294
Chapter 55: **The murder trial** 302
Chapter 56: **Never open the door to a murderer** 307
Chapter 57: **Death at a cemetery** 314
Chapter 58: **Spooked: Tales from the other realm** 324
Chapter 59: **If it looks like a duck** 331
Chapter 60: **Call me brave** 344

PROLOGUE

Sydney 1993

I picked up the landline. A voice—smug, like it got a kick out of wrecking someone's day—hit me straight in the gut.

'Do you know where your husband is right now? You might want to contact him. His workmate's just been arrested.'

Then, click. The line went dead.

In that split second, my world flipped upside down. My heart raced, my breath caught and it felt like the walls were closing in. That phone call wasn't just a wake-up. It was the start of a horror I'd never invited, a chain reaction of chaos, secrets and lies that wouldn't let go. It was like, kiss, kiss … run.

Months later, I found myself staring down horrors I couldn't unsee, pulled into a courtroom battle that pushed me to the brink. They tried to break me, but I'd survived too much to let that happen. My so-called gullibility became my strength; a shield they couldn't penetrate.

But this wasn't just about a triple murder case. It was about uncovering the pieces of me that had been buried under years of trauma, lies and misplaced love. And here's the kicker—it wasn't in the courtroom that I found my strength. It wasn't even in the thick of that case. It was in the last place I ever expected to find it: the sex industry.

The women I worked with, the moments we shared, the insatiable men—their needs a hunger I'd learned to feed but not feel. But feelings have a way of slipping in when you least expect them. It wasn't for nothing. Decades later, it finally made sense.

Life has a twisted sense of humour. Somewhere between love, loss and temptation, I was forced to confront the woman I truly was. And in that whirlwind, I began to rise.

Operator 56? She was just the beginning. I wasn't just surviving anymore. I was becoming someone new. Someone I finally respected.

CHAPTER 1

Beautiful trauma

Life didn't exactly roll out the welcome mat for me. Chaos felt like a birthright, or maybe the universe just had a twisted sense of humour. My parents' love story felt like an endless struggle, with sarcastic laughs thrown in for good measure. In 1957, my father left Abruzzo, Italy, chasing a dream—or maybe an escape—in far-off Australia. My mother followed three years later, hauling a trunk of keepsakes, two young boys, and a boatload of nausea across the seas.

That voyage was no pleasure cruise. Seasick and exhausted, my mother leaned on the kindness of a stranger to keep my brothers, seven-year-old Ivano and eight-year-old Costanzo, alive and kicking. One month later, they landed in Sydney, ready for a fresh start. She reunited with my father, the man she'd followed halfway across the world, and for a fleeting moment it seemed like everything might be okay, until life yanked the rug out.

Within months of arriving, she found out she was pregnant. Abruzzo, with its rugged mountains and ancient hilltop towns, had been her sanctuary, but this unfamiliar land felt more like a trap. Financial strain wrapped around them like a straitjacket, choking any chance of relief. Desperation even led my mother to attempt to end the pregnancy, hoping it might ease the burden. When that attempt failed, things only got worse.

Reality hit hard soon after. My parents and brothers were packed into a three-bedroom weatherboard house with another family of four in Auburn, Sydney. It was suffocating—no privacy, no room to breathe. Then I came along. With a newborn in the mix, it was pure chaos.

Two years, later they sold the house, split the cash with the other family, and moved to their own place in Granville. It was old, but it had the basics: an outside dunny and a patch of dirt for veggies. The rest? Concreted, like any good Italian family home.

With a mortgage now hanging over their heads, both my parents had to work. They had no choice but to leave me in the hands of women they barely knew. Those women? Cruel doesn't even begin to describe them. Their abuse left scars that still haunt me decades later. But I don't blame my parents. How could they have known the hell I went through? To me, that life was just … normal.

Even as a small child, survival was in my blood. That's when the real story begins, because if there's one thing I've learned it's that life loves to throw curveballs. And I've always been ready to take a swing.

My earliest memories from around the age of three and a half are shadowed by a childminder who treated me more like an unwanted animal than like a child. She would leave me by the back door on a pile of crumpled newspapers. The harsh glare of the sun was my only comfort, forcing me to shut my eyes against the world and escape into the only peace I could find—sleep.

Then there was another woman from the neighbouring street, who I believe turned a blind eye to her two teenage sons' continual attempts to harm me.

They subjected me to harrowing ordeals. One time they locked me inside an old, rusted metal trunk, much like the one containing my mother's treasured possessions that she had brought with her from Italy. Those boys pounded on the trunk's top and sides with heavy objects, the noise reverberating inside, terrifying me. Their sadistic amusement continued when they hoisted me onto the wood-and-chain-link fence in front of their house, taking turns shoving me into the thorny rose bushes below.

In those moments, I would escape into an imaginary world of wonder, shutting out the madness around me.

My mother was oblivious to the abuse inflicted on her daughter, or perhaps, in her desperation to keep her job, she chose to ignore it. To her credit, she did question my carer about the bruises and scratches that covered my body, but to no avail. The carer blamed me for being reckless during play. That evening, my mother cleaned my broken skin with methylated spirits and the sting made me cry.

Within a short time, the brothers' actions grew worse. I was sitting on the cold lino floor in the back room, happily playing with a doll, when they came in. Each grabbed one of my small hands and led me outside. Their sinister intentions were hidden from my innocence, but they were deeply rooted in their cold hearts—chilling, like the winter frost that day.

Without saying a word, they led me across the wet grass towards the shed—a place I did not like. It was dark and smelled of petrol. I'd been there before. A pile of wooden boxes gave me many splinters, and rusty nails inflicted searing pain. I didn't understand why they were doing this to me. I'll spare you the worst of the details. Those boys were not mere bullies, but agents of darkness. Their actions etched scars upon my body, and worse, upon my soul—scars that have never faded.

I was not in that woman's care for long. By spring, when the flowers began to bloom and the warmth caressed my face, my mother found another childminder who lived at the end of our street. Maria was a kind, larger-than-life woman from Naples, her plump face adorned with an ever-present smile. Her ample bosom felt soft and comforting whenever she enveloped me in her arms, making me feel happy and safe. Her compassion filled the void left by the others who should have cared for me. I believe her love and generosity, combined with my own experience of lacking affection, inspired me to work with children many years later.

She was the local dressmaker. She fed me the most scrumptious home-cooked meals, and was forever washing my dirty face and hands, which often had traces of fresh wet soil on them. I would accompany her husband, Giuseppe, a short, soulful man who loved his chickens and his garden, in the backyard. He reserved a small patch of dark, fertile earth just for me, a gift that felt like my own secret world. With gentle hands, he showed me how to press my tiny fingers into the cool soil and place a seed inside.

Whenever I was there, I would rush out to the garden and crouch down at my little patch, waiting for my seeds to sprout, my excitement willing them to grow. When they finally bloomed, vibrant flowers of every colour seemed to smile up at me, a surprise that never failed to fill me with wonder. I would look up at Giuseppe with my big blue eyes filled with joy. Giuseppe would gently pat my head, his Italian accent thick with affection: 'Gooda job, bella Lucia.' His words wrapped around me like a warm blanket, filling me with pride.

He delighted in sharing with me everything he nurtured, always inviting me to taste the fruits of his labour. I loved the way the ripe, sun-warmed tomatoes burst with sweetness in my mouth, the juice trickling down my chin. It was as though the garden had come alive and I was part of its magic. Giuseppe, like his wife, was a good soul—one whose quiet kindness made me feel seen, safe and special in a world that often felt too big and harsh. He was one of only a few men who showed me kindness and respect. For that, I will always hold memories of him dear.

Jino, their son, was older than me; around eight. He teased me sometimes, but he was a good boy, who never meant any harm. Jino taught me how to play marbles, though somehow, he always ended up winning. I stayed with his mother for a year before school and then, in 1966, just before my fifth birthday, I started attending the same school as Jino.

Every morning, one of my brothers would drop me off early at the school grounds. After school I'd go home with Jino, where Maria would care for me until one of my brothers came to pick me up. Maria always told Jino to take good care of me, and he made sure I didn't dart into traffic, never letting go of my hand. We crossed three streets and a busy main road to get to his house and all the while I'd feel his grip, solid and steady.

Back then, neighbours sat outside watching over their kids. A quiet assurance hung in the air, as though everyone was keeping an eye on you. Life felt predictable in that way—at least for a while. There was always a friendly, trusting face smiling at us as we walked by, some even handing out confectionery. Musk sticks and Choo-Choo Bars were my favourites, though my mother disapproved of my black tongue after indulging in the chewy liquorice bar.

Jino and I looked forward to these treats. If we were really lucky, we'd stumble upon a Gobstopper—a prized find. It filled my entire mouth and took days to savour, layer by layer. I'd carefully wrap it in my handkerchief and tuck it into the pocket of my school dress to enjoy the next day.

When Jino took me home from school, I'd play with him under his mother's watchful eye. Maria saw me as a delicate little flower, knowing boys could play rough. I missed those times, especially after everything changed when I turned eight and my parents decided I was old enough to be left home alone. Eight was a 'big kid's number', the age of independence—at least, that's what my parents thought.

In the beginning my brothers would drop me off early at school, so I was left to fend for myself, waiting alone on the desolate school grounds. The morning air was crisp and the emptiness around me grew heavier as the minutes ticked by, the silence broken only by the distant rustle of leaves or the creaking of an old gate. It was okay for a while—well, until the nuns caught on.

The Catholic school felt oppressive, run by nuns dressed in long black tunics with stiff white collars hugging their necks and heavy rosary beads clinking against their belts. To my young mind they resembled penguins, but without any of the warmth or playfulness—just rigid, silent figures who exuded a coldness that chilled me to the bone.

Arriving early always meant being put to work, as though my very presence was a nuisance. I'd scrape weeds from the cracked, uneven paths with a dull butter knife, the cold metal awkward in my small hands. The weeds resisted, much like I did, but I kept going, my fingers aching as I worked. My reward? A glass of warm, often sour milk that I forced down, my stomach churning with each sip, the smell lingering in my nostrils long after. As soon as those brides of purity, in their habit-clad glory, were out of sight, I spat that shit out, gave them the good old two-fisted Italian salute, and whispered, *'Vaffanculo'*—meaning 'go fuck yourself'—a useful phrase I learned from my potty-mouthed family.

I soon wised up and claimed refuge in the dim, echoing toilet cubicles. The smell of disinfectant mingled with damp concrete filled the air as I huddled inside, heart pounding, praying that I wouldn't be found before the other children arrived.

Kindergarten children were separated from the older primary kids. We had a large classroom with its own eating and play area, even a wood and metal side swing where several of us could sit and sway from side to side. But sitting on it was forbidden until everyone had finished their lunch. Patience was never my virtue, so one day I climbed onto the swing and pushed it hard, making the sides lift off the ground. Naturally, Sister Cornelius noticed and decided to make an example of me with the cane. The sting on the back of my legs was so sharp that I wet my pants and, without thinking, shouted a profanity at her, as only an Italian child can do. Yes, that one *'Vaffanculo.'*

That, of course, earned me further punishment—a wet bar of soap shoved into my mouth. Yet I couldn't help but find amusement in it, blowing bubbles and causing the other kids to burst into laughter. That didn't sit well with Sister Cornelius either and, I got another swift strike of the cane. Although I had been defiant, this time I stood frozen, silent, until I was told to move. I was naughty, but not entirely stupid.

Kindness was about as common as a unicorn in that place. My memories were more about terror and getting punished for the crime of simply being a kid. The nuns ruled through fear, and I couldn't help but wonder if that was the whole point. Their treatment left me feeling worthless, a feeling that dug in deep and stuck around like an unwanted guest.

That said, not all of my school days were a cloud of gloom. I had friends—loads of them—and I was usually the one leading the charge into all kinds of mischief. It was enough to earn me the reputation as the most disobedient and 'un-Christian-like' child; a title I wore with an odd sense of pride.

Although it might seem odd today, in the 1960s it was normal to be left home alone during school breaks. I was, unless I tagged along with my parents to the factory where they worked, the Egg Marketing Board in Lidcombe. There I got to see a different side of them; a rare glimpse of happiness that never quite showed up at home. Among their colleagues, who shared the same background, they seemed lighter, more relaxed. It was their little slice of community, their sanctuary, a far cry from the tension and exhaustion that ruled our house.

My childhood home echoed with the chaos of my father's drunken rants and the constant bickering between my parents. It was normal to see him knock back a glass of wine every morning to wash down his Bex—a weird mix of aspirin and caffeine. Then, he'd grab a flask of wine for work and sip it with his lunch. I still don't know how he managed a day of hard labour. After the factory job, he worked for the Water Board, digging ditches all day. Maybe that's why he was always so thirsty.

Despite his flaws, there were moments I actually loved, like when he'd bring home stray kittens, frogs and even turtles. My mother wasn't exactly thrilled, but my puppy-dog eyes somehow convinced her to let us keep them. Our house turned into a wild menagerie of animals—some we loved and some we ate, like the rabbits and chickens.

But I also remember the dark moments, like watching him chase my mother with a piece of timber; a four-by-two, to be exact. We always had building materials lying around the place. Her screams filled the air, and yeah, that was terrifying—but I had to hand it to her, she could outrun him. Maybe it was his trauma from the war that pushed him to drink. Still, despite everything, I adored my flawed parents. When their fighting got too much, I'd retreat into my imagination, just like I had when I was younger. I could pretend they were the way I wanted them to be kind, loving, and whole.

My father never laid a hand on me, maybe because he knew my mother would end him if he did. But those frowning eyes of his? They could freeze me in place with just one look.

And his roar of a voice was enough to send me into full-on panic mode, making me retreat to my room like a little rabbit trying to escape the storm.

I can't remember my father ever hugging me or telling me he loved me, but when he was sober—which wasn't often—he'd spend time with me in the garden or pull off magic tricks that left me in awe.

As for my mother, she could scream and hit without hesitation if I pushed her too far, which, let's be honest, I often did. She made sure my needs were met, but love was never part of the vocabulary.

Affection and love were what I craved most, yet they always felt just out of reach, elusive and distant. I found more warmth in my older brothers, who often took charge of me during my parents' long, arduous work hours. Their presence brought a sense of comfort and security, a stark contrast to the emotional void that lingered at home.

As a first-generation Australian, my parents viewed me through an Italian lens, often treating me as if we were still in the old country. I often fantasised that I was an Australian child adopted by these foreigners.

At the tender age of twelve, I barged into my parents' bedroom in the early hours of the morning, only to find my mother in her nightgown, jumping furiously up and down on my father, whose legs were twitching like he'd been zapped by a live wire. Was she ... killing him?

The truth didn't come out until months later in a sex education class at school, complete with sketches of how good Christian mums and dads reproduced, all while a nun, a nurse, and a priest looked on. That was screwed up. I was filthy angry then, believing my parents wanted another child. There was no way in hell I was going to share my room with another sibling.

I did the only sensible thing any twelve-year-old would do: I packed my oversized, hard brown school case, the kind we all used in the 1970s, with its clicky metal latches at the front and covered with groovy stickers, a testament to my attempt to express myself. I only made it to the end of the street before my mother dragged me back home, her grip tight on my long ponytail. She tugged at it occasionally as we walked, delivering a few hard slaps across my face for good measure. The shame of being seen by my friends in the street made me abandon those thoughts, and I never tried to run away again.

My attitude towards sex after that was pretty skewed. I mean, who in their right mind would willingly get into that kind of mess?

Two years after that petrifying lesson at school, my best girlfriend, Joyce, gifted me a book called *The Joy of Sex*. She was a year older and a bit more experienced in the mysterious ways of human coupling—she read a lot. Joyce thought this book would erase the horrifying mental images I couldn't shake and prepare me for the mating ritual of dating. It was filled with sketches of all sorts of sexual positions. Definitely not the ideal way to change my mind.

I had a lot to think about after that, but I still wasn't convinced people had sex because they wanted to. The whole thing felt like some mythical ritual. Every married couple with kids got the death stare from me—I was sure they were all secretly indulging in this primal act.

At that stage, I didn't need any more mental chaos. My messed-up family was enough; arguing and hitting each other like it was a contact sport. I figured no one ever told them they could 'use their words', like they taught us at school.

All I craved was to blend in like my Aussie friends, whose homes were peaceful havens. I sensed my parents struggled to cope and their frustration seeped into our lives, leaving little room for peace. I got used to the chaos; it was like training for a future in managing drama. And, of course, I was being primed to cater to a man's every whim, because, naturally, men were the superior beings in my world—or so I was taught. Lucky me.

I was determined to defy my parents' cultural expectations and break free from the toxic environment. Their tight grip on their ethnic identity drove me crazy, and I fought back by pushing every button I could find, constantly testing their patience just to see how far I could go.

Lesson: Sometimes, without realising it, the trauma we experience helps us heal, building empathy that allows us to support others in their darkest days.

CHAPTER 2

Misfortune twists

If ever there was someone who acted on impulse, it was me. Feeling hopeless about my future, I saw marriage as my only escape. At just fourteen, driven by romantic notions and blind to the crucial details, I made a grave mistake: I got engaged. And as if things couldn't get worse, it was to the wrong brother.

I met Massimo, a twenty-one-year-old Italian, at a family function, along with his younger brother, Tommaso, who was nineteen. I sat between them playing cards, and though I flirted unknowingly with both, I was immediately drawn to Tommaso, a dead-ringer for Sylvester Stallone.

As was customary back then with some Italians, a highly respected head of the community came to visit my family home to discuss my betrothal to one of the brothers. As usual, I wasn't paying attention; all I knew was this was my chance to escape my family.

Two weeks later, on the day of my engagement, I waited anxiously in my parents' hallway, longing for my love's arrival and our affectionate gaze to meet. But instead of Tommaso, it was Massimo who greeted me with a smile and kissed my cheek. I was bewildered. I scoured behind him for my intended, only no one was there.

Amid our families' applause, we were ushered into the room for the celebrations. Dazed as if by a stun gun, I struggled to comprehend what had just happened and went with the flow. The confusion stemmed from a misunderstanding of the word 'big' in Italian, which can have different meanings. While I interpreted it as referring to the taller one, in Italian culture it referred to the older one. Clearly, something was lost in translation.

What the hell had I done? What was supposed to lead to freedom and happiness had become my own little apocalypse. I was promised to marry the wrong brother, a hooked-nosed man, and have little hooked-nosed babies. It felt like destiny was laughing in my face.

I kept quiet about my mistake; embarrassment had me in a chokehold. But after seven months of kicking myself inside, I finally caved and told my brother Costanzo the truth. He had returned home after his divorce, which caused many an Italian mother's tongue to wag—especially since his son was born only two months after his wedding. Both of my brothers had married young, but I was thankful Costanzo was on my side.

With his unshakable words, he stood up for me and argued with my parents, who were mortified that people would shun them even more now. But honestly, who cared? Our family was already blacklisted by half the town, so what difference did it make at this point? Costanzo went above and beyond by helping break up my engagement to Massimo, using his persuasive charm, flexing his muscles and delivering staunch words, liberating me from a future I never wished for. I loved my brother for that.

Deflated after that incident, I dropped out of school after Year 10, while my friends went on to Years 11 and 12. Instead, I found myself stuck in a mind fog, working at a drapery store on the business side of Granville.

That same year, a fire in the neighbouring takeaway fish-and-chip shop brought Chris into my life. He caught my eye as I walked past the burnt-out shop. There he was, fixing the electrical repairs—a handsome young man with dark curly hair, a sleek moustache and long, thick eyelashes that could've doubled as paintbrushes. Before the fire, I'd often bought my lunch from the owners—fish cocktails and crunchy chips, saturated in salt and vinegar, wrapped in newspaper, my absolute favourite. During the repairs, Chris and I would exchange flirtatious smiles, which eventually led to a date.

We had a lot in common. His family was Cypriot, mine Italian. Both our older brothers had married Aussie girls and, like mine, his parents often clashed. His father had passed away, and though his mother was still around, they'd always seemed mismatched, fighting more than they spoke. My parents weren't much different.

We clicked, bonding over disco nights at War and Peace in Parramatta and The Boulevard in the city. Within weeks, we were in bed together. That's when I discovered his real age. I'd assumed he was younger, but nope, Chris was twenty-five. I was bonking an older man, fabulous! That must mean he was serious about me. But if my family found out, I'd probably lose my right to wear white at my wedding—ah, a minor detail.

A month in, Chris gave me his house key so I could meet him after work whenever we felt like getting it on. Being the good Catholic girl I was, I convinced myself we'd get married someday—typical teenage delusions.

In my lover's haze, I decided to shower him with gifts, so one day I snooped through his room to find his clothing size. That's when I found it, tucked inside a nudie magazine under his bed: a letter on blue overseas stationery, sealed with an airmail stamp. I should've walked away, but nope, I read it.

Was I Chris's guinea pig? Every time we had sex, he'd quiz me about the particulars like I was some sort of experiment. Then, out of nowhere, he casually mentioned we should 'practice' for when we'd marry someone. *Someone? Who the hell was that?* I thought I was his someone. Turns out his mother had already picked out another woman for him: a woman from Cyprus who was being shipped over to marry him. And how did I find out? By being inquisitive, of course.

Despite the blow to my self-esteem, I convinced myself I wasn't worthy of anything better. After all, I was no longer a virgin, my upbringing forbade sex before marriage, and clearly I wasn't good enough for an Italian man. So, yep, no chance of wearing white now. I was stuck in a bad situation. It would have to be Chris, or maybe an Aussie man would settle for a 'tarnished' woman.

From the letter, I learned that Chris's future bride had found his mother unbearable. Still, she flew out from Cyprus to Australia. I guess it was a free trip, so why not?

It was the first time she and Chris actually met in person. Up until then, he'd only seen a photo of her. But once she arrived, things quickly unravelled.

They didn't see eye to eye on much, especially not the idea of living with his mother until he could afford a place of his own. That same week, they called it off. And just like that, Chris and I were back together within days.

As curious as I was about what really happened between them, whether they kissed or what gritty details went down, I held back from asking. The truth was, I didn't want any more drama. Being with him felt safer than being without him, especially with my little not-a-virgin-anymore secret hanging over me. So, I bit my tongue and let it go. Maybe I just felt lucky he was back and that the secret would stay buried.

Life carried on, until the day it didn't. The day everything changed was the morning of the Granville rail disaster.

It was a Tuesday morning, 18 January 1977. I'd headed to work at the drapery, right across from Granville train station. That day, I witnessed absolute carnage. Just after eight, a commuter train, that had started its journey from Mount Victoria in the Blue Mountains earlier that morning derailed at Granville station. It slammed into a steel-and-concrete pillar supporting the Bold Street bridge, causing the structure to collapse onto two passenger carriages.

I reached the shop twenty minutes after it happened. By then, emergency services had swarmed the area, sirens wailing their haunting urgency. People rushed into our store, their pale and frantic faces desperate for cloth to help the injured. Hands trembled as they searched for fabric to wrap wounds, while others, shocked and in tears, stood frozen.

Amid the turmoil of that sorrowful day, I witnessed an outpouring of humanity. I was in shock myself, wrestling with my emotions, questioning why such tragedies occurred. Why here, where I lived and worked, and why weren't people safe travelling to work? Anxiety gripped me for a long time afterwards. I spent countless hours consumed by fear of what could happen on my way home or at work, feeling guilty for being alive while so many had died within metres of where I stood.

It was one of the worst rail disasters in Australian history, claiming eighty-four lives, including an unborn baby, and leaving two hundred and thirteen others injured. The rescue operation quickly transformed into a grim recovery mission, stretching from Tuesday morning until dawn on Thursday. Our store remained open for business as usual, but it felt goddamn disrespectful. I didn't want to be there, but our bosses insisted it was good for us. 'More foot traffic,' they said.

That harrowing memory etched itself into my mind, this tragedy that forever altered Australia's approach to rescue procedures. Many injuries and fatalities stemmed from crushing; some victims, though conscious and speaking to rescuers, succumbed to crush syndrome once the weight was finally lifted from their bodies. This devastating reality prompted significant changes in emergency protocols for such disasters.

They say even the worst storms leave something behind—lessons, warnings, or just the guts to move forward. Maybe this tragedy did too. Perhaps lives were saved in the future because of the hard-earned knowledge learned that day. As heartbreaking as it was, it sparked changes that mattered—life-saving changes. Even in the darkest moments, there's always a flicker of light. For me, that light wasn't just hope, it was change.

Chris and I were officially a thing, and by our first year together. I decided it was time to level up. I handed in my resignation and enrolled in business college in Parramatta, just a stone's throw from Granville, where I lived.

My teacher, Miss Hermanus, was the butt of many jokes, but we quickly bonded. She was only a few years older than me and we'd swap stories about our boyfriends. Parramatta became my lunchtime playground, spent with my girlfriend at the shopping centre. It was the golden era of fashion—flared trousers, dresses in bold, geometric patterns, and flowers draped around our necks. The whole scene screamed vibrancy and life. Some rebels went all in, painting their faces with colourful lightning bolts, channelling their inner David Bowie. My girlfriend? She rocked a pair of jeans with cut-outs that left her bum cheeks on full display. Talk about risky—plastic bottoms barely holding it together. If only I had the guts to pull that off.

At times, I wore my hair full and flared out at the sides, just like Farrah Fawcett—every man's pin-up girl. It was the disco era, where wild mixes of colour and creativity were the norm. The allure of non-conformity was tempting, but I knew my limits with my parents. So I simply embraced the spirit of the time—blowout hair and floral pastel flares became my signature.

Upon graduating at sixteen, I landed a job as a typist. Six months in, I found myself pregnant. I was scared shitless, knowing my parents would lose it and I'd be the one taking the heat. But what I really wanted to hear from Chris was, "It's going to be okay. I love you. Let's get married now." Instead, he was a massive disappointment.

Under Chris's influence, I made the gut-wrenching decision to terminate the pregnancy. He threatened to deny it was his, leaving me feeling trapped and overwhelmed by the consequences for my family. I thought I had no choice. Burdened with a crushing sense of shame, I kept it all a secret and faced that day alone. Meanwhile, Chris walked away without any consequences, and it felt completely unfair.

A day later, back at work, I was called into the manager's office. Shocked, I learned that the doctor's note I submitted indicated I had undergone a termination. I was mortified, and feared I'd be labelled the office whore. By week's end I resigned. It didn't take me long to land a job at a camping outfit company but, of course, I managed to screw it up by using the wrong template and wasting fifty pieces of material. My disastrous reputation had clearly preceded me and with my head hung in shame, I quit.

At seventeen, I reminded myself of the lesson drilled into me: men only married virgins. So I married Chris. Before the wedding we met with the priest, a man with a glass eye who explained the tradition of veiling the bride's face to symbolise her purity. My inability to suppress my laughter during this conversation earned me a disapproving look and a startled reaction from the priest—his glass eye nearly fell out. His words only reinforced how ridiculous I found male supremacy.

After we married in February 1979, Chris's dominance and instability became painfully clear. His turbulent relationship with his schizophrenic mother led to frequent outbursts directed at me, ranging from verbal to physical abuse.

Having endured similar mistreatment in my own childhood, I felt compelled to tolerate his behaviour, which left me disheartened and resigned to years of submission.

We lived rent-free in my sister-in-law's father's home, basically housesitting, and I returned to the city for work that year, which offered a brief escape from the uncertainty awaiting me at home. I never knew whether Mr Nice Guy or Mr Arsehole would greet me.

I treasured the fleeting moments of solitude when Chris worked weekends. During those times, I bonded with our elderly neighbour's grandson, Jessie. Both being eighteen and carefree, our conversations flowed effortlessly. We'd play records and dance in the living room like teenagers.

However, one day while dancing, things took an unexpected turn. What I assumed was his bubble-gum stick pressing against my thigh … wasn't. After that incident, I avoided him and pretended not to be home. Eventually, the knocks on the door ceased.

Then, one day while I was in my backyard, he walked out of the back door of his grandmother's house, and through the missing fence pales, our eyes collided. He looked down and walked straight back inside without saying a word. My heart sank and I was devastated at losing a friend. If only I had not married so young, if only I had recognised the importance of being with a partner who uplifted me, my life might have taken a different turn.

By late 1981, we moved into our own home in Ryde, and not long after, in February 1983, just before my twenty-second birthday, I gave birth to our first daughter, Violet—a precious little jewel. Motherhood radically transformed my sense of purpose and perspective, infusing my life with newfound significance.

My beautiful little girl became my everything.

Yet, as I realised my child depended on me, anxiety crept in, with no one to support me as a young mum. It was stressful being alone with a screaming baby, not knowing what the hell I was doing. Motherhood was supposed to come naturally. Like hell it did!

By that stage, my father had become paralysed and bedridden, leaving only my mother to care for him. So, I stepped in to help. With a newborn baby, I would take two buses and a train. Back then, Granville Station had many steps. How I never lost control of the stroller was beyond me.

Chris never allowed me to use the car; he needed it for work. But on the odd occasion he drove me home in the late afternoon, I felt like I'd won the lottery.

Being a first-time mum was no piece of cake. I was juggling responsibilities while feeling like a ghost—defined only as someone's daughter, someone's wife and someone's mother. I was lost in a sea of labels with no real sense of who I was as an individual.

Lacking the life experiences of a single woman, a creeping regret gnawed at me, making me yearn for the adventures and freedoms that most of my friends enjoyed before they settled down. But I pushed those feelings aside and, after six months, dived back into an office job in the city, placing my daughter in care to ensure she was well looked after.

Although I worked hard, there never seemed to be enough money for our bills. Countless times I found myself counting coins or selling off treasured pieces my mother had given me, all just to scrape together enough for the essentials. Chris was hopeless—for real, he was the worst provider.

Three years later, in 1986, I gave birth to our second daughter; a chubby little one whose smiles never failed to delight me. I was so in love with my two girls, spending hours playing with them.

Despite the joy they brought me, life wasn't without its challenges. Twelve months after her arrival, I needed to work again, and I chose a home-based childminding job over the demands of a traditional office role.

I met other mums during backyard playgroups within my daughters' daycare service. It sparked my appreciation for education, as I realised that pursuing further studies would make me more employable and open doors to better roles.

Eager to grow and learn, I enrolled in evening classes in early childhood education, which took four years to complete. Here I was again, juggling work, study, and family, but somehow, it worked.

Despite the happiness my daughters gave me, my husband brought me grief. I felt ashamed of how we lived, always scraping by. He had no business sense, and as a self-employed electrician, he never seemed to bring home enough. My earnings kept us afloat; without them, we might never have made ends meet. I could feel the weight of our financial struggles every day.

Meanwhile, he was out weeknights with male friends, off to so-called 'business meetings'—whatever that meant. Sometimes, he'd come home with little packets of matches advertising nude women on the front, even though he didn't smoke. It didn't take a genius to figure out where they came from—he was out at bars in the city.

Whether it was a deliberate act to provoke me or not, I couldn't be certain. But I began to develop a great distaste for my husband and at times, I couldn't give a shit. My mental state deteriorated, worsened by his constant demands for help with his work—often after hours and on weekends. By that stage, my father had passed, and I would ask my mother to stay over; otherwise, I took my daughters along, all the while questioning why I stayed in the marriage.

That's when my mother began to notice things about Chris. She attempted to talk to me about his inexcusable behaviour, having witnessed him strike me and yell. I think it must have hit her hard, reflecting on her own relationship with my father. Yet, I made excuses for my husband, ashamed of the entire situation and not wanting her to worry after all she had gone through with my dad.

Chris thought it was a great idea to throw me into dangerous situations; crawling under houses, climbing ladders, doing electrical work I had no training for. The worst? While I was heavily pregnant with our third daughter, he had me stripping copper wiring and wiring power points like some clueless apprentice. This went on for years.

After our fourth daughter was born, he left me with all four kids—our youngest just twelve weeks old, so he could chase a $36,000 payday in Nimbin. The job? Setting up lighting for a hydroponic weed farm run by some bloke named Kai. Of course, I never saw a cent. He blew the lot in three months—probably smoked half of it.

He'd show up every second or third weekend like he was doing us a favour, never bringing home money, just more stress. I was raising the kids alone, drowning in bills, scraping by with help from Mum. And when he did return, he was volatile, mocking me, slapping me, then laughing like it was all a joke. It wasn't. It was cruel and humiliating, especially in front of others. Like he enjoyed tearing down whatever was left of me.

Then came his next act: sucking up to 'important' people. He joined the Masons and buddied up with Peter, a council bigwig. Word was you could get council approvals if you handed over free services and gifts. I didn't believe it—until Peter had us working on his house for nothing. And Chris? He backed Peter's political campaign like it was our ticket to greatness. Dragged me into it too. We both ran on his council team. What a bloody waste of time.

But karma got busy. Peter was caught. He was nearly jailed, but got a two-year correctional order instead. Typical.

Maybe that's what pushed me towards something of my own. I started making quirky handmade gifts for a local shop. Between the job, my studies, and four kids, life felt like a tightrope. I was constantly on edge, chasing hope while holding everything together.

I didn't make a fortune, but I was proud. Every item sold. I got paid on consignment. For the first time, I felt like I was doing something that was mine.

But that small smile didn't last. One moment changed everything—and landed me tangled with the law.

Lesson: Sometimes, in life, the journey from hardship to resilience becomes a path of self-discovery, learning from our experiences.

CHAPTER 3

Triple murder—Hit me with your best shot

We were like each other's umbilical cord, Dorothy and me. We shared countless happy moments when we became next-door neighbours in Granville, a very Anglo-Saxon suburb. I was four and she was three. Thirteen years later, I got married, and two years after that, so did she. We lived just a few suburbs away and stayed in constant touch.

By 1992, she had six children—all sons—compared to my two, though I was heavily pregnant with my third, unaware it would be another daughter. We joked I'd keep having girls so they could marry her boys, locked in for life as family.

Daniel, Dorothy's husband, shared a similar cultural background with Chris and me, but his family took any excuse to throw a party. Lucky for me, I lived for it—dressing up, eating too much, soaking in the chaos. They were tight-knit and wildly affectionate. His mum couldn't pass me without yanking me into a bear hug like I was hers.

He ran a construction business, well, sort of, and every now and then tossed Chris a few electrical jobs to keep him busy. Chris, naturally, lapped it up. Ever the self-important one, he loved strutting around anyone he thought was a real-deal business type, like hanging with them somehow made him one too. I reckon he thought having mates like that made him superior—like, bullshit it did. He was missing one key ingredient: brains.

Even though he was self-employed, he knew Centrelink had his back, so working hard was never really on the agenda. I mean, who actually chooses to scrape by on government welfare when they're perfectly capable of working, just can't be stuffed, right?

Chris would chuck money and time at get-rich-quick schemes that went nowhere. Honestly, if they worked, we'd all be stinking rich. He even tried roping Daniel into some dodgy money-making scams. Whenever Daniel came over to see Chris, they'd yak about it, but listening to their waffle bored the absolute shit out of me. To keep the peace at home, I slipped into a blissful haze of ignorance just to tune it all out.

Aside from all that crap, we still got together as families for picnics at Lane Cove National Park—kids tearing around while the blokes talked business. Dorothy and I would chat about motherly things, like the best playgrounds for our kids or the perfect shade of lippy. Those moments felt normal. Her life looked picture-perfect: stay-at-home mum, always something new. But behind the smiles things weren't so shiny. I didn't realise until her husband asked Chris for a four-thousand-dollar loan—massive at the time. Apparently, she'd maxed out their credit card. We didn't even have one.

I was furious when Chris took half the money from our children's bank account and never replaced it. That burden fell to me years later when I finally saved it back up. We were financially strapped ourselves, and I had worked hard for what little we had. That was our savings—there was nothing more. Of course, I questioned him about giving them the money, but that was a mistake. Any sign of defiance would earn me a verbal dressing-down and a backhander. How dare I question the all-knowing Wizard of Oz?

Despite my resentment, somehow Dorothy and I kept darting

between houses like nothing was wrong. She seemed oblivious to the fact that Daniel had borrowed money from us to pay off her credit card, and it was pretty clear he wanted to keep it that way. I guess things weren't going quite as well in business as he always bragged.

Still, on the surface, everything seemed normal. Her extensive social circle and Daniel's work connections meant their home was always buzzing with new faces. I loved meeting people and soaking up their stories.

It was at one of those get-togethers in 1993 that I met a young man named Jordan—an undeniably handsome twenty-five-year-old—and his parents, Theresa and Otto, both in their sixties. A few weeks later, I saw the parents again during another visit. They were polite, painfully normal even—the sort you'd pass at Woolies and forget five seconds later. Our conversation barely scratched the surface, filled with nothing more than pleasantries and comments about the kids. Nothing that hinted at anything deeper—or darker.

Then, during another one of our visits, a man named Harvey turned up—mid-forties, a bit rough around the edges. He worked as a labourer for Daniel, but the way he greeted Otto and Theresa, all casual nods and easy laughter, made it clear they'd crossed paths before.

The men grouped in the lounge, chatting in low tones, while the women stayed at the table enjoying a few munchies as the kids played outside; so typical, so completely ordinary.

Back then, Harvey gave me a weird feeling. It wasn't that he didn't talk—he did, in these quiet, measured tones, but there was something in the way he watched, like he was sizing everyone up. He'd hover just outside conversations, never fully part of them, yet never out of place either. I caught him staring a few times, eyes flat—like he was somewhere else entirely.

I vaguely remember someone mentioning their son Jordan had gone AWOL for a while, but it didn't strike me as a red flag. He was a young guy—guys do that kind of shit, right?

Then, sometime later, that ordinary day turned into one I'd never forget. Everything changed in an instant.

Otto and Theresa's bodies were discovered dumped like rubbish inside a metal shipping container at a remote tip, discarded without a second thought. The sheer callousness sent a cold shiver down my spine.

Jordan's body was found some time later, decomposing in a similar container at the same spot—clearly killed before his parents, the timing chillingly calculated. It seemed the killers wanted to wipe out every trace of them. The silence that followed was deafening, an emptiness that stuck in the back of my mind.

When the news broke, it hit me like a sledgehammer to the chest: sudden, brutal and unforgiving. I was raw, terrified and desperate for answers that never came. The air felt heavier after that. Everything around us shifted. Nothing felt safe anymore.

I was lost for words, still reeling from the shock. My husband mentioned 'execution-style.'

I pretended to understand but honestly, I had no clue what it really meant at the time.

It was unimaginable; I had spoken to them not long before, and now they were gone. Why?

My 'all-knowing' husband insisted it was a bikie-related murder, but honestly, back then, everyone seemed to be pointing fingers at the bikies. I always saw them as cool dudes in leather, living for the open road on their Harleys and Choppers, waving like rock stars every time we drove past in the car. They were heroes, not killers.

Maybe I was too naive to understand the depths of the situation, but in a way, it was a blessing I didn't realise at the time—something that would help me later.

Daniel and Harvey were arrested, accused of the murders, and held on remand. My world spiralled. Daniel, my friend, was suddenly at the centre of something horrific. And Harvey, the man who'd built my garden bed? He was a strange bloke. I tried to steer clear when he worked at our place, but my husband always insisted I give him food and drink. I hated every interaction.

Just think: he was accused of butchering people. And I had no clue.

How close was I to a completely fucked-up situation?

The court case dragged on for years; endless investigations, hearings and a media circus that wouldn't quit. Chris couldn't help inserting himself into every twist and turn. He knew someone, then someone else. His obsession strained our marriage to breaking point.

But things took an even darker turn. My husband's connection with Daniel didn't end with their past work before the arrest. Daniel's younger brother, Ben, had also been working with Chris, and in my husband's mind, that somehow made Chris part of their family—and the whole messy situation. Chris's work with Ben just poured petrol on the flames. One of those lovely shitstorms hit while Daniel was still locked up.

It happened on a weekday while I was running my childcare business from home. The landline rang and I knew, no doubt, it was the police. They held a serious grudge against anyone who sided with Daniel.

A voice—smug, like it got a kick out of wrecking someone's day—hit me straight in the gut.

"Do you know where your husband is right now?" You might want to contact him. His workmate's just been arrested.'

Then—click. The line went dead.

My heart raced. Confusion, fear, dread—they all hit at once. Was Chris in trouble too?

He was supposed to be working with Ben that day, but I later found out he'd been sent to a different site. Meanwhile, Ben was pulled over, caught with a gun and arrested—another name on the growing list of suspects.

That call from the police didn't feel like a heads-up. It felt like a warning. Chris could be next, just for knowing Ben and Daniel.

I never truly grasped how far the law could reach—until it crept into my life, turning everything into a waking nightmare. I kept looking over my shoulder, bracing for the next blow. Somehow, my cluelessness became a shield, helping me stumble through it all.

When the case went to court, I was called to give evidence, which meant meeting with Daniel's defence lawyers and their team. At the time, I was extra cautious. One of the children I looked after had parents who were both police officers. I had a strong feeling they had no idea I was involved in the case, but just the thought of it sent my anxiety into overdrive.

Then there was the day I had to meet Chris Murphy, a big-name defence lawyer who'd taken on Daniel's case. Before that, I'd only seen him in the media, so I was nervous as hell. But to my surprise, he and his colleague were so genuine I felt like I'd just met old friends. They treated me with calm, measured professionalism—no arrogance. Somehow that took the edge off and made the madness just a little more bearable.

It was my first time stepping into a legal setting, but it sure as hell wouldn't be the last. With the kind of luck I seemed to attract, it felt like I was walking around with a neon target strapped to my back, practically daring the universe to throw more chaos my way—*'Come on then, hit me with your best shot!'*

On top of everything, Daniel's family hired an investigator—I'll call him GS, an ex-cop turned private detective. He'd left the force after some of the shit he saw go down—couldn't stomach it—only to wind up on the other side, working for the defence. Go figure.

He showed up at my place with manila folders bursting with documents. During our meeting, one slipped off the table. My hand shot out to grab it, but it slipped through my fingers and hit the floor, flipping open like it had a mind of its own, spilling out unimaginable photos. I couldn't look away. I just froze.

Black-and-white photographs stared back at me—sharp, haunting, and each one worse than the last. They were images of Otto and Theresa, their bodies twisted and cramped inside a large trunk. The sight carved itself into me like a cold, sharp knife: jarring, gutting, soaked in a sadness so heavy I could barely breathe. I wanted to throw up.

That trunk, those bodies—like something out of a nightmare. It dragged up memories of the metal-and-timber trunk I'd inherited from my mother, brought all the way from Italy. Suddenly, childhood trauma I thought was buried came rushing back. I couldn't keep that trunk anymore. It had turned into a bad omen, a haunting reminder of those bodies stuffed inside a similar one. Honestly, I was thankful I never saw photos of their murdered son.

Meanwhile, Dorathy was under police protection, going by the name Cindy Crawford—because sure, using a supermodel's name won't draw attention. Despite how close we'd been, I never saw her again. I blamed Chris. He took Daniel's side and let the case swallow him whole, turning me against Dorothy with stories that she was out to ruin Daniel just for believing the cops.

The case consumed us. My hatred for Chris only grew. He didn't just destroy my friendship—he drove a wedge between me and my family with his self-righteousness. They distanced themselves from the mess. Chris had a knack for stirring the pot, especially between Mum and my brothers. Rude and inconsiderate—but at least he was consistent. He treated everyone like shit.

And then came the whispers. Missing money.

$275,000 to be exact. Where the hell did that go?

Good question. But first—court.

The day I gave my testimony in court, I somehow managed to fluster a respected police prosecutor, all thanks to my natural ability to confuse people without even trying.

Before I even stepped into the courtroom, our solicitors noticed the prosecution team looking rattled. They'd seen me outside, calmly reviewing a copy of my witness statement—the one I'd highlighted in bright yellow like I was cramming for finals.

What they didn't realise was that I wasn't holding my official court copy. That clean version was tucked safely in my handbag, which my husband held onto when I took the stand. The highlighted one? That was Chris's copy to hang on to while I took the stand.

He planned to glance at it during my testimony, just to see how well I held up under questioning.

I'd marked it up because I was nervous, and my memory's never been the best. I wasn't rehearsing a script, I was just trying to reinforce the key points. But the prosecutor saw it differently. To him, it looked like I'd been coached. And when cross-examination started, he pounced.

'Do you have your statement on you?' he asked.

'Nah, I don't,' I said casually.

The judge raised an eyebrow. 'A simple "no" will do, madam.'

'Sure thing, Judge,' I replied.

Once it was confirmed I had the statement in my bag, it was retrieved and handed to me. I opened my bag and pulled it out.

'Do you have it now, madam?' the judge asked.

I gave a quick thumbs-up towards the gallery. 'Yep, now I do.'

'Just answer yes or no, madam,' the judge sighed again.

I took that as the universal sign for—we're good to go. Then I handed it to the court officer, who passed it to the prosecutor.

He fumbled, tearing through each page like he was on some kind of mission.

Then came the final attempt. 'Is this the only copy you have?'

I smiled. 'Yes, it is.'

Technically, it was the only one in my possession. The other one was still in my husband's pocket, but technically it was his, and he wasn't under oath.

The judge called a break and during the adjournment, Daniel's defence lawyer walked over, grinning.

He clearly knew something I didn't.

'You were brilliant in there,' he said. 'I've never seen a prosecutor that flustered.'

'Oh ... I'm sorry?' I replied, genuinely confused.

He laughed and gave me a pat on the back. 'No, kid, you did good. This'll be talked about for a long time.'

On the way home, Chris explained what I still hadn't fully grasped: that in under ten minutes, I'd somehow made a seasoned prosecutor look like an amateur and entertained the courtroom gallery in the process, all without even realising.

Despite the confusion, I couldn't help but feel quietly proud of myself.

Not long after, while Daniel was still incarcerated, I unexpectedly fell pregnant with my fourth daughter. By February 1995, motherhood had wrapped its arms around me once again.

Was I a rabbit? How did this even happen? At thirty-four, I was juggling four daughters, from a sassy twelve-year-old down to a squishy newborn. Daunting? Absolutely. But each one added her own splash of joy to the beautiful chaos. Somewhere in the thick of family madness, I realised I could still claim a little corner of life for myself—if I could just work out how to balance the bloody lot.

During that time, and over the next few years, my husband insisted we visit Daniel in jail. He was oblivious to how tough it was to take our children, especially a breastfed newborn, into the high-security section of Long Bay jail.

The screening process was a drawn-out nightmare and when a baby needed feeding, it didn't care about delays. It just wanted a breast in its mouth. I hated taking the kids even though I loved our friend. It felt unfair for my husband to expect so much from me.

At some point, Daniel was moved to a jail too far for us to visit. I couldn't shake the feeling it was deliberate, to cut him off completely. We passed messages through a relative, clinging to what little connection we had. My gut said Daniel was innocent. He knew too much and got swallowed by something far darker than any of us realised.

When he was finally moved back to Long Bay, he was a shell—mind and body unravelled. It was heartbreaking.

By early 1998, money was tight, so I started working nights on the sex lines. After that, everything blurred. I lost track of who I even was. And my memory? Started slipping, fast.

As usual, Chris, full of his so-called 'inside info', claimed to know 'privileged' details about Daniel's case, though I never knew what was real and what was just his wild imagination.

Then, in July, he came home pale-faced, saying Harvey had confessed everything to the prison psychologist: names, methods, reasons. But days later, the psychologist was quietly taken off the case.

Not long after that, Harvey was dead. Knifed in the eye, but that wasn't what killed him. Then Daniel was found hanging in his cell. 'Suicide,' they said. But nothing felt certain anymore.

What terrified me the most was the timeline. I still can't get over it. I had Harvey, an accused killer right in front of me—and wild as it sounds, it wouldn't be the last time.

How crazy is that? I still get chills thinking about it.

And then came the money.

That $275,000? Vanished without a trace. One of Chris's dodgy mates who was barely tied to the case claimed Daniel was laundering cash for Otto and Theresa through his building business, stashing it in his ceiling.

The cops tore the place apart, but found nothing.

So where the hell did it go? Was money the real motive all along?

Did Harvey and Daniel turn on Otto and Theresa for it, deciding a few hundred grand was worth the blood on their hands?

Or was someone else lurking behind the scenes, someone who walked away with the money and the secrets, and left everyone else to clean up the mess?

I felt like I'd been dropped into a badly written crime novel—twists, lies, bodies, and no bloody resolution. A million questions hit me at once, and they didn't let up.

I mean, for real, how does that much cash just vanish? Someone took it. Someone lied. But who?

Turns out, fate wasn't done screwing with me. Years later, I'd find myself tangled in even more bizarre cases, because clearly, drama and I were in a committed relationship.

Lesson: Never underestimate what you're capable of.
Sometimes, your hidden strengths step up just
when life decides to flip the script on you.

CHAPTER 4

Battlefield

Sometimes, life's curveballs are just the thing you need to trigger a total transformation. Just when I hit one of my lowest points, fed up with my husband's behaviour and about to lose my friend to a tragic death in jail—everything changed. My life veered in a whole new direction.

It happened one night in early 1998, while Chris and I were out with our friends Craig and Tony. We ended up at a lively gay bar in Darlinghurst. I spotted a bowl of individually wrapped sweets at the bar and asked Tony if they were free. With a cheeky grin, I grabbed a handful and tucked them away for later.

The evening was incredible; we danced, our bodies reflecting dazzling splashes of kaleidoscopic light from the ceiling. On our way out, we passed The Tool Shed, a sex shop. My curiosity was heightened, so we went inside. My mind exploded like a confetti-filled balloon—it was like stepping into a candy store bursting with pleasure.

Breaking away from our respective partners, Chris and Craig explored the shop together, while Tony and I revelled in our pursuit of nude male magazines. It wasn't surprising to discover that we shared the same taste in men. After all, I had harboured a secret crush on my gay friend for years. We always found similarities, even in the way we squealed at the perfectly sculpted male physiques featured on every page. Briefly tearing my gaze away from the magazine, I noticed Chris and Craig both holding something that resembled oversized black curtain-rod ends.

Tony saw my puzzled look and, without raising an eyebrow, casually said, 'Butt plugs,' then went back to scanning the pages. My mind raced as I contemplated how that plug would fit in someone's rear end. Tony remained composed, playing it cool. Suddenly, he burst into laughter, fully aware that my curiosity was getting the better of me. He proceeded to fill me in on the details of how those rubber plugs were used in preparation for an onslaught of sex.

I appreciated my friends for their openness; our conversations were unrestricted, frank, and thoughtful. I gained valuable insights and surprisingly, my connection with that store didn't end there. Somehow, I caught the attention of the man behind the counter with my gift line ideas. He suggested I present them to the owner. All I heard was, 'Bring them in.' Despite the daunting task of creating forty unique feather tantalisers in a week, I couldn't resist the challenge. After all, 'challenge' was practically my middle name.

The following week, I bought feathers, beads, and other necessary items. After packaging, I labelled my creations as 'sensual body ticklers' and the smaller ones as 'fanny ticklers'. I earned four hundred dollars for a week's work, which was good money at the time. As for those free sweets from the bar, they turned out to be an assortment of coloured and flavoured condoms. I'm glad I didn't try eating them.

That was my grand entrance into the sex industry; you could say opportunity knocked and kicked down the door, forever changing my trajectory. Just a few months later, I found myself honestly considering leaving my husband—talk about a defining moment!

His erratic mood swings consumed him, and my life felt like a war zone, filled with upheaval and obstacles. At times, it seemed like I was on a self-destructive quest for an escape from my troubles, and here I was again, deliberately marching into battle. As I stepped off the bus with my youngest daughter, I clung to her tightly, shielding her from the careless rush around us.

Overwhelmed and out of place, my mind drifted back to my early school years. Despite being just like every other little girl, the strict Catholic school made me feel different. My ethnic name seemed to irritate the nuns, who insisted on using the English version, cementing my sense of not belonging. But then again, I did everything I could to deliberately annoy the shit out of them.

I returned to the present. Just a short distance from my destination, I focused on the numbers on the buildings, quickening my pace to escape this hazardous speedway. Arriving at the entrance, I stepped into the foyer and paused, taking in the chaotic scene of people sprinting about.

It resembled a battlefield; instead of blood and guts, there were boxes overflowing with cables and telephones. I took a few more steps towards the receptionist desk. As I looked up, our eyes collided. My mouth gaped open, and blood rushed to my cheeks, embarrassed at being caught with my opinionated thoughts on the disorganised clutter.

I judged as others judged me; I had no right to. I should have left my prejudices outside, just like jurors in a courtroom. It was obvious by the expression on her face that she knew what I was thinking. With a raised eyebrow and a tilt of her head, she smiled at me and said, 'Yes, it's a fucking mess.' I smiled back awkwardly, grateful that her frankness had broken the ice.

'Come on, I'll take you to meet the supervisor.'

With that, she led me into a corner of the room that may have previously had walls erected, and there before me stood a stunning woman. She was flawless, with long brown hair cascading past her waist, delicate strands falling over her immaculately sculpted brows.

I stood like a stunned mullet, gazing in amazement at this

well-put-together woman. That's when I caught a whiff of a fragrance I knew well, Chanel No. 5, one of those luxuries I couldn't afford. Whenever I entered a department store, I would spray a little on my wrist and let its scent engulf me. I was more in the eau-de-toilette price bracket.

Her sheer elegance made me forget why I was even there. But the truth was ever-present: at thirty-seven, I had four responsibilities—my daughters. My beautiful Violet, my eldest at fifteen, headstrong and independent since she was twelve, working at a local fruit shop. My gorgeous Katya, twelve going on twenty, my little truth-seeker and prankster, always leading her two younger sisters into trouble, but thankfully, she kept an eye on her sisters and entertained them. Then there was our sweet Nila, the kindest girl you'd ever meet. She loved with all her heart, whether it was our cat or a pet rock; her passion knew no bounds. And, of course, there was tiny, adorable Luna—my baby. She was a tornado in human form, leaving a whirlwind of mayhem wherever she went, but I wouldn't have had it any other way. She was my lucky charm, an unexpected gift I was endlessly grateful for.

My duties were overwhelming to say the least, but they were mine, and I stepped up, even though I often wished my husband would take on more responsibility. But he didn't, and we were always struggling. Oh, how I wished he was like the other husbands I knew, kind, strong, full of warmth. Instead, he was a wildcard—sporadically insane, a dirty little secret I kept hidden from the world.

My daughter's weight leaned into me, and I shifted slightly to relieve the pressure. The woman in front of me could surely see straight through my discomfort. What must she have thought, me showing up with a small child in tow? But what choice did I have? I had to make this work.

'Hello, Lucia, is that correct? My name is Suzette.' Her voice was firm yet melodic.

My vocal cords strained to get the words out. 'Ah, yeah, that's me.' I couldn't have predicted how anxious I would feel; this was unfamiliar territory, and I lacked confidence.

Luna, my littlest jellybean, seemed oblivious to my emotions and was fully immersed in the delight of the commotion taking place. Her head bopped around from side to side, making sure she didn't miss anything. She stopped every now and then to look at me with those wide, magnificent eyes and smile. I acknowledged her with a nod of my head and a smile back.

Looking at this beautiful little girl in my arms, I realised my husband's insistence that I contribute more financially was the nudge I needed to re-evaluate my life. The truth hit me hard: I was here for her and her three sisters. I had to be honest with myself—I couldn't let my daughters' lives mirror mine. My life wasn't what I dreamed it would be, all because I let others impose their will on me. I was in a rough spot, and it was time to change things, no matter what it took.

I knew my daughters carried with them parts of their father and of me, but not all were the pieces I wanted them to adopt as their own. They needed to see what normal could be like, and I wanted to ensure they did not become accustomed to having violence in any form as a part of their existence.

Being here was a blessing in disguise—one I didn't recognise at the time but desperately needed to set me on the right path. I stood there, fingers crossed, hoping to return home with good news. After all, it was my husband who unearthed this opportunity for me, and with his persuasive nudging, I finally took the plunge and applied.

Suzette showed kindness towards my daughter, smiling at her as she leaned in to meet her eyes. Fascinated by her attention, Luna giggled back. Suzette complimented me for having such a beautiful little girl, one of my proudest moments. She also acknowledged that it was okay to have brought her with me.

I was directed to sit on a sofa, where I settled Luna, who

immediately pulled at my bag to get out her juice box and treats. She was happy to munch away as I turned my attention to Suzette, who indicated the business was moving offices, a little closer to Circular Quay, hence the mess.

She then clarified what was expected of me in my role, and honestly, it sounded easy. Answer phones, talk dirty. I took the job. But the very next night, I would find out just how foolish I was to think that.

My first shift would start at eleven in the evening and finish at five the next morning. This would give me enough time to get home and possibly sleep for a half-hour before getting up for the children. It was going to be tough, but I believed I could manage.

The strange thing was, my sexual experiences to date had only ever been with Chris—well, apart from witnessing some spontaneous combustion between inmates and their partners during visits to Daniel at Long Bay Jail. Maybe that was my unintentional training for the role I now had to play.

Picture this: a sterile concrete room, sitting on cold metal stools, leaning on tables bolted to the floor, with a front-row seat to some interesting interactions between inmates and their female visitors. One woman had her hand planted firmly between a guy's legs, working it like she was churning butter. A moment later, she crumpled a white handkerchief and casually tucked it into her pocket like she'd just done her weekly shopping.

And it wasn't just her. I saw more of them at it, like a row of milkmaids hard at work, except for the poor guys stuck in those one-piece overalls with zippers up to their necks. Even with guards all around—it was like they had selective vision.

Oh, and let me tell you about the time they organised a special Christmas event for families. Daniel's wife and sons had no contact with him, so, of course, my husband insisted we go, dragging our youngest daughters along. Thank God Violet was working that day.

We were ushered into this open concrete area, surrounded by a high wall with a few sad patches of grass. The kids, bless them, didn't seem to care about the grim surroundings. They were off, happily playing with their gifts, while I was left wondering how I ended up in the middle of this holiday spectacle.

Adults paired off, men sitting leaning against the wall and women sitting on their laps, either facing them or with their back against the male's chest, moving rhythmically side to side. Now I knew why all the women dressed differently than usual; in full skirts or dresses, a detail that initially escaped me until my husband explained. It was a bizarre mix of family fun and unexpected romance! I was shocked but also captivated; it seemed I had a lot more to learn about sex, and the call centre was going to be the place I would earn my degree.

I thanked Suzette, we said our goodbyes, I packed up my daughter, who was covered in crumbs and happy with a full belly, and made my way home. Except this time, I walked as close as possible along the buildings to avoid contact with others.

Once inside the safety of the bus, I relaxed, focusing my attention on my daughter sitting on my lap, bouncing around as the bus drove along. Her wide eyes took everything in like a sponge soaking up water. I wished I could see everything as exciting as she did, instead of fearing what was to come.

Lesson: Taking a chance on yourself is never a wrong move —try it and you just might surprise yourself.

CHAPTER 5

The Establishment's new recruit

That fear of the unknown took me somewhere I never imagined—The Establishment, as I called it. A place where sexual fantasies weren't acted out, just whispered, twisted, and teased over the phone. I mean, honestly, why would a man pay to talk dirty and get off on it when he could just visit a brothel and have actual sex with a real, live woman? Made no sense to me… at first.

It was on Young Street, just a short walk from Circular Quay. The building itself was simple—brick and concrete. The office was on the eleventh floor, and I remember how convenient it was to find free street or laneway parking. You'd enter through these glass doors right at street level.

Outside regular hours, the main entrance was locked, prompting the use of the side door, a wooden thing a dingy shade of chocolate brown. Unfortunately, it bore the unpleasant scent of urine, courtesy of inebriated men who used it as a urinal. Despite the less-than-ideal conditions, the side entrance served as a welcome escape route, offering a brief respite from the confines of the building.

Usually I stepped out the door without incident, but for some reason, chaos seemed to gravitate towards me. On one occasion,

I pushed the door smack-bang into an unsuspecting man, causing him to bounce off the door onto the ground. 'Whoa!' was all I could say. In an attempt to be helpful, I extended my hand to assist him, only to swiftly retract it when I noticed his exposed penis in a collapsed state on his wet pants—although I did do a double take at its impressive size. The unpleasant odour of alcohol indicated that I caught this intoxicated man mid-stream during his impromptu relief break.

In the flurry, I tried to step over him to get past but instead stepped on his hand, making this more awkward than it already was.

He cried out something inaudible, which sounded like a shrieking banshee.

'Oh fuck, sorry, sorry,' was all that came out of my mouth. They were my go-to words for everything. With that, I hurried down the street to Macca's, the great American golden arches, where food was aplenty. On my return, he was gone, and so was the colour from my face as I was still in shock, but at least in a safe space where I could not possibly cause any more harm.

The call centre was comprised of a sizeable open area with a reception desk in the middle of the room, featuring two telephones. One was a standard phone, while the other was used for transferring calls to specific women.

The main room could accommodate about sixteen booth-style tables, each partitioned on either side to provide a sense of privacy. While a basic padded metal chair was designated to sit on, it was seldom used for that purpose, such was its lack of comfort. Each booth-style table was placed against the wall, and our link to the men who called in was a telephone attached to the wall via a cord. If you were not facing a window that overlooked another building, the blank wall was your friend for the night.

On my first night, I noticed some women had notepads, just like the one I'd been given. At first, I thought they were for doodling during slow moments between calls. A few days in, I realised they were much more than boredom-busters—they were client cheat sheets, used to jot down notes about regulars and the quirks that kept them coming back. Keeping track of specific desires and fetishes was apparently part of the job.

During busy nights, up to fifteen women might be on the phones at once. The noise made concentrating nearly impossible. I'd often find myself crouched under my desk, trying to hear clearly. *A strange way to earn a living*, I'd think, whispering sweet nothings while hiding under a table.

Off to the side was the chill-out room, everyone's favourite hangout—a cosy spot with cushions, beanbags and phones scattered on the floor. Perfect for long calls, especially with regulars who seemed more interested in running up their phone bills than getting to the point.

Clients often asked for specific women they'd spoken to before. If their favourite was busy, they'd either chat with someone else until she was free or we'd pull off the old switcheroo—passing the phone mid-conversation. Men rarely noticed. A quick swap, a few moans and sighs, and they were none the wiser. Honestly, those calls felt like hitting the jackpot.

Sometimes, I'd hand off my phone if one of my regulars called while I was tied up. If I needed a break, I'd tell him to chat with another woman for a bit. Strangely, they didn't seem to mind paying by the minute just to wait for me. The logic? Still a mystery.

What stood out most was how the women always had each other's backs. Sure, some stretched out calls for the bonus, but most of the time, it was just about passing the night. No denying it—we had a talent for making the absurd endearing.

Of course, there were men who found it exciting to talk to a different woman. It was like having two for the price of one—not a bad deal. There was always the possibility that, by handing over a call, the man might prefer speaking to the new woman. In that case, I ran the risk of losing them as a regular client. That was the gamble I took.

Each woman used an alias, which served to hide our real identity. Back then, I wasn't entirely in touch with my true self, so I fashioned a character, perhaps one I secretly desired to become. Our alias names helped callers easily find us when they called back.

Women became acquainted with each other's telephone persona and their specialty. We knew who to direct a caller to if it seemed we were losing their interest during a conversation. If a man called asking for a specific woman who wasn't available, the manager had a roster and could inform the client about the woman's next scheduled shift.

Why men believed they shared a special connection with any of us was bizarre. However, it kept them calling and loyal. Some men held onto hope of one day meeting. Although not always effortless, I did what was necessary to keep men on the phone and exerted extra effort for a bonus.

Many times, my voice would go hoarse as I pushed for those few extra dollars in my pay packet. The typical duration of a call was five minutes. On a landline, it cost $2.95 a minute, and on a mobile, it was $7.95 a minute. This was an insane amount of money, yet they paid it.

It was a twenty-four-seven operation. I could only imagine how much money the company and the telephone provider were making. What a prime investment!

I was paid an average wage of eighty dollars for a six-and-a-half-hour shift, with bonuses of five dollars on top for every man I lured into talking for thirty minutes. If one of us was on a call leading up to a bonus, we would usually work through until the call ended, regardless of the shift hours.

When the phone rang, women greeted callers with variations like, 'Hi, I'm Mandy. Who am I speaking to?' or 'Hi, babe, glad you called tonight, I was getting lonely.'

The night manager transferred clients to the right woman, handled calls, assisted as needed, and helped manage rosters. Serving as our personal cheerleader, she informed us when we were close to a bonus, saying, 'You're on twenty minutes; try to keep him on another ten.' Annoyingly, some clients abruptly hung up just shy of the bonus mark, sometimes by mere seconds.

During peak times with a shortage of women, we juggled answering multiple phones simultaneously, attempting to satisfy two callers at once. It was a frantic effort where every minute counted, though it was often a comical scene.

In moments of need, whether for a brief break or assistance with a call, colleagues and the manager stepped in to help, fostering close bonds among us through shared stories, advice, and even providing rides to and from work.

At times, I gave lifts home to two co-workers who lived near my suburb. Sometimes, I'd wait for them to finish their calls, especially if they were close to hitting a bonus. If I got too tired, I'd nod off under my desk until they were done, and then we'd drive home, giggling about the array of sexual techniques we'd used to get men off that night. Moments like those—the little ways we had each other's backs—gave me a sense of belonging that still means the world to me.

While occasional competitiveness did arise on the phones, this experience taught me about the resilience and supportiveness of women. Women have a unique ability to uplift, care, and speak the truth without pretence.

During breaks, we'd dash out for a quick smoke or hit up Macca's. Sometimes, I'd scout a corner store for something with more kick than coffee—especially on those nights when sleep wasn't on the cards. One supervisor, though, gave me more than just job advice; she put my problems into perspective and made me realise my own worth. I learned to hold onto hope and keep pushing forward. But for now, there was that little thing called 'on-the-job training' to tackle—oh, and my first shift.

Like a virgin stepping into the unknown, there I was, my first time as the master of sex.

Honestly, I felt like an uninvited voyeur—there but not really. Scribbling notes on something I hadn't done? Weird. These conversations were anything but standard chit-chat. But over time, that notebook became gold, full of insights I needed to handle clients.

The women manning the phone lines formed a diverse and intriguing group. Among them, the youngest, barely out of her teens, wore jeans and a cropped white t-shirt, her hair pinned up in a bun, casually rolling gum between her fingers as she spoke. Her participation, a chorus of sighs and murmurs, was unremarkable until the last thirty seconds—a mind-blowing eruption of explicit language well worth the wait.

As she hung up, another call came in. She grabbed the handset, shook it vigorously, clenched her teeth, and muttered profanities under her breath. Then, with composure, she addressed the caller as if nothing had happened. Great, I thought. *I just nailed my first memo: shake phone, grit teeth, and deal with it.*

Although that call must have bored her, a few minutes in, she flopped her head on the desk with the handset barely beneath her ear, closing her eyes as if in a comatose state. Someone plonked a cup of coffee on her desk, reviving her.

I decided to approach the woman seated across from me, who looked a bit intimidating, with a physique that could've belonged to a sumo wrestler. But the moment she opened her mouth,

I was so stunned, I literally fell backwards. The melody in her voice, paired with a subtle accent, was both soothing and sexy. Her words had this sensual edge without the vulgarity.

This was worth paying attention to. Silently, I thought, Tell me more.

When her call ended, she stood up, leaving the handset off the hook, and shouted to the supervisor at the end of the room, 'I'm taking a fucken break before my arsehole shits itself.'

That enchanting vocal melody vanished somewhere between ending the call and standing up—maybe it disappeared into the folds of her bum. Shocked, I quickly figured out that I'd need to improvise and use whatever acting skills I had, even if they were minimal. With that in mind, I felt a little more prepared as I made my way to the supervisor, who led me to my partially partitioned desk.

'You'll be operator fifty-six, and you'll need a name the clients can use to identify you when they call back,' the supervisor informed me.

From that moment on, my persona was that of a young, sexy woman named Dominique.

Lesson: When women team up, we're unstoppable. Competitive? Maybe. But we rise by lifting each other—stronger and sharper. Every moment's a lesson, whether from a chat or life's curveballs. Stay sharp and catch them.

CHAPTER 6

Maiden voyage

Leaning over my desk, I pressed my face hard against the windowpane. The cool glass was refreshing, easing my nerves. I scanned the laneway below. The streetlights threw beams of light, revealing rats the size of cats scurrying along the gutters. Yuck! I guessed that was to be expected. I mean, there were restaurants nearby.

Looking out at the apartment block across from my booth, I felt like a voyeur. Suddenly, the phone jolted me back to reality. My first call on a sex line—like a maiden voyage into uncharted territory. I drew in a deep breath.

'Mmm, hi, my name's Dominique. Who am I speaking to?'

Oh, gosh—wild thoughts flooded my mind, my head buzzing with words, spinning like a tornado of madness.

Before I could process anything, he introduced himself as Angus. His voice was calm.

'Where are you from, Angus?'

'I'm from the Northern Territory. I live on a cattle station.'

'That's different from where I live. Do you live alone?'

'Just me, the cattle, my horses and a few dogs.' He paused. 'First time calling one of these numbers. The first time talking to a lady.'

All those whirling thoughts melted away at the word 'lady'. It was nice—sounding prim and proper, civilised. 'Glad you got me, Angus.'

'Why's that?'

'Because I'm feeling lonesome and need some company.'

He cleared his throat and asked where I was. I exaggerated, telling him I was in my apartment in Sydney, overlooking the harbour.

'By yourself, are you?'

'Yes, I am. Actually, I'm lying on my bed, wishing you were here next to me, Angus.' I couldn't believe how easily those words rolled off my tongue.

'Wish I was, too. So, what are you wearing?'

I glanced down at the reference paper I'd been given earlier. Nope, nothing about that. I shoved the useless paper aside. *Guess I'll wing it from here.* The next words that came out of my mouth were sensual, lingering.

'I have on the sheerest red negligée. What about you?'

'I'm wearing my hat and boots,' he said. 'And I'm holding something I think you'd like.'

I innocently asked, 'What's that?'

'My throbbing cock.'

Oh, boy, I wasn't expecting that! He definitely got my attention. His voice was hypnotic, pulling me in right away. Beads of sweat started to form on my inner thighs. I wanted him to picture me there with him. For some reason, I lowered my voice, almost like a male baritone, and said, 'Oh, I want your cock so bad.'

'You okay?'

Oh, shit. I've ruined the moment. That's fine—I know how to fix it.

'Sorry about that, Angus, but I've never had a cock as big as yours in my mouth.' Thank fuck. I rectified the situation, and now we were back on track.

'Angus, would you like me to bend over for you?'

'I don't just want to look; I want to taste you on my lips.'

'Oh, yeah, I'd like that, too.' That part I actually meant—if only.

His little pleasurable moan told me he was stroking his cock. The thought of him touching himself made those beads of sweat evaporate into steam.

'I'm going to sit on your face so you can taste me.'

'Mmm, you like the feel of my tongue?'

His voice was captivating, and for the briefest moment I imagined he was pleasing me instead of the other way around. I was really getting into this. Maybe I'd missed my calling as an actress.

'Oh, baby, that's it, deeper. I want you so bad.' Was that too much? Nah, how could it be—this was a sex line, after all.

'Yeah, that's it, now suck my cock.'

Wow! Angus seemed well acquainted with Mrs Palmer and her five daughters, it appeared.

He moaned, then I moaned several times. I told him I needed him inside me.

'I'm going to bend you over,' he grunted, as if thrusting hard. 'Can you feel how deep I am inside you?'

This might be Angus's first time on a sex phone line, but he certainly wasn't a novice. I pleaded with him to do it harder and faster. He must have liked that a lot—unexpectedly, he gave one last moan, and that was that.

Shit! That was too quick. I mean, the idea was to keep him on the phone as long as possible.

Guess I forgot that detail. Oh, well, next time I'd do better.

Angus, a true gentleman, thanked me and expressed a desire to meet me, reaffirming his loneliness. He told me I sounded like a really nice lady, and there it was again, that word, '*lady*.' It was a term I had never associated with myself before, suggesting a sense of dignity I had never felt. That single call planted the seed of an idea: perhaps I was that indeed.

He mentioned calling back, but that call never came. Not that it bothered me. His words had already given my confidence a serious boost. That chat with Angus, along with a few others that followed, made me consider that maybe, just maybe, I deserved respect.

It also made me realise how far from normal my husband's treatment of me really was. I'd been so wrapped up in my fears and confusion that I hadn't realised what I'd been missing—trust, dignity, and the simple decency that should've been mine all along.

Though it was a positive start, the job did take a toll after a while, making me question my worth. Not all callers were decent. *Are all men like this?* I often wondered. *How many women know what their partners are up to?* It left me feeling resentful of men, but at the same time I couldn't ignore the role they played in my transformation. It was a serious head trip.

Despite all that, there were things in my life I was grateful for. The solitude during my commute offered a sense of freedom and excitement. The bustling city was always alive, full of anticipation, and I loved being part of it. I felt independent driving in alone, relishing the simplicity of finding free parking in Bridge Street or Loftus Lane.

The journey back home had its perks, too. On one occasion, I saw a small aeroplane being transported on a large trailer across the Iron Cove Bridge with its wingtips bent upwards.

Quite the sight.

Of course, there were times I despised my husband when he wouldn't let me use the car, leaving me stuck on public transport—even in the middle of the night. I could never understand why he wouldn't want me to get home safely in a car instead of braving public transport at odd hours. What a total fuckwit, no joke!

After my morning shift, I often had to wait for buses to start running, then walk home from the bus stop down a dark alleyway. If it wasn't my thoughts haunting me, it was the crazy dog next door, barking its teeth off and gnawing at the fence posts. I'd run like an Olympian to get home. And while home wasn't ideal, it was all I had—temporary, sure, but a place to clear my head when I was alone. A place he couldn't penetrate, where I could start working on my escape plan—kind of like the 1963 movie *The Great Escape* with Steve McQueen. He never gave up, and he was courageous enough to face the challenge.

Lesson: Open your mind to the possibilities of what can be when you change your perspective.

CHAPTER 7

One-armed bandit

Ellen, with her distinct laid-back Aussie slang, had me at, 'Hey, mate.' She triumphed over personal challenges from an early age, which instilled a profound appreciation for the lighter side of life. I saw in her a persistence to overcome any obstacles in her path, and for that she earned my respect. We teamed up on the phone lines, using whatever means possible to keep men on the line. I affectionately referred to her as the 'one-armed bandit'.

In her twenties, she stood tall with a lanky frame, a cascade of strawberry-blonde hair, and freckles that painted her entire face. When she smiled it was as if her freckles danced. Her constant happiness was admirable, but it was her vivacious personality and warmth that truly mesmerised everyone around her.

The first time we met, she looked me straight in the eyes, smiled, and raised her arm, saying,

'So I guess you're wondering what happened here, hey?'

Embarrassed, I realised she had caught me staring at her absent forearm.

Her eyes twinkled. 'Well, you see, it was like this: I had a fight with a croc over a fish, and he won.'

Ellen had a remarkable ability to make me laugh, even in situations that weren't inherently funny. The truth behind her missing forearm was poignant. As a child, Ellen had a passion for horses and riding. Unfortunately, several falls led to multiple operations. Despite efforts to save her arm, the nerves were beyond repair. With no movement from the elbow down, her parents faced the agonising decision to have it removed.

Sadly, it's often those who love you most who must make the hardest decisions, the ones that break your heart but can't be refused. I couldn't fathom how distressing that time must have been for Ellen. Yet she had a remarkable way of lightening the situation, often saying, 'At least it wasn't my good arm,' always bringing a smile to my face.

She once described it to me by saying, 'My arm was like a floppy dick—useless. Although it made for a good flyswatter.'

To truly comprehend the strength of laughter, one must have faced grief. I supposed she, like me, used laughter to overcome pain. This aspect of resilience became something I deeply appreciated and incorporated into my own coping mechanisms.

On evenings when she assumed the role of supervisor, everything became more enjoyable, making the passage of time swift. Her leadership left a lasting impression, inspiring me for decades. When I became a leader, I integrated aspects of her approach into my own style. She was one of those rare, exceptional women who led by example, always ready to assist with any challenge.

Ellen possessed this incredible talent to evoke laughter and tears simultaneously, to the extent that I almost wet my pants—which was not hard to do after four pregnancies.

One night, as I arrived for my shift, Ellen raced over with a huge grin and said, 'He did it, he did it to me.'

Confused, I asked, 'Did what?'

'He touched my stump, what'd you think?'

Ellen had been dating a guy who always avoided touching her

arm—until one special, romantic night. As he tenderly caressed her face, shoulder and arm, he naturally embraced her stump.

Phew, I thought. Thank God that's all it was. As much as I loved her, I didn't want to hear some kinky, blow-by-blow account of her sexual escapades and how she'd used her stump on him! But instead, it was a pretty special moment in Ellen's journey, showing a raw, emotional side I hadn't seen before. I was honoured she chose to share such an intimate moment with me.

After that, Ellen openly shared her story with me and even with male callers, talking about losing her arm with real courage. She'd mix in humour too, like her unforgettable crocodile tale, which always lightened the mood. Sometimes, when she was on the phone, a man would urge her to touch herself. She would wittily respond, 'Hang on, mate, I'm not a bloody contortionist, I've only got one arm, you know.'

Callers reacted with everything from shock to laughter. It wasn't just about keeping them engaged; it was Ellen's coping mechanism. When men doubted her story, she'd hand me the phone for backup. I was amazed at how quickly their attitudes changed once they realised she was the real deal. It was a refreshing reminder that not all men were insensitive morons.

One night, a drunken caller phoned in, eager for a risqué chat. I introduced him to Ellen. It took some effort to break through his dense understanding that Ellen had lost an arm. Astonishingly, he even suggested that Ellen should have retrieved her arm after the crocodile attack. Ellen told him she let the croc have that one and wasn't stupid enough to try and get it back.

The story took an unexpected turn when he asked us both to participate in sex with him. So there we were, both on the phone, with Ellen playfully pretending to screw me with her stump.

At one point, he urged Ellen to get in deep.

'I'm up to my shoulder, and if I go any further, I'll be swallowed whole,' she crowed.

This triggered a fit of giggles from both of us, and a huffy question from the caller as to why we were laughing.

'She's ticklish,' came Ellen's response.

This was quintessentially Ellen—a sharp sense of humour and quick wit. On another occasion during a call, a man asked her for a hand job, and I must say, she handled it with finesse. The first time I witnessed this, I couldn't help but mouth the words, 'What the hell are you up to?'

'I'm giving him a hand job, can't you tell?'

The other women and I were left in hysterics at seeing her stump moving like it was conducting an orchestra. At times on the phones we were unaware of how deeply we were immersed in fulfilling requests.

Another time, a client requested for Ellen to perform oral sex while simultaneously rubbing his balls. I happened to be sitting next to her that evening when suddenly she looked over, smiling. That's when I knew this was going to be well worth watching. In the middle of her conversation, she said, 'Would you mind if I ask my girlfriend to hold the phone for me?'

He must have asked why, because she responded with, 'Well, I only have one arm, so I can't rub your balls and hold the phone at the same time.'

I couldn't help it—I burst into laughter. The conversation quickly shifted from naughty to questions about Ellen's arm. Ellen flipped the situation like a pro, snagging a bonus and a regular caller in the process.

I often think back to my time with the women I worked alongside, especially Ellen. She taught me not to take myself too seriously and to grab every opportunity. Most importantly, she made sure I'd never let anyone dim my shine.

***Lesson:** Just let others try to underestimate your abilities, then prove them wrong.*

CHAPTER 8

The hunk from the club

I encountered him on the dance floor—tall, handsome, and undeniably younger than me. By day he worked as a concreter and by night he transformed into a male entertainer. His robust arms enveloped my entire body as we danced. I let myself feel the electricity between us, allowing him to kiss me, or perhaps I encouraged him to do so. I might have avoided this situation if it weren't for the persuasion of a group of women I worked with on the phone lines. They swayed me to join them at a club and of course I took advantage of this newfound friendship circle, meeting up with the ladies at Tattersalls in the city.

We had several hours before our shift began, so we enjoyed a few drinks and a quick bite to eat at the bar and grill, then hit the dance floor. The women laughed as I demonstrated some of my well-known moves—the ones that never failed to make my daughters cringe. As the music transitioned into a slow dance, we started to make our way off the dance floor. Out of nowhere, a hand gently rested on my shoulder, and there he was: Blair. Undoubtedly the most attractive man I had ever laid eyes on, boasting a chiselled jawline and a body to match.

'Can I have a dance?'

I looked around. Nope, nobody there, he was definitely talking to me.

I gazed straight into his piercing emerald eyes, captivated and eager to lose myself in them.

Without uttering a single word, I simply nodded, feeling like a giddy teenage girl. He took my hand in his and encircled my waist, gliding his hand up and down the tender curve of my back as we swayed intimately. I placed mine on his shoulder.

By the second song, he embraced me even closer, which I didn't think was possible. There was a conversation, but I missed parts of it, mesmerised by every aspect of him, including his husky voice. I did remember he worked for a concreting company in Pyrmont, a detail that probably caught my attention because I drove past it to and from work in the evenings.

Why he chose to dance with me was a mystery. I didn't see myself as an attractive woman, yet I enjoyed the attention. It could be that he sensed my fun personality as he watched me with my friends, or maybe it was the fact that my breasts were on display for all to see in a skimpy sheer white shirt, which I had deliberately unbuttoned, revealing my lacy white bra.

He looked down at me and told me I had the sweetest smile he had ever seen. That's when I felt the pulsating hardness of his cock pressed against me. I wasn't sure if it was my face or tits he was actually staring at, but it didn't matter at that stage. He then swept my long hair to the side, exposing my neck, the touch of his hand sending electric charges over my body. His lips seemed to engulf themselves around mine, lingering forever. It was the most perfect kiss.

I was lost in the moment, unaware anyone was watching, but when our lips parted, I noticed one of my friends staring. Embarrassed, I pushed myself away from Blair and told him I had to go. He pulled me back into him and asked if he could buy me a drink. Without a thought, I agreed, and turned around with my arms whirling. Smack! I accidentally slapped the front of his pants.

If that wasn't bad enough, when I looked back at him, he was grinning like a Cheshire cat.

'Glad you know how I feel about you,' he said.

I fluttered my eyelids and shot him an innocent grin. Oh yes, I did—I couldn't miss the start of a bulge in his pants. I returned to the table where my friend Selina was sitting. She smiled and said Blair was cute. I apologised, calling myself an idiot. She shook her head and said, 'No, you aren't. You're just enjoying yourself.

Remember, a little attention goes a long way!'

Blair walked over with drinks, introduced himself to Selina and joined in on the conversation, all the while placing his hand on my leg as if we were a couple. After a short while Selina checked her watch and informed me that she would gather the others. We had about forty minutes before the start of our shift and the walk was about twenty minutes.

Before we parted ways, Blair handed me a card with his work details and phone number. I promised to call, but never did. If nothing else, that moment gave me a feeling of positive self-perception, seeing myself as desirable and attractive for the first time in a long time. I never spoke about him or that event to anyone after that evening; he was my beautiful secret. That encounter revealed to me that the women I worked with were not judgemental, and even if they were, I shouldn't give a damn. I cherished being around women who didn't criticise and genuinely seemed to understand; most likely, it was because they themselves had experienced similar situations.

If any of my family or friends at the time had known about my activities with other men (yes, there were others after Blair), they might have labelled me a whore and sympathised with my husband. However, they either didn't know Chris the way I did or chose to ignore what they knew he did to me.

Chris was my living death, and despite my desire to leave, I feared what the future held. I knew I would have to rely on myself and

I didn't feel prepared for that yet. It would be a few more years before we finally parted ways. In the meantime, while working in the sex industry, the cycle of dreamy interludes persisted.

Lesson: For the sake of your own self-preservation, you may need to create happy moments.

CHAPTER 9

Survival hacks

When I first plunged into the sex industry, I was terrified of what others would think, so I told no one. I thought they were all better than me. But over time, I grew resentful of those who looked down on women in non-traditional jobs. To protect my daughters, I spun a tale about being an evening office worker handling phone calls. It wasn't a total lie—I really did take calls at night—I just skipped the spicy bits.

Things stayed smooth until a Mother's Day celebration at my daughter's school. I walked into her classroom and saw her drawing—a big smiley face in a tiny window, surrounded by stars in a black sky. It almost unravelled me. Other kids drew mums cleaning or typing at desks. Some mothers asked about my job, and I casually replied, 'I work nights, manning the phones for a security company.' If only they knew.

I lied to avoid admitting my husband was a shitty provider. Graveyard shifts were brutal, but it was honest work. Easy money? No way. Being the voice behind a sex call wasn't all sultry whispers. I juggled personalities like a pro. Funny, shy, sweet, sophisticated—you name it, all logged in my trusty notebook.

Some calls made me feel like a therapist without the credentials. Others were pure filth. Then there were the men just seeking connection, or a safe space to explore their sexuality. Of course, a few were downright disturbing, I ended those calls faster than you could say 'paedophile.' But I reminded myself it was just a job. A fucking job. A means to an end.

Every call felt like Russian roulette—would I win a regular or scare them off?

The relentless hours turned me into a zombie. At first, I thought the 'boosters' we passed around were all natural. A doctor's visit shattered that illusion when my liver protested the caffeine-loaded meds. After that, I stuck to straight caffeine.

Living like an owl was not as glamorous as it sounded. The exhaustion messed with my head. I worried I wasn't enough for my daughters. Ballet, gym, playdates—the endless list haunted me. Sometimes I'd collapse for a nap, leaving them glued to the TV. Don't judge me! Ask any sleep-deprived mum—working late nights while raising kids wasn't pretty.

Despite the chaos, the job gave me unshakable confidence and taught me to value myself. My upbringing and my marriage had twisted my view of womanhood, but this work forced me to see women differently. I developed respect for all careers, even those that society misunderstood.

But the cracks in my marriage grew wider. Resentment and anxiety gnawed at me. I didn't want to stay with Chris, but leaving felt impossible. Desperate for relief, I started collecting phone numbers from other men. I told myself it was harmless—just chatting, no sex. But it only made things messier and cranked up my mental mayhem.

Opening up to my co-workers helped. They'd been through it all—bad marriages, kids, toxic exes. Even the night supervisors lent an ear when things got too crazy.

The job wasn't easy, but it proved I had grit. I survived one hurricane after another, rolling with the punches. I thought I had it all figured out, until Alex entered the picture and turned everything upside down.

Lesson: Life's hard times can kick you in the pants and open new doors, but if you want real change, you've got to quit chasing someone else's dream and make room for your own.

CHAPTER 10

The meet-ups

If not for the women I worked with, spilling their stories like we were all at some boozy confession booth, I might have spiralled into a guilt-induced meltdown. Turns out, sharing the chaos of our lives—and our weirdest phone clients—was the therapy none of us knew we needed. Some of those men filled emotional gaps; others delivered lessons that stuck like gum to a shoe. Tough? Absolutely. But pain tends to be the best teacher.

The women had their reasons for meeting clients, and I wasn't about to judge. Take Freya, for instance, a knockout Dutch model with wild auburn hair and a laugh that could captivate an audience without even trying. She fell for a client who spoiled her with gifts and fancy dinners, breaking the company rules faster than you could say 'policy violation'. But love—or lust—could make us all a little reckless.

Eventually, his obsession went from cute to creepy. Freya had to shut it down, but he wouldn't stop calling until the night supervisor stepped in, risking her job to tell him Freya had moved on. To avoid more harassment, Freya switched her phone name and shifts. Some rules weren't just for show, but the allure of what *could* be was sometimes too tempting—even for me.

Then there was Jen, a sweet-looking twenty-year-old who couldn't stop talking about her long-distance boyfriend in Molong. She convinced me to let her use my empty house for a weekend. Chris, the girls, and I were crammed into a granny flat while saving up to rebuild, so it felt good to help. Or so I thought.

Jen left on Monday, but not before trashing my house, leaving used condoms scattered across the bed. Turns out her so-called boyfriend was a client she'd met on the job. I felt like an absolute fool. When I tried to talk to her, she shrugged it off. That was the day I learned that empathy had an expiry date.

Nancy, on the other hand, was in her thirties—fairly average-looking, but she had confidence, and a body built to turn heads. Not that the men could see that over the phone, well, not until she decided to meet them. She milked the phone calls for all they were worth. She didn't care if the relationships were fake, as long as the perks were real. If a guy didn't seem worth her time, she'd promise to meet him in the city for a quick 'preview'. If he didn't meet her standards she'd vanish without a second thought. And somehow, the guys she'd left hanging always came crawling back for more.

Lexi was a stunner—a tall, blonde, busty lesbian who could've graced the cover of *Vogue* if she hadn't chosen stripping and backup dancing instead. She made serious cash teasing men with promises she never intended to keep. One night, she swooped in when I was fumbling through a call with a female client. Lexi took over and spun the kind of sensual magic that had me questioning whether I was on the wrong team.

Her connection with that client didn't end on the phone. Lexi met her—a wealthy, lonely woman in her late forties who lived in a Mosman mansion. Her businessman husband was always travelling, and she rationalised her fling with Lexi as 'not really cheating' because it wasn't with a man. Lexi walked away from that rendezvous with a stack of cash and a new appreciation for her own charm.

And then there was Danni, a thirty-year-old Persian beauty studying psychology. She had a magnetic voice that could talk a cactus into blooming. Danni never met clients in person—she believed some things were better left to the imagination. 'Otherwise, it might change how you see things,' she once told me. Her words stuck with me, especially as I began to question my own perceptions of the people I met.

Some women hoped to find real connections with clients, and I couldn't blame them. On the phone, some men sounded genuine, almost like a Hallmark card come to life. But reality had a way of slapping you in the face once you met them.

As for me, I kept searching for something outside of myself—an identity, a purpose. What I didn't realise was that the thing I was chasing was already within me. As I would find out, I didn't need a man to complete me. Who knew?

Lesson: To discover who you really are, focus on what matters most to you—your values and beliefs. Ignore the distractions and outside opinions. Trust your gut and let your instincts guide the way.

CHAPTER 11

Reckless rendezvous

Alex took me to the next step—one I could never come back from. It happened so fast. While my choices often led me astray, I had been chasing something elusive that was now crystal clear: I wanted to be someone's priority, not an afterthought. What I didn't expect was that I would earn a bad reputation along the way.

Sure, diving into flirtations wasn't the smartest way to figure things out, but it distracted me—until my mind hit a breaking point. I convinced myself that chasing passion was the answer to filling the void. But real relationships needed balance without fear or losing yourself.

Looking back, my upbringing messed up my ideas about relationships. I thought women had to settle, stay quiet, be insignificant. Breaking free from that mindset was empowering. I understood women could do anything—we choose it, and we own it.

After marrying Chris, I realised what I really wanted was a kind partner. Naturally, I was drawn to guys who seemed that way—like Alex, my first lover. A younger guy who didn't call the phone lines for sex talk, he just wanted to chat.

Alex, a businessman with mobile phone stores in Sydney and Canberra, became a regular during his travels. Our conversations ranged from random trivia to deep philosophical debates—not what you'd expect from a sex line, but I wasn't complaining. He challenged my old ideas, opened my mind, and made me feel heard. While my marriage crumbled, Alex felt like my ticket to freedom from my husband's grip.

Pretending I was heading to work, I met Alex at a motel near the Rosehill racetrack. He greeted me with a bouquet of flowers, kissed my cheek, and whispered, 'I want you badly.' The walk to the room was intense. Once the door closed, he undressed me sensually, kissing every part of my face and body—even the scars below my belly. He made me feel desired.

Over the next two months, we met a couple more times at a beachside motel. It was a short-lived arrangement, but it gave me the connection I needed to reclaim my power. It fed my soul and nourished my mind.

I'd had enough of Chris's unpredictable moods and violent outbursts. I never knew when he'd yell or strike, so I decided to shake things up. To ruffle Chris's feathers, I hatched a plan to meet Alex, in front of Chris, at the Paragon Hotel. By this stage, I couldn't have cared less.

Before we left, in the hope of driving Chris away for good, I told him I'd met someone through a friend at work. To my surprise, Chris didn't react. He suggested we talk about our issues away from the kids—as if he cared! I guess he didn't believe me, probably thought I was bluffing. Without missing a beat, I blurted out that he was my only problem. Suddenly, I felt like the hunter, and he was the prey. I didn't know what had overcome me, but there were moments of pure audacity on my part. I didn't care; it was like I knew I'd either get a backhander or he'd fall into his stupid, clouded mindset, afraid to lose me.

Not long after we arrived at the Paragon, Alex and his friend walked in—perfectly timed for our showdown. Alex flashed that charming smile, and I tilted my head, half-expecting a kiss.

'Hello, Lucia! What a surprise! Lovely to see you here.'

'Hey, Alex! Great to see you, too!'

I shot a grin at Chris, whose eyes widened. In that risky moment, I felt a mix of fearlessness and foolishness. This was my way of reclaiming power after enduring Chris for so long.

The conversation was quick, just niceties. Alex played his part perfectly, then casually strolled to the bar with his friend, promising to catch up—making sure Chris heard every word. As he walked away, a brief wave of apprehension washed over me, but I shoved it aside and turned to Chris. 'See? I wasn't kidding. I met someone.'

Chris threw in a few jabs about Alex's ethnicity—he was Pakistani—and acted like losing me to 'someone like him' was no big deal. His emotional cluelessness cranked up my frustration.

Honestly, could he be any more out of touch?

But within a week, Chris reeled me back in with flowers, heartfelt notes and sappy letters. He played the 'think of the family' card, using every emotional trick in the book. He painted himself as the victim, and I fell for it.

Then, as always, he turned the tables. My bravado petered out and I caved in, unsure of what to do. This back and forth had me feeling like I was losing my grip—no one to turn to for understanding. Everyone would just label me a whore.

Chris's manipulation didn't stop. He'd say, 'No one else will want you once they know the truth about you.' Meanwhile, he boasted about all the women supposedly throwing themselves at him. My mind was a mess. Was he right, or was I completely losing it?

Fear of the unknown held me back from leaving, yet I clung to the hope that Chris would change, convinced that leaving would only make things worse. I ended it with Alex and never heard from him again.

As for my bad reputation, Chris started spreading rumours. He told his friend I was a cheat—called me a trollop! One minute I was his queen and the next, I was a total strumpet. Why would he stay with me if he was out there spreading that kind of garbage? Was I missing something, or was he in training to become a garbage collector? Hell, what did I care? I just had to keep surviving until I could figure this all out and get the hell out of this goddamn mess.

Lesson: If you find yourself stuck in a situation you can't stand, don't just leap into the unknown—make a damn plan first. Trust me, you'll thank yourself later, and you won't end up face-first in another mess you can't escape.

CHAPTER 12

Thelma and Louise

A month into working the phone lines, I met Sandra during a night shift. She was ten years younger than me, a sweet yet sassy firecracker who lit up the dreary hours. Sandra quickly became the Louise to my Thelma, my kindred spirit in this bizarre new world. Like Geena Davis and Susan Sarandon's iconic duo, Sandra was Louise—bold, blunt, and never shy about calling things as she saw them. Meanwhile, I was the clueless Thelma—stuck in a dud of a marriage with my useless husband. We clicked like kindling meeting a match. She brought the blaze, and I didn't mind burning a little.

Originating from the quiet country town of Orange, she now lived just one suburb away from me. This arrangement worked out great; I could give Sandra a lift home whenever we worked together, making the trip enjoyable and safer than driving home alone and sleep-deprived at five thirty in the morning—or so I thought.

On a frosty winter morning, while driving home with Sandra fast asleep in the passenger seat, I dozed off for a millisecond—literally one street away from her block of units. Suddenly the car came to an abrupt stop, jolting our bodies awake. We were a little stunned, but then we burst out laughing. Maybe exhaustion had overtaken us and we were too delirious to cry, or maybe we were just in shock and didn't realise it at the time.

After a moment, we glanced at each other and Sandra bellowed, 'Damn, what are you doing, a Thelma and Louise?', alluding to that iconic cliff scene. That's when I noticed I had careened over a speed hump, slap-bang onto the wrong side of the road, missing the wall of the local leagues club by mere centimetres.

Everything inside the car had flown around and landed in all the wrong places. My trusty lippy—never went anywhere without wearing it—had somehow made its way up above my lip and nose. Perfect. Glancing at Sandra, I noticed a gash on her temple, small, yet bleeding like a crime scene. Her seatbelt was tucked under her arm, so when the car finally jerked to a stop, her head had hit the dash.

As for me, I took a hell of a knock to the chin, right on the steering wheel. Luckily it just bruised up, though my jaw ached like crazy for days.

We were too tired to get checked out, even though the hospital was only a two-minute drive away. Instead, we decided to head home and sleep it off. What absolute imbeciles we were. That little incident necessitated a wheel alignment, but more importantly, it taught me a hard lesson. I never let myself doze off at the wheel again. From that night on, I cranked the air conditioner full blast to stay awake, no matter how freezing it was outside.

Looking back, I realised how lucky we'd been not to end up in the morgue. It hit me hard—life was short, and I wasn't living it the way I should. For days after, a cloud of dread loomed over me, as if my future had already been stamped with 'nothing to show for it'. But Sandra wouldn't let me spiral. Her zest for fun turned every moment into a mini party.

At work she became my go-to for everything, especially on the phone lines. Sometimes we'd even have threesomes over the phone with men, only to laugh about it afterwards. We formed a close bond, often joking with clients that we were partners in crime. Sandra was assertive, meticulous, neat and independent—everything I wasn't but wanted to be.

She had a profound impact on me, nudging me towards change. Slowly but surely I noticed little shifts, from my appearance to my attitude, a transformation I welcomed with open arms. I stopped hiding behind the invisible shield I'd constructed to protect myself and began trusting my decisions. Shedding the irrelevance my husband had saddled me with felt like breaking free from chains I didn't realise I'd been dragging.

It wasn't an overnight miracle. Like a record stuck on repeat, I kept stumbling over the same lessons until they finally sank in. But Sandra was one of many people who left their mark on me, helping me see myself as someone who mattered—someone worth more than the scraps my marriage had left me with. Her influence, along with the lessons I'd learned from others, gave me the push I needed to keep moving forward.

Living under Chris's control made me painfully aware of how stifled I was. His ridiculous expectations, imposed on me since I was fifteen, started to crumble. Raising daughters forced me to consider not just my own future, but theirs too. The idea of staying married for security lost its appeal, especially since financial stability had always been a foreign concept to my clueless husband. Let's just say he was no John Rockefeller.

Opening up to Sandra about my life was like flipping through the pages of a book I hadn't dared to read before. She was my missing half—intelligent, tough, and grounded. I admired her deeply and wanted to carry a piece of her strength within myself.

Before Sandra, I was as naive as a lamb when it came to talking to men, tolerating whatever nonsense they threw my way. But Sandra's fiery spirit rubbed off on me and soon enough, we realised we were more alike than I thought. We both had a heart wrapped in care and kindness, but Sandra had a hell of a lot more sass.

Before I knew it, I was adopting her resilience. When men called and hurled insults, I held my ground. Their words didn't rattle me like they once did. The things they said were often immature and downright rude. Some men called just to verbally abuse women, proving they were nothing more than playground bullies stuck in a 1950s time warp. Narrow-minded idiots with teeny-weeny brains.

Whenever I'd had a hellish day at home, she'd spot it the second I walked in. With that sly smile, she'd say, 'Come on, wild child, here's your chance to let loose. Give those motherfuckers what's brewing inside you.' It was her way of telling me to unleash my inner lioness and make damn sure men knew they couldn't talk to me like that.

Sandra didn't just leave me with memories, she gave me a stunning rose-pink quartz crystal pendant. At first, I refused. It was too gorgeous! I wasn't used to receiving gifts. But she insisted, saying her time with it was over and it was meant for someone who needed it. At the time, I didn't understand the significance of crystals. Now I know rose-pink quartz is all about restoring trust, healing wounds and inviting love—from others and ourselves. I couldn't help but think she knew I needed a little extra love and peace.

Our paths crossed for a reason, even if just for a brief time, and it changed my way of thinking in ways I never expected.

Lesson: Don't settle for a second-rate life—grab the wheel, broaden your perspective and enrich your journey. Life's too short to be a backseat driver in your own story!

CHAPTER 13

Liquorice Allsorts

Having female friends who weren't afraid to speak the truth gave me a sense of camaraderie I couldn't ignore. These remarkable women, my partners in crime in the phone room, revealed their strengths and struggles just like I did. We were all striving for a better life, united despite our differences. Like a bag of liquorice allsorts, we were a colourful mix of personalities, each with our quirks, yet connected by our shared goals.

We were a diverse group. There were the quiet, intense ones, like black liquorice, and the lively, colourful ones, full of energy. Each added their own texture to the mix. Together, we formed an unexpected yet perfect balance, creating a dynamic that was as surprising as it was satisfying.

We all tried to balance our lives, finding flexibility in our work on the sex phone lines, often stretching beyond our six-and-a-half-hour shifts, because who didn't love a little overtime? The job was challenging and sometimes mind-numbing, like trying to find a needle in a haystack—while blindfolded, of course. But we persisted, chasing elusive bonuses that slipped through our fingers when clients hung up just as we were about to clinch that extra five bucks.

Some of us got downright creative, turning side hustles into mini business ventures. Coordinating private calls with men? Check. Going on dates with clients, hoping for more than just a dinner? Double check. For some, the dream was a connection—maybe even a man who saw us as more than a fantasy voice. The perks were fancy dinners, glittering gifts and that fleeting thrill of feeling valued. But to be honest—it often left us feeling more like a punchline than a queen. We tried convincing ourselves it was something more, but deep down, we knew better. If this job taught us anything, it was how to play the game. But the mind games it played with us in return? That was a whole different story, and not the kind we wanted.

On a positive note, each woman imparted valuable wisdom. Even though I didn't always grasp it immediately, when I finally did, it stuck with me like gum on a shoe.

There was Chelsea, a beautiful Māori woman who seamlessly blended business with pleasure. She met phone clients in person and had them call her at work to rack up bonuses.

Ingeniously, she played these men, tantalising them just enough to leave them craving more. In return she received leather jackets, dinners and jewellery—all without the company owners catching on to her little side hustle. Chelsea's story was a masterclass in human behaviour—resourcefulness, seduction and risk-taking.

Margaret, a lady in her fifties, hid her childhood trauma behind a jolly facade. She met men for sex as a way of punishing herself. She blamed herself for the sexual abuse she had suffered, telling me, 'I let it happen.' Hearing her speak about it triggered memories of my own childhood abuse at the hands of those two young boys. I had buried it all those years, denying myself the chance to mourn the loss of innocence.

Margaret was never to blame. She never let it happen. Whoever did bad things to her instilled fear and convinced her she was the cause. They flipped the guilt onto her, as most abusers do. I finally understood that I needed to give myself compassion and time to heal so the cycle of blame and guilt tied to childhood trauma could finally dissolve.

Not every woman's story was one of sadness, though. Take Bethany, for example—an absolute stunner with a curly mane of blonde hair, piercing green eyes and a determination that could move mountains. When she was eighteen, she started working in strip clubs and brothels, and quickly saw the potential for bigger earnings with a little enhancement in the chest department.

'The bigger the tits, the bigger the tips,' she'd say with a grin.

Now at age twenty-two, Bethany took on extra shifts on the phones, diligently saving for a breast enlargement. She had a clear goal in mind and wasn't about to let anything stand in her way. With the money she saved, her ultimate objective was to establish a women's lingerie line, because why not turn her experiences into a business? She had witnessed the lucrative potential of the industry. Bethany's drive for financial stability at such a young age was commendable, a path I had considered but ultimately hesitated to pursue. Sixteen years her senior, I lacked confidence yet admired her boldness.

One of her regulars at the strip club caught her attention. One evening, he bought her a drink and before she knew it, she found herself at his place. There, he proposed an opportunity for her to make some extra money. He was a submissive crossdresser. All she had to do was dress him in lingerie and take on the role of dominatrix.

Bethany loved playing the dominant role and raking in the cash. Soon she harboured desires to become a professional dominatrix. It was her ticket to financial independence and a stepping stone towards her ultimate goal. I left the phone lines before I could witness Bethany's dazzling transformation with her new breasts, but I was sure that, with her determination, she would go through with her plan—after all, nothing stood in Bethany's way! She opened my eyes to what could be. While it took me forever to find my own independence, women like Bethany sped up my crash course in what was possible.

Bethany got me—she understood my encounters with men but never passed judgement. She saw it as part of my journey and always reminded me to never lose sight of who I was. Her sharp eye and old-soul wisdom were priceless. She knew exactly what to say at the right moment. She even taught me to stop belittling myself for my choices, reminding me that every decision was a bold leap others might not have the guts to take.

Bethany's words stuck with me and carried me through some of my toughest days. She proved that wisdom wasn't tied to age—the young could teach us just as much as the old. Who said you couldn't learn a thing or two from a woman who'd just started paying her own bills?

Lesson: Hold your head high—doing what it takes to survive is a badge of honour, and not everyone has the guts to wear it.

CHAPTER 14

Valentino and the escort

Valentino's voice had a magnetic quality that drew me in with every word he spoke. Each inflection stirred a sense of excitement in me, making my skin tingle. I craved the thrill he brought into my life. Envisioning his breath on the side of my neck, I was captivated from the moment he uttered that first word. Or maybe I was just plain horny that night. Whatever it was, it felt good!

He stood out among the handful of men who genuinely engaged with me on the phone, complimenting my secret uninhibited nature.

By this point, I had been working the phone lines for about six months and sensed a change within myself, allowing me to speak openly with certain men. I could never be my true self around my husband, let alone express my opinions without facing mockery—especially after the Alex debacle.

In a sense, the opportunity to connect in intimate conversations with men was helping me in my process of self-discovery.

Despite knowing this was a fantasy phone line, I was undeniably drawn into Valentino's web. A euphoric feeling washed over me each time he flattered me, making me wish our conversations could go on indefinitely. Even though his stories made him sound like a player,

I still found myself devouring every word. He became my fantasy, my secret desire, occupying a special place in my thoughts—one no one could invade. As he recounted his erotic tales of passionate lovemaking-sessions, a pulsing, rhythmic beat stirred between my thighs and I wished he was right there with me. I indulged in fantasies about Valentino having me; his stories were the highs of my night. If only my husband knew the effect this place was having on my thoughts!

Although one specific story made me doubt the validity of his account, it also sounded like something a man might do, so I accepted it. During a business trip, his corporate partner in Tasmania arranged for a high-class escort as a welcome gift. In the back of my mind, I thought, *Aren't men so considerate of each other?* If only we women felt as comfortable doing the same!

Valentino portrayed the escort as an incredibly beautiful woman with long red hair cascading over her ample breasts. Hearing his vivid description sparked a hint of jealousy—perplexing, considering he wasn't my lover. I assumed I felt a strong connection to him, secretly hoping he saw me in that light. It might sound ludicrous, but there I was, feeling envy over a man I had only ever spoken to.

He recounted how he shared an intimate hour with the woman, and when his allotted time was up, she willingly extended it at no cost. Supposedly, she enjoyed the sex so much that she wanted more. According to him, by the time she departed, she was shaking all over from the multiple orgasms.

'Why keep pleasing her?' I asked.

'I get pleasure from seeing women get pleasure from me.'

Well, fuck me, I thought, *what a refreshing concept*. My husband had led me to believe that women were meant to be a man's servant and exist solely to please them. The notion of a man intentionally and genuinely wanting to bring pleasure to a woman, prioritising her needs, intrigued me.

I probed him further, eager to understand what he did to make her so happy and why she insisted on staying longer. He believed it was the way in which he connected with her.

'Oh, that's a novel idea,' I told him.

He let out an almighty laugh. 'I believe it was the way I caressed and kissed her. Even a working girl deserves attention, and besides, being able to please her makes me feel satisfied.'

After hearing him say that I felt like a complete fool. Here I was, working in the sex industry, making jest of a subject to which I could relate. 'Okay, you have me there. I get it; I apologise.'

He already had my full attention, so I asked him for details. He told me he would start by kissing her neck, then move to her lips, kissing them gently. First the top of her lip, then the bottom, then top and bottom together, ensuring he lingered while softly touching her bare breasts. He enjoyed sucking and nibbling on them while he slid his hand between her thighs, probing her gently, then slid his fingers inside her, pushing them back and forth until he made her wet.

'I have enormous hands and fingers, you know.'

I imagined they were like ten miniature cocks on the end of his hands. But, then again, I have seen men whose dicks were as small as ladies' fingers. I was beginning to think this woman must have thought all her Christmases had come at once with his fingers as big as cocks.

I wished I was that woman. It didn't sound like straight-up sex; this was more like sensual intimacy—the kind of romantic interlude I craved.

I interrupted and asked if she was doing anything to him—after all, it was part of her job description.

'No, she was enjoying everything I was doing to her, so why spoil it.'

Oh my fucking fuck, was all I could think. I wanted to reach into the handset, drag him towards me, and ride him hard. After taking a moment to regain my composure and adopt a more ladylike demeanour, I allowed him to continue.

He liked being on top of a woman, he said, so he would lay her down and put in half of his cock to tease her.

'Only half of your cock, how big is this damn thing?'

'I guess about average for a man my size, say fifteen centimetres.'

I chuckled. 'That's about average.'

'I suppose on the slack, and then it grows to over twenty centimetres or more and becomes fatter when I'm deep inside.'

'What? Holy shit, what do you mean it grows fatter when it's inside a woman?'

Amused, he responded, 'It grows thicker in width.'

I was gobsmacked and took a moment to pull myself together.

'I've never had one that big inside me, I don't think it would fit. I'd need to put a couple of doughnuts on your dick to stop it from penetrating so deep. But, knowing me, I'd get hungry and eat the damn doughnuts.'

He was in hysterics. 'I would get you so wet, and make sure it slid in easily.'

'No, thank you, that would send me insane,' I politely replied.

'Well, I need to make a woman have multiples.'

'What do you mean—multiple orgasms?'

He assured me it happened, but only if a woman was really turned on. That's why it was important to ensure any woman he had was fully satisfied.

Now I really felt like I was missing out on something amazing and needed to find it.

'I can stay hard for hours without coming. It's a tantric self-control method to prolong the journey.'

'I don't understand what you're saying. What's this tantric stuff you're talking about?'

'When I feel close to ejaculating, I stay still for a few moments and concentrate on my breathing, almost putting myself into a meditative state.'

'Yes, please, I'll have some of that.'

He offered to meet up with me, and I did seriously contemplate it but decided against it.

I knew that if everything I fantasised about him came true, he would have been hard to give up. I didn't want to get a taste of ecstasy and then let it go. Then again, he could have been blowing smoke up my arse. I would have been disappointed. So I let the dream live on.

Lesson: Sometimes, the best lessons come from the most unexpected places—like a phone conversation with a guy who thinks he's the next tantric guru.

CHAPTER 15

1300 Advice at your service

My official job description was as vague as a politician's promises, but one thing was certain: I had to keep callers on the line for as long as possible. This meant I could dish out any advice I deemed useful—or completely off the wall—when they asked for it. Each call was like a new challenge, and they were all unforgettable. I was like that friend who always listened, the unofficial shrink for anyone looking for answers.

It was just before my shift ended when twenty-something Marcus called for advice on how to break up with his clingy girlfriend. He felt platonic towards her and, despite the guilt, craved new experiences.

Not being an expert, I suggested he be honest: 'How hard can that be? If you don't want a committed relationship, why lead her on?'

'Wouldn't it be easier to just say you're having a fling?' he muttered.

I pointed out how cruel that sounded and questioned why he called if he already knew the answer. After a moment, he agreed to consider her feelings and abruptly ended the call. No bonus for me, still, at least I helped some poor woman dodge a heartbreak bullet from Mr Clueless!

Next up was Bradley, a thirty-something guy with an awkward vibe, grappling with a similar issue. I guided him on how to end things with his long-time girlfriend—without my help, he might have ended up married with a dozen kids, thanks to his indecisiveness.

It hit me that the advice I gave to others also applied to me. When I suggested he be honest, he unexpectedly broke down and revealed, 'I'm gay, and my name is Matteo, not Bradley.'

Yikes! I felt terrible for the mix-up, especially knowing the societal pressure Matteo faced as an Italian man. Being Italian myself, I understood the weight of his revelation, but I really could've been more tactful in my response: 'Come on, Matteo, find your balls and get some courage.' He chuckled, sniffling a bit, and I added, 'Put yourself in her shoes. Not knowing the real reason for the break-up would be torture—you owe her that.'

Sure, confronting his girlfriend could have repercussions, but he'd be staying true to himself. I marvelled at how I was hitting my bonus half-hour mark while having such a heartfelt conversation. Was it insensitive to think about making a little extra cash during this serious chat? Nah! This was my job, and I needed the money.

Matteo's plan was to spill the beans to his girlfriend, hoping she wouldn't be too upset about wasting her time. A week later, he called with an update: she took it well and empathised with him. But here's the kicker—she spotted him with another guy who just happened to be her ex! They eventually laughed about the idea that she had turned them both gay.

I told him she probably said that in jest, and he should thank her next time they met. He should tell her that people were drawn to her beautiful nature, and it had nothing to do with her influencing anyone's sexuality. Words were powerful, after all—they could cut deep or help heal.

Then came Thomas, a thirty-three-year-old guy from a small town who tragically lost his partner in a motorbike accident. He felt utterly lost, especially since he had just moved to the country five months before to be with Brad. Everyone thought they were just flatmates, but he feared they'd be ostracised if people found out about their relationship. Now he was contemplating moving back to Sydney, feeling torn between leaving and betraying the love he shared with Brad.

This was quite the pickle. We chatted for over an hour, diving deep into how Thomas could move forward. I validated his feelings, and he realised that no matter where he lived, Brad's love would always be tucked away in his heart. Our conversation opened my eyes to the fears people faced about being judged for their sexuality. It also reminded me of the biases I felt, worrying about what people would think of me if they knew I was talking dirty to men for a living.

Thomas's call snapped me back to reality. Yep, even on a sex line, I was helpful and valuable. Apparently, my words and listening skills counted for something and, as weird as it might sound, it allowed me to actually appreciate my job. Who knew?

Lesson: Don't sell yourself short! Celebrate who you are, because what you bring to the table could really change someone's life for the better.

CHAPTER 16

Lace up your bootstraps

Before I could get a word in, the man on the other end of the line barked, 'What's your name, sweetheart?'

'Dominique. My name is Dominique.'

'Well, Dominique, I hear the same crap from you women every time I call. So, what makes you special? What can you offer me that I haven't heard already?'

Without skipping a beat, I fired back, 'Well, for starters, I could teach you some manners.'

He snorted. 'By the way, my name's Dick.'

Of course it was. 'Well, Dick, you're really living up to it.' He nearly choked on his own laughter.

'To be honest, Dick, we do our best to keep things interesting, but some men, well, they're just impossible to satisfy.'

He let out a chuckle. 'I've got to say, you've got spunk. But when life gets tough, you just pull up your bootstraps and stop complaining, you know?'

'Nope. Not a clue.'

'It's a metaphor, my dear.'

'A metaphor?' I raised an eyebrow. 'Well, aren't you just a human thesaurus.'

'It's a figure of speech. You're the first woman I've talked to with the guts to say what's really on her mind. I'll stay on the line. Let's chat.'

'Well, I appreciate that, Dick. So, what exactly are you after tonight?'

'Nothing, just wanted to hear your sweet voice and give you something to think about.'

I rolled my eyes so hard I nearly saw the back of my head. Classic arrogance. Yet, his words lingered long after we hung up, like glitter that refused to be vacuumed up. Most nights, I dragged myself through the exhaustion, keeping guys on the line just long enough to hit that sweet bonus. And I was surprisingly good at it. As much as I hated to admit it, there was something about that brief conversation with such an assertive guy that stuck with me.

I'd handled my fair share of tough clients before. Pushing through those unpredictable calls became my nightly workout—equal parts stamina and sheer will. Even when a pack of guys joined forces, talking over each other like hyenas competing for the title of Most Obnoxious, I handled it. Honestly, their nonsense was so absurd it was almost entertaining. Almost.

Some callers burned money like they were at a Vegas strip club; others barely qualified as functioning humans. And then there were the stoners—so baked they thought their own echo was riveting. Then again, I wasn't here for a motivational seminar; I was here for the bonus.

My secret weapon was determination and maybe a little spite. Outsmarting these clowns felt like winning a game. Dick's advice about 'pulling up my bootstraps' wasn't so bad after all—ugh, I hated that he was right. When things got too dicey, I'd signal one of the girls for backup. Together, we'd tag-team the chaos. My personal therapy? Smacking the handset on the desk like it owed me rent.

It was a battlefield, and I had my armour: wit, sarcasm and the ability to not take it personally. Well, most of the time.

One evening, a pair of intoxicated buffoons decided to treat me to their version of a roast. 'Slut' was the word of the night, spat with all the creativity of a wet sock. I'd handled name-calling before, but this time it hit a nerve. What gave these losers the audacity to think they were superior just because I worked on a sex line? Oh, they could have their fun on the weekends, but tearing me down made them feel like real men? Please.

After the call, one of the guys had the nerve to call me back—this time, to apologise for his buddy's idiocy. Go figure. We ended up having a surprisingly decent chat that earned me a ten-dollar bonus—a nice little cherry on top of an otherwise rotten sundae. He even asked what I looked like and why I worked the phones, then casually threw out a date proposal. Bless his heart. I suggested he keep calling if he wanted to get to know me better, but deep down, we both knew there wasn't a date in his future.

In this business, it wasn't uncommon for men to try their luck, hoping to turn phone chemistry into a real-life connection. Sure, it stung a little when one of my regulars decided to chat up a different operator, although, sharing clients came with the territory.

Except for Bambi. She wasn't just good—she was a phone line assassin. With her smooth voice and quick wit, she snatched up some of my best clients like it was a sport.

Lesson: Stay positive, roll with the punches and keep your eyes on the prize—because in this game, cash is king.

CHAPTER 17

The zookeeper and me

Okay, so today wasn't winning any awards for best mood. Everything felt like it was piling up, especially after a heated argument with my husband. I drove to work feeling a bit down, maybe it was just the universe testing my superhero skills. Who didn't love a good challenge?

As I let the phone ring a bit too long, my supervisor gently reminded me to, 'Pick up the damn phone.'

'Hey there, you're speaking with Dominique! What's your name, gorgeous?'

'The name's Maloney.'

'Well, Maloney, you're definitely the sexiest voice I've heard tonight!' Little did he know I said that to everyone … and he was my first call of the night.

His laughter was the perfect icebreaker, and the banter flowed like water. I learned all about Maloney and his real-life zoo in Mildura, a beautiful part of Victoria. Just like that he became a regular, calling twice a week.

Eventually, our phone fling escalated. We swapped private numbers and I even vented about my marital drama. Things got real when he sent me a huge bouquet and a stuffed gorilla with a sweet note.

Luckily, they showed up before Chris got home. I trashed the note, hid the gorilla in my children's toy box, and spun a tale that the flowers were from a colleague who appreciated the rides home.

Strange as it sounded, a connection was building as he started revealing personal details about his life. One day, he sent me a VHS recording of a car commercial featuring a panther from his zoo. In it there was an interview showing his three-year-old daughter casually playing with a fully grown lion in her bedroom. The absurdity of it had me hooked. His openness made it feel like he was falling for me.

This became my escape from the daily struggles with my husband. After a month of phone calls, our attraction jumped from late-night chats to meeting in person—a choice that turned out to be both the best and worst decision of my life. If nothing else, it taught me two things: boundaries were crucial, and my heart had a flair for turning emotional chaos into a full-blown soap opera.

By this point I was desperate to change my circumstances. Chris had crossed a line with a disgusting sexual attack, and that was the final straw—I had to break the toxic cycle. The fear of telling Chris I didn't love him anymore disappeared, replaced by a boldness likely fuelled by all the lessons I'd soaked up on the phone lines.

I hit him where it hurt, confronting him about all his shady behaviour—his mysterious three-month trip to Nimbin, his get-rich-quick schemes, and every way he'd let me and the girls down. I pushed harder than ever, making it clear I was done tolerating his nonsense. To top it off, I told him I needed a week off to think things through. Bold move? Sure. Long overdue?

Absolutely.

Of course, I didn't tell Chris the whole truth about Maloney. Instead, I whipped up a story about how he'd bought some of my creations from a store in Sydney and wanted to stock personalised goodies in his zoo shop, which I would take to him in person. Not a total lie, but honestly, who cared at that point? I was done playing nice.

His response? No shouting, no slapping, just a weak, 'Okay, take your break.'

At first I was confused, even felt a twinge of guilt, but then it hit me—he was playing mind games. So, I kept my face stone-cold, refusing to give him any satisfaction.

I had already organised this with Maloney a few weeks earlier, making these creations at work during breaks. He eagerly agreed to stock my quirky handmade zoo-themed finger puppets—think Old MacDonald's farm, but with a twist. Instead of a farmer, I made Maloney the star, surrounded by his zoo animals. This felt like a promising new chapter, a real chance to achieve some financial stability. But in the back of my mind, I couldn't shake the feeling that Chris was agreeing a little too easily. Maybe he thought if he played nice I'd forget about leaving him.

I knew better. Chris no longer deserved my love, kindness or forgiveness. I was ready to experience real love and in my mind, I'd found that with Maloney. His charm was impossible to resist; he made me feel wanted with every word he spoke.

Once I decided to leave, things moved quickly. Within the week I was packing for a solo interstate journey. I loaded up personalised cups, coasters and those quirky finger puppets. I was confident my daughters would be in good hands with my mother there, bunking up in their bedroom. She never warmed to Chris. He caused too many family squabbles. She knew he was a dick.

To everyone else it appeared I was focused on setting up my own business, which, in a way, I was. However, I also needed to explore whether there was more to this connection.

I left on a Wednesday, scheduled to return on Sunday. Chris insisted on driving me to the airport. As I stepped out of the car he handed me an envelope and urged me to open it on the plane—a two-page handwritten letter.

Immediately, I recognised his intent: to evoke empathy. But I had grown weary of his manipulative tactics. Why should I buy into his attempts when he had never treated me with anything other than disdain, viewing me merely as his plaything to be ordered around? Memories of how easily he degraded me in public—yelling, belittling, and even slapping me across the face when he wanted to shut me up, not to mention forcing himself on me—were still vivid. His letter, full of lies to make himself seem humble, didn't fool me for a second.

Upon arriving at Mildura in a small light aircraft, I walked off the tarmac to be greeted by Maloney holding a massive bouquet of flowers. He didn't attempt to kiss me, and while I initially thought it was out of respect, I now wonder if he was concerned about who might have witnessed such an act.

He drove me to the cabin I had booked for my stay, ensuring I was comfortably settled with food and drinks he had stocked in the fridge. Later that afternoon he returned to take me to his home for dinner.

Maloney's home had a glass partition wall between the dining and kitchen areas, offering a view of lush ferns and large, deep-green emu eggs speckled with bluish hues scattered on the ground. It was a magical sight, unlike anything I had ever seen.

That night felt comforting and familiar, reminiscent of our conversations over the phone, instilling a sense of hope for the future.

The next day Maloney gave me a tour of his zoo, and I handed over my handmade items for him to sell. He also introduced me to a woman in her twenties who worked in the cafe. Over the next few days, I found out they had an on-and-off casual thing. Her body language screamed uncertainty, like she saw me as competition. A pang of jealousy hit me, but I quickly reminded myself that whatever they'd had was over. I was here now, and if there'd been anything between them it was ancient history.

On my second night there Maloney took me to this fancy restaurant owned by Stefano de Pieri—you know, the guy with the cooking show everyone was obsessed with back then. As a surprise, he gave me Stefano's cookbook, *A Gondola on the Murray*, and even arranged for me to meet the man himself. Stefano signed the book, and I was floating on cloud nine, thinking nothing could ruin this night.

Just outside the restaurant, Maloney pulled me aside and pressed me against a sandstone wall. It felt so primal, so raw—it set me on fire. I could feel his heart pounding, our bodies melting together like butter on hot toast. The anticipation nearly killed me, but his kiss … totally worth the wait—gentle, yet with enough force to keep it interesting.

Afterwards, I buried my face in his chest, inhaling his sweet scent like it was the best cologne I'd ever smelled. His hands slid over the back of my neck, lifting my chin as he whispered that I was beautiful. And just when I thought it couldn't get any better, he kissed me again. And again. Like he didn't want it to end, and honestly, neither did I.

The next morning Maloney dropped me off at my cabin and I spent the day exploring the area. I took a paddleboat ride on the Murray River—just me, the water, and my thoughts.

The third night was different. Maloney's friend Jim invited us to a barbecue on his houseboat. Stepping aboard, I was shocked to find it was more like a floating home than a boat—complete with all the comforts. On the deck, when Jim offered me a beer, I politely turned it down for a glass of white wine. That's when he casually pulled a rope from the side of the houseboat and—voila—a six-pack of stubbies appeared. Beers rising out of the river. I couldn't believe it. I always thought they came from a fridge, not the water.

I must have appeared astonished because Maloney laughed at me, saying I was cute, and then he made a joke about it, which made me feel stupid.

The men swiftly consumed all those beers and then some more. All the while I slowly sipped my single glass of wine.

Once the seafood was cooked we gathered around the dining table inside, enjoying the meal and conversation. Jim seemed genuinely interested in the business I was attempting to launch—or so I thought.

After finishing the meal we returned to the deck, where the guys indulged in more beers. Concern crept in, as Maloney had to drive us home. When I expressed my worries and suggested they take a break from drinking, all I got was an agitated response from Maloney, who told me I could drive instead.

I shot back, 'I can't drive a manual, especially a big four-wheel drive, and I don't know how to get us home!' He ignored me, which only upset me more.

Before I knew it, the men had stripped down to their undies and jumped in the water, asking me to join them. I told them I had no swimmers. They jeered, insisting I strip down and jump in. Discomfort twisted my gut. I refused, and then it began to sprinkle, so I went inside and started packing up the table. That's when Maloney and Jim climbed back onto the houseboat.

I was stretching out to reach the plates on the other side of the table when Maloney came up behind me, dripping wet, kissing and touching me in front of Jim. I was annoyed and demanded he stop, telling him I wanted to be taken home.

In a joking manner, Maloney apologised, saying it was just a bit of fun. I didn't know what to make of it all, and then the bomb dropped. Jim started asking me questions about the phone lines and what else we women did. I became furious. Maloney had told him all about me and how we met. From there, the conversation went downhill.

Jim alluded to how much fun a threesome would be. That was it for me. I cried and yelled at the top of my lungs to be taken home. I was thinking I might possibly have placed myself in a bad situation, and it was my fault.

Both men looked panicked, doing their best to calm me down. Maloney told me we were going.

In the car, I leaned my head against the window, feeling the agonising silence stretch across the entire drive back, broken only by the occasional sob I couldn't hold back.

When we got to Maloney's place, he apologised—like, really apologised—and asked me to stay the night, saying that he wanted to make things right. He poured himself a whiskey, then another. I stuck with water. His intentions quickly became obvious as he leaned in for a kiss, and before I knew it we were tumbling into bed. He blindfolded me, and in the haze of it all, one thought kept circling: *Is this pity sex? Because I'm not sure I'm into this.*

Once again, I was in a predicament I should not have been in with a man I believed to be sweet when, in fact, he was not. Maloney was kissing me all over. Then he got off the bed and returned with what sounded like a handheld electric mixer coming towards me. *Surely not*, I thought, then it jittered on my breasts and slowly slid down my body.

I ripped the blindfold off to see Maloney pressing an electric vibrator, which was plugged into an extension cord, up between my thighs. *Where did this pre-historic thing come from?!*

'No fucking way are you putting that thing inside me!' I yelled. 'I'm not getting electrocuted tonight, Maloney.' With that, I rose from the bed. 'You know what, Maloney? I'm going back to my cabin. This isn't fun anymore.' My words spilled out as I stumbled about searching for my clothes. 'You put me in an awkward position back there with your mate. What the hell was that about?'

Maloney offered a feeble excuse, claiming he thought I was more open-minded and would enjoy the attention. 'You do work on a sex line anyway,' he added.

My jaw dropped. 'And what's that supposed to mean, mate? Just because I talk dirty to men for a living doesn't mean I'm everyone's sex object!'

In that moment, it hit me, Maloney was way more hammered than I'd first realised. His words were slurring, and he was in no condition to be behind the wheel. With the hour creeping into ridiculous territory and a cab probably as likely as a unicorn sighting, I made the call to stay the night. I set up camp on the farthest side of the bed, like the Grand Canyon was between us. Boundaries, my friend, boundaries.

The next morning Maloney's mood had shifted, like he was trying to dodge me. He was all business—rushing to make coffee and toast, then dropping the bomb that he was 'too busy' to hang out and would drive me back to the cabin. His sudden distance was as clear as day. I could feel it.

So, I grabbed my sketchbook and spent the day by the river, drawing trees and mulling over my life's mess. It didn't take long to realise that sticking around was a waste of time. I called my husband and booked a flight home. No more waiting around.

I rang Maloney to let him know I was leaving. I told him how he'd made me feel like an afterthought during my stay. He was taken aback, apologised, and even offered to drive me to the airport the next morning.

On the drive over, we made some peace. He apologised again, admitting I was a great lady but that we just didn't click. *Please*, I thought, *our 'clicking' was not the problem.*

I decided to leave him with one last piece of advice: respect boundaries, and don't forget women have standards.

'Next time you're with a lady, treat her like one,' I urged him.

He nodded, taking off his favourite cap and bowing his head. Seizing the moment, I grabbed the cap and declared, 'It's mine now.' Surprisingly, he allowed me to take it.

Our parting was marked by a final kiss goodbye. I inhaled one last whiff of his scent. As he walked away, gradually blending into the crowd, I couldn't contain the tears. It wasn't because things didn't work out, but because I felt foolish for harbouring the belief in the possibility of happiness. The realisation that a man I had met through a phone line perceived me as nothing more than an appetiser added a layer of sorrow to my emotions.

Strangely, Maloney and I stayed in touch over the next month, chatting about all sorts of things. I even sent a birthday gift—a Barbie doll—to his little girl. At home life went on as usual, with thoughts of breaking free from Chris temporarily pushed to the backburner. Honestly, my attempts to plan a getaway seemed to flop every time. What was I doing wrong?

Maloney and I eventually stopped speaking. I think it was the thrill of the unknown that had fuelled our initial interest over the phone, and after that semi-disastrous trip, all desire had fizzled.

Meanwhile, Chris was biding his time, acting nice and waiting for me to feel secure in our relationship before reverting to his usual self.

Lesson: *The wrong relationships teach us what boundaries we need to set, leading us to the right one.*

CHAPTER 18

The Viagra conference

I arrived at my accountant's office just as the receptionist's perturbed expression made it clear I wasn't expected—especially since it was closing time on a Friday.

'Hello, I'm Lucia. I'm here to see Freddo.'

She flipped through her diary with a pointed air.

'I don't have an appointment, but I spoke directly with Freddo, and he promised he could fit me in after hours.'

Her eyebrows shot up in disapproval. 'I wish I had been informed about these arrangements.'

I smiled and shrugged. She frowned, muttered something about leaving, and instructed me to wait until Freddo's conference ended. She gathered her things, slammed the door behind her, and I figured she was headed out for a well-deserved drink.

Seated on the couch, I heard Freddo's voice in Italian. Though I didn't speak it fluently, I could make out enough to catch him bragging about his Vegas trip. *Typical little fucker*, I thought. When he switched to English I knew he was watching his language with the receptionist around.

Freddo boasted about all the 'arse' he'd scored and how careful he had to be not to bring home a 'souvenir' for his wife. I assumed that meant an STI. *Lucky wife*, I thought cynically.

After a decade of knowing Freddo, his deceitful nature was finally coming into focus—married with four young kids, a stay-at-home wife, and more disposable income than sense. He never grumbled about her endless spending on the home renovations, and I finally understood why.

He'd forgotten our appointment, so I shifted on the couch, trying to grab his attention. A few subtle noises didn't do it, but things got interesting when Freddo started talking about taking Viagra with his wife. He hoped it'd boost his performance—spoiler, it didn't. Instead, it made things worse. I wondered how many guys were in the same boat, going on about the dizziness and swearing off the stuff for good.

I heard what sounded like an old guy bragging about his four-hour erection in Vegas. He'd hired two escorts, but apparently, they couldn't keep up with his so-called stamina. *Oh, gross*. I couldn't help picturing those poor women. If he needed Viagra, odds were he didn't have much to work with in the first place.

I thought I'd heard it all until some guy started ranting about a 'slut with big tits', claiming she wanted more after everyone else had her without payment. Honestly? Why did men feel the need to slap labels on women they were clearly paying to fulfil their own desires? Sex workers would never refuse payment—it was their job. A transaction, plain and simple. These guys were delusional.

Honestly, even though I was only thirty-eight at the time, I wanted to bust in there, channelling my future Italian nonna, slap them about the head, and call them '*stupidos*.'

Each man tried to outdo the other with tales of sexual escapades. It was a game to them, but I was sure none of them could attract a woman on their own. Truth be told, I felt grateful for the women in the industry. They were heroes for dealing with these idiots day in and day out.

I decided I'd heard enough. I got up and slammed the front door, feigning my arrival.

'Hello?' I called out.

It worked! Freddo emerged with a smile, assuring me he wouldn't keep me waiting long. The three men stepped out of his office. Let's just say oil paintings they were not. They scrutinised me as they went—well, my tits, at least—and exchanged a few words in Italian.

Freddo was clearly trying to keep things discreet, hoping I didn't catch what they said.

In his office, Freddo apologised for the comments, blaming it on typical male behaviour around a good-looking woman. I bit my tongue and brushed it off with a sarcastic smile, although I did want to say, 'No, please enlighten me, dickhead.'

In the middle of our discussion, Freddo casually commented, 'What those guys said about you is true. You have amazing breasts.'

I froze. Did he really just say that? I just smiled, though I wanted to kick him in the nuts to repay the compliment, my style. He was taking things too far.

Then he suggested I come back to sign some paperwork once he finished up. As I stood to leave, he leaned in, saying he'd love to kiss me 'just once.'

I frowned. 'You're kidding, right?'

He wasn't. I had a few choice words for him but didn't bother. I was done.

A few weeks later, his secretary called, asking me to come in and sign the paperwork. I told her to send it. I had no intention of letting Freddo harass me again.

But he tried—calling me, texting me for months, suggesting we could 'just be friends'. Was I wearing a neon sign flashing *Please fuck me*? That was the last time he got my business.

Lesson: Don't be afraid to stand up to anyone who disrespects you.

CHAPTER 19

Josie and the Pussycats and other fun tales

Peering down at the street through the massive window eleven storeys up on a Saturday night wasn't the grand life I'd pictured for myself. Far from ideal, sure, but at least I had a view to remind me the outside world still existed. I watched as people strolled by, soaking up the intoxicating buzz of Sydney. Just a concrete wall separated me from that vibrant energy, where life seemed more alive than my own.

Instead, I was stuck in a room with a group of women, waiting for the phone to ring. Every now and again I'd let my mind drift. I'd imagine myself down there, heels clicking on the pavement, brushing past someone who might spoil me rotten for a night. Because honestly, a little pampering never hurt anyone, right? That was my secret—the thing that helped me survive those long nights and kept my head in the game.

That wave of melancholy hit me right at the start of my shift, but it didn't last long. A quick glance around the room at the familiar faces snapped me out of it—we were all in the same boat.

There was Jane, rocking faded jeans and a crisp white off-the-shoulder midriff tee. Her beach-bleached waves tumbled over her perfectly shaped breasts, and yeah, I couldn't help but wish mine were that perky. Four babies later, I was relying on underwire to boost their visual appeal and help me deal with the idea they would never be the same.

Most of the women on the graveyard shift dressed for comfort—trackpants and tees, like they were gearing up for a movie binge, not to talk dirty to strangers. How bloody weird was that? Talking dirty to a stranger. But it paid the bills.

I chose something in between—jeans and a snug-fitting top. If only the clients knew their late-night fantasies were coming from women in casual gear, not the sexy lingerie we described on the phone. What would they think?

There was Josie, irreplaceable and unapologetically unconventional, sitting next to me. At thirty, she was the definition of a free spirit, with long dreadlocks twisted at the top of her head like some artsy bird's nest. She wore her usual getup—a worn-out, pale-brown leather jacket over a vintage cotton dress dotted with tiny pink flowers, paired with men's work boots. Mismatched, but somehow, it all worked. It was so … Josie.

She lived in a tiny studio apartment behind Wynyard station. I didn't even know people lived in the city. I swear, I must've been the most naive woman on the planet back then.

Josie passed the time sketching as she spoke to men on the phone. The filthier the language, the more intensely her pencil moved across the paper. Watching her work was like being on a hallucinogenic drug; it was intoxicating. The end results were large, orgasmic abstract images of beauty. Josie was ahead of her time, producing art unlike anything I'd seen.

She lugged in her art tools, cranking out pieces so detailed they belonged in a gallery. One day she proudly showed me a magnificent dragon, painted so meticulously it looked like it was about to slither off the paper. I was in awe. Every page of her sketchbook outdid the last, filled with shimmering blush tones and almost three-dimensional swirls of pastel pinks, yellows, and browns. She urged me to feel the painting, which had this oddly satisfying mix of silky-smooth patches and raised rough bits. I had no clue what the painting was supposed to mean, but I didn't care. I enjoyed gliding my fingers over it in a figure eight.

Josie giggled. 'You're rubbing a pussy; you know that, right?'

We burst out laughing. I nicknamed her Josie and the Pussycats on the spot. Once I looked a little closer, there it was: a vulva in all its glory. I flipped through her sketchbook again, this time really taking it all in. Every page was a dazzling tribute to vaginas—each more stunning than the last.

Josie instantly joined the growing list of women who inspired me—bold, creative, and fearless.

Just then, reality kicked in as the calls started pouring in, and it was pure bedlam. The witching hour for horny men had arrived. Picture the frenzy of shoppers racing through a department store on sale day—except instead of hunting for bargains, we were answering calls. One call would end and another would start almost immediately. Even the supervisor got caught up in the madness, taking calls like a seasoned pro.

The room felt alive, like a whirlwind. We bounced from desk to desk, each of us frantic not to miss a single call. Women's voices cut through the chaos, and I heard, 'Hey, it's your regular, Daniel!' signalling for me to scoot to another booth.

The pace was relentless. Cords from handsets twisted into a tangled mess, resembling a poorly made spider's web as we scrambled between calls. We relied on our trusty stimulant—coffee—to stay awake and manage the endless stream of men getting off to the sounds of our voices.

Things took an interesting turn during an intimate conversation with a regular caller. I felt a tap on my shoulder. It was Sandra, the Thelma to my Louise, signalling for a double. She traced a figure eight in the air, then pointed two fingers converging at its centre.

I got her signal but hesitated, unsure if I could juggle it while staying focused on my call. She thrust the phone at me, and suddenly I found myself with two phones pressed against my head, trying to listen to my client and guess what Sandra's was saying to her. It was like a game of charades, except no one was winning.

Sandra alternated between pulling the mouthpiece away to talk to her client and thrusting it back towards me so he could hear my seductive words. While trying to focus on my client, I told him I wanted his cock deeper. Sandra started making obscene hand gestures in front of me, distracting me even more. It was like a bizarre circus act, and I was the clown.

From an outsider's perspective, the scene must have been quite the show, but by this point I was exhausted. My thoughts were a tangled mess, and Sandra was clearly enjoying herself, listening to my increasingly nonsensical responses while relishing the chaos. Somehow, I figured out from her hand signals that her client wanted me to describe how she was licking me.

Meanwhile, my client was demanding that I tell him to pound me harder. Fatigue had set in, and I rocked back and forth in my chair, knees pulled to my chest. Suddenly, the chair gave way with a loud thump, and I tumbled backwards.

'Oh, fuck me dead,' I groaned, looking up at Sandra for help.

Her response? She straddled me while still talking to her client, of course.

When my client asked what happened, I told him I fell off the bed because he was screwing me so hard. He took it as gospel and we continued like nothing had happened.

Sandra's client asked what was going on and she casually told him she was using a dildo to pound me against the wall. With her body weight on me, it kind of felt like she was. I have no idea why he believed her, but he did. Sandra kept pretending to hump me while I stayed deep in conversation with my client.

It was absurd yet fascinating how these men truly believed the scenarios we created. We were all just actors playing our parts—and playing them well. My client was satisfied and we ended the call like old friends. Sandra and I laughed at the madness that had just taken place. We ended up earning two bonuses that night.

Later that evening Sandra asked me to help her with tanning lotion—she had a date the next night and wanted to have that healthy glow. At first, the tan didn't appear, but I was right into a conversation with my client and barely paying attention. Then, as she walked towards the exit to leave for the night, I noticed it looked slightly patchy. But I was certain it would even out in time.

Two nights later Sandra walked in and flashed me a thumbs-up. I asked her about her date, and she revealed the zebra-striped tan on her legs.

'Oh, shit,' I mouthed. 'Sorry, girl!'

She took it in her stride, saying it gave her and her date the perfect icebreaker. Turns out zebra stripes were great for a laugh, and she got to be herself. Needless to say, Sandra never asked for my help with tanning lotion again—and I didn't blame her.

Lesson: Find inspiration in others—their passion and humour can reveal our own potential and remind us not to take life too seriously.

CHAPTER 20

What's your colour?

The phone lines opened my eyes to the bias surrounding lifestyles and sexuality. At first, I let others' opinions sway me, but I quickly realised I didn't have to adopt their disapproval. I started a journey of self-discovery—one free from external judgement—and saw how upbringing, religion and culture shaped people's views. Some couldn't accept differences out of fear. While I had gay friends, I hadn't fully grasped the struggles they faced just to be accepted.

Then along came my next client, Rowan, who completely shifted my perspective. We clicked instantly, and as he shared his story, I gained a deeper understanding of love, loss, and resilience—a life filled with both joy and hardship. Rowan later introduced me to his partner, Jamie, and their openness caught me off guard. They were miners in a small Western Australian town, hiding their love in a community steeped in old-school values.

Their bravery stirred a deep sadness in me, reminding me of my own struggles to embrace who I really was. Then Jamie's revelation hit me hard, they were ready to leave the mining life and dive into organic farming, a dream they'd been building towards for months. I couldn't help but admire their courage. They had scraped together enough to buy a property but needed more to make it a reality.

As they shared their plans, I felt a twinge of envy. They were out there shaping their future, while I was stuck squinting for a glimpse of mine. If I was ever going to break free from my own oppression, I needed a plan. After all, you don't leap out of a plane without a parachute, right?

Curious, I asked Jamie how they met. Turns out they'd both worked office jobs while attending evening agriculture classes. Fate stepped in during a practical experience placement when they ended up on the same worksite. On a scorching day, Rowan held a bag of mulch while Jamie spread it in the garden. When the heat became unbearable, shirts came off, and their chemistry was undeniable.

With the homeowners away and their supervisor at another site, they seized the moment. At a luxurious Dover Heights mansion, complete with jaw-dropping harbour views and an outdoor pool shower, they had raw, sensuous sex.

I couldn't help but laugh and say I should've been the one paying them for this call. They cracked up, admitting it was the first time they'd shared that story. I could tell recounting it had turned them on, and they wanted me to listen as they got it on. For me, it was part voyeurism, part lesson in technique—a crash course in spicing up future calls. I wondered if my presence added to their pleasure. It was an odd privilege to be part of their moment, even from a distance.

A few minutes later, the phone dropped. They were blissfully unaware I was still on the line.

For the next fifteen minutes, I overheard them chatting away, laughing and carrying on. Eventually, they picked the phone back up and casually resumed our conversation like old friends. Part of me wondered if a third bonus was on the cards, but then my conscience chimed in: *Damn, girl, that's pushing it*. I fessed up that I'd let them run over time. They laughed it off, saying it felt like a weight had been lifted from their shoulders.

That call left me with something to chew on. My morals weren't as questionable as I thought. I've always been the type to accept people as they are, and I'm proud I raised my daughters the same way. They grew up surrounded by love and acceptance, like Craig and Tony, a wonderful couple in our circle of friends. I wanted my kids to form their own opinions, free from society's stuffy expectations. It was a far cry from the secrecy of the men I spoke to on the phone—guys hiding their truths out of fear.

Then Jasper called. At first, I almost brushed him off when he asked for advice about his sexuality. I didn't realise how tough it could be for a gay man to find judgement-free support, but that flipped a switch in me. I started welcoming those conversations with open arms—after all, a faceless voice on the other end of the line was probably the safest space they had.

He was curious about exploring his sexuality and wanted to talk it through. I felt like I was nailing my part. Then he said, 'I'm not gay—I've never been in a relationship with a man.'

That's a bit of a stretch, mate, I thought, but I kept it to myself. I'm glad I did, because I felt like a total bitch after what he told me next.

He was a League player, and I knew the kind of prejudices he faced in that world.

He wasn't attracted to his teammates. They were his friends, but he avoided socialising with them because of the attention they got from women. This was the first time he had admitted that to himself, and it was a big moment. He was gay, and saying it out loud changed everything.

I told him about Craig and Tony. I hoped their courage and love would inspire him. I told Jasper to find his people—the ones who would accept him, no strings attached.

I might not have fully grasped the weight of his fears, but I had learned my lesson: embrace who you are, no apologies.

I never heard from Jasper again, but as more athletes came out in the following years, I liked to think he found the courage to be one of them. I never told Craig and Tony, though, that I'd been sharing their story. If they're reading this now, well—surprise!

They embody the spirit of the pride flag—proof that love comes in many forms, and no matter the colours, it shines just as brightly.

Lesson: Step out of your comfort zone and own those fabulous, unique colours of yours. They may just paint your path to something incredible.

CHAPTER 21

Psychic women

I came across every kind of weird and wonderful in the bizarre patchwork that was the sex industry. People with stories that could rival any soap opera—and I mean that in the best way—left their mark on me in ways I didn't expect. But it was the women I worked with on the phone lines who really turned my perspective on its head.

Take Cleo, for example. She was in her fifties, had psychic abilities, and could light up a room with her energy and that big, infectious smile. You couldn't ignore her if you tried. But behind the laughs and the larger-than-life personality she carried wounds from a childhood that no one should ever have to endure.

For all her sparkle, Cleo struggled with self-esteem, constantly deflecting compliments with self-deprecating humour about her looks. Over time she let me in on her story—layers of pain and resilience that left me in shock. It wasn't until years later that I truly understood the depth of our connection, but even then, I knew she was someone unforgettable.

I believe Cleo sensed my pain and knew that by sharing her story she could help me untangle my own struggles and figure out how to cope. Despite being married to a kind and caring man, Cleo carried the weight of her childhood trauma and sought solace in relationships with other men. The remarkable part? Her husband, fully aware of her past, accepted her as she was and loved her just as deeply.

Cleo confessed that every time she got involved with another guy guilt would set in, but she couldn't seem to stop. At first, I couldn't wrap my head around how these random flings brought her any comfort, until it hit me: I was doing the same damn thing! Maybe the universe threw us together so I could finally get my act together … just not quite yet.

Cleo wrestled with guilt and self-love, treating her relationships like a form of self-imposed penance, always chasing redemption and approval from others.

One day, during a psychic reading she did for me, she held up two sealed envelopes, each containing a photo. In the first, she described a man shrouded in darkness; an ominous presence who had caused me pain. The second revealed an older woman, weighed down by mental anguish, wreaking havoc and tossing my life into chaos. She nailed it without even cracking the envelopes. One held a photo of my husband, Chris, and the other, his mother, who suffered from schizophrenia and was the source of endless anxiety in my life.

During the same reading, Cleo predicted a man would swoop into my life like a knight in shining armour—though he wouldn't arrive baggage-free. She gave me a choice: take the less-travelled path alone or walk it with him. Was she warning me about what lay ahead? Probably. Did I pay enough attention? Absolutely not. My thoughts were too tangled up in my crumbling marriage to worry about some mythical hero.

Chris still expected me to help on job sites whenever I was home and insisted we take out a loan to build a flashy new house to replace the old weatherboard one. Never mind that we couldn't afford it—he had to keep up with the Joneses, blind to the toll it took on my physical and mental health. I was constantly running on empty, with no energy left to even consider another serious relationship.

Looking back, I kicked myself for brushing off Cleo's words. Impulsive decisions had become my specialty, which only made things worse. I'd made choices out of fear—fear of being alone—when I should've channelled my inner bad-arse. Maybe then I wouldn't have been so terrified of independence. Turns out, being brave is the ultimate power move in life!

Funnily enough, the phone lines also offered a psychic service, but Cleo wanted no part of it. She didn't need gimmicks; her predictions about me were spot-on. No one else could've called it the way she did.

Anne, another psychic who worked alongside me, had her own share of childhood trauma. She painted a vivid picture of the house I would build, even predicting design changes as I went along. Ironically, neither the first nor the second designs came close to what we ended up choosing. But the last one she described? That was the one that worked. Tony, our drafter, patiently endured three revisions of the layout. Unfortunately, the house Anne predicted led to financial disaster, contributing to the collapse of my marriage and leaving us in ruins.

Both Anne and Cleo had their struggles, just like I did, which made me wonder whether the phone room was our escape or salvation. We all had baggage—was it just us screw-ups, or did everyone have their issues?

The phone lines became the perfect outlet for all the frustrations we carried, and we aimed them at the men who called. The shared struggles in the room created a sense of familiarity, helping me face my own truths.

Lesson: Own your past, but don't let it keep you from chasing your true self.

CHAPTER 22

Footgasm: The perfect fit

'What's your shoe size, sweetheart?' the caller demanded, like it was some secret code.

I furrowed my brow. 'Uh, seven, maybe eight.' 'No, you're a size six. Petite,' he insisted.

'Right, sure. I have small feet.'

His grunt screamed frustration—obviously because I didn't say 'petite'.

'Yeah, petite,' I added.

I leaned over to Tiffany sitting next to me. 'He's into shoes or maybe feet, I honestly don't know.'

She grinned. 'Go with it, exaggerate a little.'

'Tell me about your shoes. What are they like?' he asked. 'Sneakers,' I answered.

'No, no, they're red leather stilettos covered in filth.'

I scoffed. 'Sure, stilettos, whatever, but you're wrong, I keep my shoes clean.'

Tiffany snatched the phone. 'Yes, they're filthy, so lick them clean.'

I goggled at Tiffany. This clearly wasn't her first foot rodeo, and I was along for the ride now.

Tiffany handed the phone back with a devilish grin. 'Tell him your heels are caked in dog shit, and if he doesn't clean them, you'll go barefoot.'

I stared at her, wide-eyed. 'What the hell?'

'Just say it.'

I rolled my eyes. 'All right, all right, let's do this.'

Metaphorically rolling up my sleeves, I leaned into the phone. 'Lick the damn dog shit off my shoes right now!'

The groan from the other end was primal. Tiffany nodded and gestured with her hand to say more.

'Yeah, lick it, you piece of shit.' I swear, I almost didn't believe what was coming out of my mouth.

Amanda, who was close by, leaned over and casually whispered, 'You like the pungent smell? Now rub your nose in it,' then went back to her desk as if it was a regular thing to do.

The groans grew louder—my signal for anything goes. I added, 'Slap your dick on my feet until it hurts.'

Tiffany almost choked on her laughter. 'You go, girl, let him have it. Tell him to get on all fours like a dog, lick your feet from toe to heel, and if he does it right, you'll let him explode all over them.'

Well, it didn't take long after that for him to be done like a dinner.

A few nights later, I answered a call from a woman who shared a similar situation with her husband, who wanted to wear fishnets and high heels during sex.

I laughed—I couldn't help it 'Nothing wrong with that. A man in heels is sexy, like being fucked by Frank-N-Furter. You know, from *The Rocky Horror Picture Show*.' She obviously didn't appreciate that. She hung up. I didn't blame her.

That same night a newbie started on the phone lines; Brandy was her name. She overheard that short conversation, so we began talking about the weird and wonderful world of fetishes. Brandy was a walking encyclopedia. Her real-life experiences could have filled a library with the plethora of stories she had to share, particularly about her relationship with a man fixated on her feet. Of course, I was captivated and eager to explore more. It was a wake-up call. Not all fetishes were the same, and not all of them were healthy.

Then there was Sammy, who had a fling with a guy obsessed with feet and shoes. He'd pay her to do things with her feet that seemed harmless at first but got pretty strange. She didn't mind; for her, it was a bonus to have sex without using her pussy.

Sammy was, a statuesque beauty with naturally large feet, elegantly long yet slender, and she was highly sought-after. Her long toes meant she was able to rub a man's python with ease. She would use honey and oils as lubricants between her toes, then make men lick it off. It disproved my belief that only women with small feet were desirable.

Sammy unexpectedly fell in love and put an end to her secret side hustle, keeping her past hidden from her boyfriend. Her story flipped my views and gave me a reality check: when people weren't getting their needs met at home, they'd find ways to satisfy that craving elsewhere. Maybe those willing to push their boundaries could discover a world of endless possibilities. Who knew exploring could be so eye-opening?

Lesson: Embrace the weirdness and don't be afraid to let your voice shine. Every story is unique. Sharing them helps us understand each other a little better.

CHAPTER 23

The grease pit

It didn't take me long to discover my Achilles heel—men with irresistible voices, like Tristan's dreamy Scottish lilt. Our late-night phone chats were a refreshing escape from the usual mind-numbing conversations I endured. I was hooked.

Tristan had moved to Australia at seventeen to study mechanical engineering, eventually landing a job in aviation. But when life changed, he juggled a string of odd jobs, including the ultimate cliché: selling vacuum cleaners, door-to-door. Naturally, like any good travelling salesman of the era, he dabbled in flings with married women—because, well, wasn't that part of the job description back then?

By twenty-five, he thought he'd found 'the one'—a woman who'd never been with another man. They'd had three kids, a picket-fence dream … until twelve years later when she ran off with someone he knew, kids in tow. His world fell apart. Heartbroken, Tristan plunged into a decades-long spree of sexual escapades, trying to patch his wounds with a growing list of lovers while piecing together his shattered life.

At first, I felt a flicker of sympathy for the guy. But let's be real—that didn't last long. Tristan liked to brag. Apparently, he was some kind of pleasure expert, claiming he could leave a woman in tears of joy while acting like his 'selfless' efforts deserved a round of applause. Honestly? I'd heard this kind of talk before. Guys like him were always legends in their own minds. But I decided to give him the benefit of the doubt. For now.

I came to understand that some men felt completely untethered after a break-up, desperate to prove they'd still 'got it'. They'd jump from one lover to the next, patching up their egos like a bad DIY project. Maybe Tristan thought he'd failed as a husband, and all that chasing was his way of reclaiming his manhood. But honestly, how many lovers did it take to prove a point?

It made sense that Tristan didn't dive into another serious relationship, but what was with the shield of protection? I guess I still had a thing or two to learn about how people coped with heartbreak, especially when it came to love. Maybe Tristan was meant to be my lesson.

After several chats, I realised his fear of abandonment was real. Over time, those feelings started to make more sense. Other guys shared similar stories with me, and suddenly, the puzzle pieces began to fit.

While stuck in a toxic marriage with Chris, I wrestled with my own feelings of failure for even thinking about ending it. As an Italian, I'd been raised to see marriage as sacred, breaking those vows was like ripping apart my own skin, knowing it would leave scars I'd carry forever. But there were moments when my heart outmanoeuvred my brain, and I took comfort in the company of other men.

My defence mechanisms kicked into overdrive, and I projected all the hatred I felt for Chris onto men as a whole. In my mind, they were all egotistical bastards, consumed by their own needs—until someone came along and smashed that theory to pieces.

Before I knew it, I was tangled in wild, steamy, late-night talks about sex—hour after hour, night after night. My emotions flipped upside down and my sense of reason vanished, leaving me to dive headfirst into the mess like I'd been training for it my whole life.

Despite my initial negative perceptions, men like Tristan played a crucial role in helping me understand the male psyche on a deeper level. I was clearly clueless about my decisions with men. I still had a lot to learn.

As I tried to make sense of his behaviour, Tristan shared stories of his romantic encounters.

One that stuck with me was about a time he worked on a property near Cessnock.

On weekends, Tristan headed to Newcastle to meet women. That's where he met twenty-eight-year-old Krissy (he was sixty at the time). Krissy was in the Royal Australian Air Force, stationed at Williamtown, and they happened to visit the same pub for a few beers.

Sparks flew right away. Tristan gave Krissy his undivided attention, using what he jokingly called his 'man bible': a book filled with techniques and questions to charm women. I couldn't help but laugh at the absurdity of it. A man bible? Really? But Tristan swore it was legit.

Back in his early sales days, he'd been handed a manual on selling. He would attend early morning sessions with other salespeople, practicing tactics designed to charm customers into wanting whatever they were peddling. But the real kicker was the book on hypnosis and suggestion, which he said taught you how to get anyone to do what you wanted. I called that straight-up 'deliberate deceit'. Even worse, it included a section on how to approach women and seal the deal on the first try.

At first, I laughed. 'What kind of sales manual teaches you how to score with women?'

He swore it was real, written by—you guessed it—a man.

Well, of course it was. I couldn't help but feel annoyed that a book like that existed, providing tips on how to manipulate a woman into having sex. What had started as amusement quickly turned into outright fury.

'So you think it's perfectly fine to lie to some unsuspecting woman young enough to be your daughter just to get laid?' I snapped.

Tristan immediately defended himself, explaining it was just a tool and stressing he would never force anyone into anything. He went on to say that at that point in his life he was simply looking for validation, wanting to know if women still found him attractive enough to be with. According to him, when his wife left, so did his sense of self-worth.

My God, the man was sixty—he should've figured that out by now. But here I was, still judging.

I couldn't wrap my head around his method back then. Part of me wanted to hate him, but another part almost felt sorry for him. There was truth in his feelings, sure, but his actions still didn't sit right with me. They made me wonder if I was just drawn to his captivating story.

It wasn't until several years later, when I faced my own desertion, that Tristan's story crept back into my thoughts. Maybe our emotions weren't so different after all, considering the similar events in our lives.

Tristan kept assuring me his only goal was to use the book's info to become a better salesperson. It was a coincidence that it also helped him approach women. He claimed the book taught him techniques for asking the right questions in the right order to gain a woman's trust and interest—basically making her feel comfortable enough to spill her guts.

That's messed up. But then again, who was I to judge?

My view of him started to soften. Strangely enough, part of me found him almost charming, in a way that was burrowing under my skin. Maybe it was the way he expressed his emotions so openly, enjoying the chance to please a woman. I admitted to him how much I craved that but had never gotten it.

That was the wrong thing to say, because, not surprisingly, he asked me out. I shot him down with a firm 'no.' Unbothered, he kept going with his story about how he'd wooed the young Krissy.

He invited her to visit his bungalow at the farm, and the next weekend, Tristan headed into Cessnock to gather supplies for the occasion. When he returned that afternoon, he found his charming brunette waiting for him outside his cabin. Tristan was delighted to see that Krissy, a military girl with a strong sense of independence, had already set up a log fire, a bottle of wine half-gone.

As they sipped wine together, Tristan cooked steaks on a makeshift hotplate while Krissy strummed tunes on her guitar. She was quite the multi-talented gal, as Tristan later discovered.

A few drinks later, they decided it was time for bed. Krissy knew the art of the tease, dancing and stripping down to nothing while Tristan watched, his desire growing with every move. Naturally, so did his ego and his dick. What he hadn't considered was how this petite thing would handle him in bed.

After spending some time kissing and touching her smooth, silky body, he rolled on top of her, trying hard to slide inside her. Sadly for Krissy, she couldn't take in something so huge—or maybe she wasn't as into him as he thought. Women get it—sometimes we start something we don't want to finish. We are allowed to change our minds, but often we do surrender to men unwillingly.

Tristan, being the thoughtful man he was, decided lubrication was necessary. Since there was no lube on hand, he got up with his massive hard-on and grabbed the olive oil from the kitchen. His logic? It would make a perfectly suitable substitute.

Krissy was initially horrified, she felt like a car about to be worked on in a grease pit. But Tristan reassured her with his wisdom: 'If it's good enough to eat, it's good enough to go inside you.' And, just to sweeten the deal, he added that it was extra virgin olive oil, so, you know, top-tier quality.

Still, Tristan could only get half his cock inside her. All I could think was, *How big is this thing?*

It was obvious that Tristan had overlooked the fact that perhaps Krissy wasn't as turned on as he assumed. They had been drinking a lot. Tristan, true to form, exclaimed he still enjoyed himself for about ten minutes while Krissy lay beneath him with a look of exhaustion. He wanted to keep going but it was too much for Krissy, and, sensing her disapproval at the use of the oil, he felt it best to keep it short.

I didn't want to burst Tristan's bubble, but I firmly believe the mind controls the body. Once a woman's turned off there's no coming back from that. I was surprised it lasted as long as it did. My guess? Krissy was probably faking it just to get it over with—a pity fuck.

Tristan claimed he preferred prolonged sex, but he was considerate enough to keep it short if he sensed that's what a woman wanted. *How thoughtful.*

Tristan, thanks to his size and stamina, was convinced most women couldn't keep up with him. Yeah, right. I figured he was boasting. Despite being captivated by his voice, there came a point when reality hit me. He turned into a carbon copy of every other guy I'd talked to. It was like they all shared the same DNA.

Tristan's ideas about what women wanted were way off. He seemed to think every woman craved a marathon session in the bedroom. Sometimes, though, a quick shag and a cosy cuddle were all we needed. Just because a woman consented didn't mean she was signing up for an all-night extravaganza.

While I didn't buy into everything he said, our conversations were far more entertaining than the dull routine of endless moans during sex talk. I had to give Tristan credit for one thing: he showed me the importance of chasing what I wanted in life. He wanted his confidence back, and damn it, he got it.

Tristan's openness was a breath of fresh air. Those chats helped me figure out the kind of relationship I wanted—and the ones I'd gladly avoid. They opened my eyes to a whole new world of possibilities in love.

Lesson: Chase your dreams, no matter the bumps in the road, and let your experiences teach you what you really want —and where to draw the line.

CHAPTER 24

Connections

Working the phone lines was like playing a sport no one else could understand. And the team had each other's backs. Sure, we got swept up in the charm of the men we chatted with—some of us even dared to meet them. It was all smoke and mirrors, but that didn't stop us from dreaming of happily-ever-afters or, at the very least, a whirlwind romance. And oh, the allure of gifts and weekend getaways? Let's just say it wasn't exactly part of the job description, but who's complaining?

Adventures with men outside the office were strictly a personal choice. Mine? I was on a quest for a guy who'd treat me the way I deserved, like a queen, not an afterthought. I clung to the fantasy of a knight in shining armour swooping in to rescue me from my marriage and drop me into a better life. Reality check: some men had other ideas, like free sex with zero strings attached.

A lucky few did hit the jackpot. Xenia was one of them. One night, some guy and his buddies called in, passing the phone around like they were hosting a comedy show. Xenia played along, charming the lot of them so well that she snagged a twenty-dollar bonus just for the laughs. That girl could talk circles around anyone, a true master of the gift of the gab.

Maybe it was her background as a psychology student that gave her an edge, though her brilliance and beauty were equally stunning, each complementing the other in a way that made her impossible to ignore. At twenty-nine, she had this aura of someone who had life all figured out, and I couldn't help but envy her intelligence. She could dive into any conversation, no matter the topic, like it was second nature. Watching her in action taught me one of the most important lessons of my life: the power of education. It lit a fire in me, pushing me to pursue more studies myself.

One of the men she'd been talking to claimed to be a friend of a famous, wealthy Aussie, but he never revealed who. Xenia was sceptical, but that didn't stop her from being a regular on his call list. One time he invited her to join him on a yacht owned by this mystery millionaire. *Why not?* she thought. He might have been full of it, but she took the chance, hoping for a little adventure.

Her companion, a fabulous gay guy in his forties, was proof that age, gender or who you were into didn't matter in relationships. Xenia would always say, 'It's all about the connection.' Back then, I didn't fully get it, but I pretended I did—no way was I going to look clueless. Now? Not only do I get it, I also live by it.

After a fancy cruise on the yacht, Xenia and the others hopped onto a smaller boat that took them up the Hawkesbury River, straight to a jetty owned by the famous entrepreneur. She painted a picture of a giant log cabin decked out with all the luxury trimmings and high-tech toys. But what really caught her eye was the wine cellar—naturally, since she was a bit of a wine connoisseur herself. I soaked up every detail like it was a juicy soap opera.

When Xenia finally met the property owner, she recognised him instantly. The guy was a big shot, tied to all kinds of business and political circles. At the time, I couldn't care less about that stuff—his importance was lost on me—but his name would later embed itself in my mind.

As for Xenia, she knew that the men she met carried their fair share of secrets, courtesy of their social status. Funnily enough, none of them were chasing sex; they craved the company of smart women. Xenia used the opportunity to study their psychology while soaking up all the kindness they offered. She was living her best life, dissecting their minds like a true pro.

Her role? Escorting them to fancy events, scoring extravagant gifts, and occasionally pocketing a little extra cash for the perfect outfit. We're talking five-star experiences—Moët champagne, high-end restaurants, and rubbing shoulders with the rich and famous. Despite living it up, Xenia never lost focus. Practical as ever, she enjoyed the moment but stayed grounded and thought ahead—a lesson I took to heart.

I held onto some of those sensible ideas and they helped me chill out when life threw its unexpected challenges. The fears and insecurities stirred up by people who let me down didn't run my emotions anymore.

Xenia's views on education and mindset made me reassess my own reality and what my future could look like. Once I asked Xenia why she picked phone sex and escorting, and her response was pure logic: it offered insight into human behaviour for her psych studies while keeping her financially afloat.

I cheekily suggested she could just rely on male support, but she shut that down fast. Xenia took pride in carving her own path as an independent woman—something I desperately wanted for myself.

Knowing Xenia was nothing short of enlightening. She opened my eyes to topics I hadn't even realised I needed to think about. Our brief but purposeful friendship was inspiring. The saying, 'People come into our lives for a reason or a season' rings true for me, especially when I think about all the short-lived relationships that had delivered valuable lessons along the way.

Fast-forward four years to 2003, I was watching the news, and—bam! There was the famous guy Xenia had met at his place in the

Hawkesbury. It all clicked. He was now facing charges for insider trading, and, as fate would have it, he was connected to Gene, a self-made millionaire I happened to cross paths within the strangest way.

How wild was it that something so random and far-off could come full circle. The world really was small—only a few degrees of separation between us all.

Lesson: The people we connect with—whether briefly or deeply— have the power to inspire, challenge and shape our views, leaving behind lessons in their words and actions.

CHAPTER 25

The social circle

Working the phone lines wasn't exactly sipping piña coladas on a sunny beach. The booths were so cramped it was like being wedged into a shoebox with no exit strategy. Oddly though, those tight quarters doubled as my haven—a tiny bubble where the madness of life couldn't touch me. On slow nights, when boredom wrapped itself around us like a fog, the booths became our makeshift cocoons. Some of us perched on desks, others sprawled out under the tables.

When we weren't hiding, we kept each other sane by chatting between calls. Still, by the end of the shift I'd stumble out of my booth with a voice as raspy as a rock singer's and eyes that looked like I'd just pulled an all-nighter at a rave. I'd hit what truck drivers called 'the wall', and it hit hard.

Running on fumes, I'd push through the monotony, pretending I still had a shred of energy left. Tensions were high—lose your cool, lose your clients. Anxiety became my constant companion, leaving me jittery, like a caged bird desperate to stretch its wings. I'd squirm in my metal chair, my legs quivering and teeth grinding as I fixated on the clock, its hands crawling like snails.

Frustration crept into the air like an unwelcome guest. Some girls would step outside for a hit of the green stuff or pop a smiley-faced pill—the kind that made reality blur just enough to survive the night. Others stuck to less questionable methods, like pacing in the cold night air to wake up or sprinting to Macca's for a caffeine fix. Each of us had our own way of keeping it together, but by sunrise we all shared the same look—worn out and wondering why the hell we were still doing this.

Believe it or not, I once took pills from co-workers without the faintest clue what they were. Trusting? Sure. Reckless? Absolutely. But when you're desperate to stay awake, good judgement tends to take a back seat. It didn't take long for me to figure out those mystery pills were screwing with my health. Needless to say, that habit quickly got the boot.

Some nights, I'd cruise around the city like a sugar-crazed maniac, hunting for a convenience store packed with energy drinks and chocolate. Those goodies were my lifeline, keeping me upright and off my desk.

Not every shift felt like a marathon, though. Some nights were oddly calm, almost meditative. And on those rare occasions, we found ways to kill time—knitting, journalling, or burying our noses in books.

It was a bizarre scene. A room full of women whispering seductive nothings into their phones while knitting scarves or solving crossword puzzles. Multitasking at its finest! Josie, the artist, would zone out with her paints or sketchbook. Watching her create was inspiring, and I took a page out of her book during those quieter shifts. I'd scribble notes about quirky client calls, sketch designs, or even make little trinkets I sold in local gift shops.

Then there was Patricia, the queen of the side hustle. She'd sit there, casually working on leather whips, attaching silver press studs to eyelets with handheld pliers like it was no big deal. She'd whip up leather blindfolds, G-strings for men and women, and even neck restraints. Her craftsmanship was next level, and her creations found homes in sex shops, private brothels, and even with women she knew in the bondage scene. It was both impressive and, let's face it, a little intimidating.

And, of course, there was Xanthe, a twenty-seven-year-old single mum living in a shared apartment. At the time, I was married with kids and had no idea what it was like to juggle everything solo. Not long after, life threw me into her shoes, and I finally understood. Her resilience was nothing short of incredible.

With a waitressing job and the phone lines on her plate, Xanthe relied on her flatmates to help care for her son. During the day, he was either at school or with carers, while she bent her schedule every way she could to make time for him. To make ends meet, she and a friend crafted and sold hand-stitched beaded handbags at the Rozelle markets.

She was ten years younger than me, but her maturity and capability were on another level. The constant fatigue and dark circles under her eyes made perfect sense once I realised how much strength it took to keep her world from falling apart.

Claire, another phone colleague, was a fiery redhead with magnetic charm both on and off the lines. Now in her late thirties, Claire had a jaw-dropping backstory. Before joining the phone team, she'd worked in data collection, which led to her being recruited by the Australian Federal Police. Her mission? Go undercover to infiltrate a pornography syndicate in Darwin with ties to Canberra.

Thanks to my own brushes with the law, I knew better than to believe her recruitment was a coincidence—police didn't leave much to chance.

Claire's undercover role required her to dive deep into the industry, attending conventions and mingling with its players. Everything was arranged for her, and with her regular job on hold and her expenses covered, she threw herself into the assignment.

She and her husband hit the jackpot with tickets and an all-expenses-paid trip to a massive sex expo in Las Vegas. For four days, they soaked up the luxury. The expo buzzed with filmmakers, porn stars and all the glitz you'd expect. Claire's striking looks even caught the eye of a discreet adult film company, which tried to recruit her on the spot. Meanwhile her husband, in a moment of curiosity, accidentally signed up for a 'free videos' subscription that kept their mailbox entertained for nearly a year.

Because of Claire, the police made multiple arrests, taking down key players in the syndicate. Her wild adventure didn't just make for a gripping story; it sparked a passion for forensic science, which her phone job was funding.

Women were incredible—practically superheroes. We juggled tasks like pros. I mean, we could have sex while mentally planning tomorrow's dinner. Ask a man to multitask like that and his dick would probably go limp! In stressful situations, we could go on autopilot, expertly balancing priorities and getting things done.

The job pushed me to my limits, but it also showed me how resourceful I could be. That shift in how I saw myself changed everything. Some of the girls I'd gotten close to dragged me along to blow off steam. We'd hit the city bars before work, dancing, drinking and living it up. It was a slice of freedom I'd missed out on in my younger years. For those few hours I got a glimpse of what normal might feel like, even if it was all hidden from my husband. Not that the dickhead deserved to know, considering how he treated me.

Just around the corner from work was the Paragon Hotel, a spot we hit one night to celebrate Zander's twenty-ninth birthday. She was a tall blonde bombshell with curves that could cause a traffic jam. After grabbing a drink, she stuffed her change into her bra and dragged me onto the dance floor. Before I knew it, I was sandwiched between her and another well-endowed woman, her coins dropping to the floor like confetti from the heavens.

Zander kept dancing, downing her drink like it was water, unbothered by the cash spilling from her cleavage. Meanwhile, the rest of us were crawling around on all fours, scooping up the coins like drunk treasure hunters. It was chaos—a full-blown comedy show—with people tripping over each other as we tried to snag the change.

Another night, we made our way to the Slip Inn Bar on Sussex Street—you know, the same place where Mary met her prince and became the Queen of Denmark. Feeling cheeky, I printed a dozen black-and-white photos of my phone alias, along with the call centre number and a sultry message: 'Call me, Dominique.' With military precision, I slipped those photos into the pockets of unsuspecting men throughout the night. Some actually called! Would you believe it? A few even became regulars, proving my little stunt was worth every second.

We found our laughs where we could. Such as at Christmas, when the workplace turned into a festive feast, complete with bubbly and enough food to forget our troubles for a while. But no matter how much fun we had, the phones never stopped ringing. The job was tough, but those pay packets, and the sisterhood we built, kept us coming back. Somehow, together we made it through.

On slow nights, especially when the footy had all the guys glued to their TV sets, we'd sometimes head out for food. One night, three of us were all set for Macca's but we took a detour and stopped at the pub around the corner. While the ladies knocked back shots, I nursed my single one like an English rose sipping tea.

'What the hell are you doing? Scull it, for God's sake!' they laughed.

So I did … and then had two more. Ten minutes later, we stumbled out of the pub, but damn, I felt proud.

I quickly discovered that the saying 'Sharing is caring' was alive and well among the women in the industry. Take Maria, a woman in her fifties, who told me a story about her husband, Albert, and his two mates. One afternoon, while they were at a barbecue, Maria overheard them chatting about trying Viagra. One of them even bragged about using his dick like a sledgehammer.

I'd heard this kind of nonsense before. Maria's husband proudly chimed in, saying he didn't need any help to satisfy his missus. But then, flashing a wicked grin, Maria recounted the one and only time he actually took the stuff. It made him dizzy and he had to sit down. She laughed, explaining that Albert typically lasted a whole three minutes—just enough time for her to plan the week's menu!

I'd heard plenty of women claim they'd perfected the art of multitasking in the bedroom, too. Maria nodded, clearly on the same page. She wasn't really into sex anymore said it felt more like a chore these days.

Then there was Frida, in her sixties, who had a boyfriend addicted to Viagra. Since it took a good half-hour to kick in, he'd have her do a striptease to get him revved up. Then she'd inevitably be left high and dry. He'd just get on top, piston away, and ignore her needs.

That pissed me off—his ridiculous expectation that she had to strip for his entertainment. It made me realise just how self-centred some men could be, and it marked the beginning of my own emancipation from my husband and his self-serving ways—or, at least, I thought it did.

Lesson: People drop wisdom, whether we want it or not. The real takeaway? Don't let anyone—man or woman—make you feel indebted to their selfish needs. Stay true to yourself.

CHAPTER 26

Conversations with Murphy

After my 'friendship' with Maloney was dead in the water, a new man swooped in on his cordless phone like a knight in shining armour.

Murphy pulled me in with his deep life stories. The twenty-year age gap? Honestly, I didn't care. His tales were too good to resist. And we both had Italian roots and weird name changes—his from Marzano to Murphy, mine from Lucia to Lucy. It felt like fate intervening, and maybe for a damn good reason.

Murphy, a widower aching for the love of his late wife, entered my life when I was craving that deep connection, even though I was married. The more he opened up, the more he tugged at my heart-strings. Money wasn't a concern for him; he'd made his fortune in what he called the 'rag trade', starting as a fabric merchant before becoming a clothing manufacturer. I could relate, having worked at a drapery store back in the 1970s. Another bond between us.

In his twenties, Murphy married the love of his life. Though they couldn't have children, he found true happiness with her, affectionately calling her 'my girl'. To him, meeting her had felt like stumbling upon a treasure he never knew he was searching for.

But Murphy lost his girl shortly after his thirty-eighth birthday.

'The day my girl left this earth was the day the sun vanished from my world.' It was one of the saddest things I'd ever heard—raw and achingly beautiful in its own way. My heart cracked wide open for him, and I couldn't tear myself away from his words, each one heavy with the weight of his grief.

His stories offered deep insights into love, revealing layers I hadn't fully grasped before. Hearing Murphy talk about never finding a love like that again made me reflect on my own life. There were pieces I hadn't even acknowledged. He put his wife before himself. I'd never experienced anything like that, but his words made me wish I had.

During his sabbatical from the world, Murphy tried to recapture intimacy by diving into desires he'd missed, with new lovers. He spent his days chasing happiness through pleasure, not love. Fate took a wild turn when he ended up in a month-long sex marathon with a beautiful young woman.

'There were days we only left the bed to shower and eat,' he said, making it clear that it was just physical, never about love. His blunt honesty was refreshing, unlike most men I'd met, who often spun tales about their relationships to look good when they were anything but.

From where I stood, Murphy dodged commitment in those brief relationships, likely out of guilt and a sense that he did not want to betray his first love. I figured that when you faced trauma like his, you've got to heal before you can move on.

He admitted that, while he was physically drawn to these women, the emotional connection was always missing—until a woman who reminded him of his wife unexpectedly stirred up his feelings. And so he chose to let her go.

At the time, I wasn't totally conscious of the difference, but Murphy cleared it up. He explained that for him, sex was about lust—an outlet to satisfy his cravings for pleasure.

Love, on the other hand, was the hidden, vulnerable part of him, still tangled up in his grief.

I couldn't remember ever feeling such deep emotion for anyone, and that made me sad.

Maybe, just maybe, I'd never truly been in love.

I developed a fondness for Murphy, and with each passing week, my desire to meet him face-to-face grew stronger. Our connection was magnetic, and I eagerly anticipated his calls.

Murphy began to invade my dreams, turning into my secret fantasy. I wondered if he could sense my attraction through the playful questions I tossed his way during our chats. One evening, he shared his contact details and we made plans to meet outside of work. Unsure of what to expect, I hoped that meeting him might stir up some new emotions within me. We kept it casual—just a drink and a chat.

Leading up to our meeting, whenever Murphy called my workplace, we steered clear of discussing our plans, aware that our phone conversations were sometimes monitored. I assumed no one had noticed, since no one ever brought it up.

On the day of our date, I stopped by work to change and freshen up, adding a bit more lipstick and perfume than usual. We decided to meet outside the Paragon, near Circular Quay—familiar territory for me, just a five-minute walk from work.

When Murphy and I finally met, it felt like reconnecting with an old friend. It was incredible. My mental image of him was spot-on; standing tall at six feet, he towered over me. His jet-black hair, speckled with grey at the sides, was neatly slicked back. With a warm smile, piercing blue eyes, and a sturdy build, he was impeccably dressed in a crisp white shirt, navy trousers, a black belt, and polished shoes.

Despite recognising each other instantly, we exchanged formal introductions. At nearly sixty, Murphy was undeniably handsome. As he clasped my hand and leaned in for a sweet kiss on my cheek, his eyes never left mine. The fragrance of his cologne sent shivers up my spine.

We sat side-by-side at the bar, close enough for our legs to touch. Murphy ordered my favourite drink, a Brandy Alexander, showing he had listened to me, while he opted for a double Scotch on the rocks.

He made me feel like the most important person in the bar. Despite the beautiful young women passing by, his gaze remained fixed on me the entire time. That was significant to me. Chris had a wandering eye and always made sure I knew when he noticed a pretty woman walking by. He was a real jerk that way.

We chatted easily, and each had another drink. Before I knew it, I had to leave for work. He walked me all the way to my workplace, stopping at the skanky doorway next to the building. But I didn't care; for once, that doorway felt like the most beautiful place in the world, despite the lingering odour of piss from the drunks using it as a toilet stop. I felt reckless and didn't mind being seen. He embraced me with surprising strength, pulling me firmly against his body.

His eyes bored into mine. 'You are absolutely beautiful.' I could feel his breath on my forehead. He placed one hand behind the nape of my neck and kissed me with such passion that my entire body tingled. Thoughts raced through my mind. I yearned to make love to this man at that very moment. He was hot, and I was on fire. That kiss seemed to last forever—well, long enough for me to feel his rock-hard cock pressing against me. It felt huge, like it extended from the top of my thigh to above my belly button. The harder he pressed, the more my desire for him grew. I stood on my tippy-toes, rocking my body slightly from side to side, letting out little sighs of desire every now and again. Damn, he was hot for an old man.

Finally, our lips parted. I was shaking all over. The last thing I wanted was to go into work and talk dirty to a bunch of horny men. My body was desperate to be with Murphy.

He took my hand, holding it tightly, kissing it, and expressing his desire to see me again. I placed my free hand on my chest, attempting to compose myself before responding. I knew he could become addictive and difficult to let go of. It stung to say it, but I had to keep my head on straight. I told him I wasn't sure it was a good idea.

Squinting at my wristwatch, I struggled to focus, my eyes glazed with perspiration. The hands indicated it was ten to eleven. We had spent two hours together, and I needed to get upstairs before my shift started. 'Sorry, gorgeous man, I really am. I need to run; I'll be late.'

As I stepped towards the door, he pulled me back in and planted another kiss on my lips. I had to push him away or I would have stayed there forever.

'I'll call you. I need you.'

Damn, why did he have to be the one that shook the earth beneath my feet? He kept to his word and called within a few minutes of us parting.

Time spent with him had me convinced there was something better out there. For real, he was the hottest man I hadn't yet had the pleasure of sleeping with. He left me with an unquenchable thirst in my throat—he was the drink that could've satisfied it.

Murphy kept calling, but his calls got fewer and farther between. We never saw each other again. Still, that euphoric feeling he left me with never faded. Maybe fate sent him my way just so I'd have something to hold on to when the world felt like it was falling apart.

Lesson: Never underestimate your worth—your current circumstances don't define who you are.

CHAPTER 27

The golden stream man

Just when I thought I'd heard it all, a man's voice came through the phone: 'You do golden showers, beautiful?'

I tapped Sandra on the shoulder. 'What the hell is a golden shower?'

'He wants you to piss on him, babe. Hope you've got a bladder full.' Sandra chuckled and went back to her book.

Well, that was unexpected. Still, I supposed I could figure out how to piss on someone over the phone—what's life without a little challenge?

With a confident smirk, I leaned into the call. 'Sure, catering to men is my specialty.' Even if it wasn't.

A breathless groan came from the other end. I covered the mouthpiece and whispered to Sandra, 'Got any tips on how to convincingly simulate pissing on him over the phone?'

Rolling her eyes, Sandra muttered, 'Fucken weirdos and their fetishes.' All she wanted was to get back to her book, but I really needed her help—she was my go-to person.

I scrunched up my nose, giving her my best pleading look.

She shot back, 'I guess a girl's gotta do what a girl's gotta do to make a buck. All right, let's piss on this guy big time.'

We shared a quick, silent giggle, knowing this would be an Oscar-worthy show. I was still puzzled—why would anyone pay for an imaginary piss session over the phone?—then again, I was in it now. Little did I know, this scenario would become all too familiar during my years in a different workplace … but we'll get to that.

Sensing the urgency in his voice, he begged me to hurry—apparently, he'd already stripped down and was sprawled out on the bathroom floor.

Men really are strange creatures, I thought. Sandra handed me two plastic cups of water, positioning them near my phone. The plan? Speak dirty to him while she poured water from one cup to the other, simulating the sound. I had to admit, it was a genius move. How had I not thought of this earlier?

I described how I was pissing on his balls and the client moaned, clearly enjoying the sound of water trickling into the cup. Sandra, ever the perfectionist, poured the water extra slowly to draw it out. Surprisingly, it did sound realistic, to the point I felt the urge to go.

'That's it, now move up to my face and piss all over it.'

I leaned towards Sandra and whispered, 'Oh, man, this guy has no idea—I've had a couple of energy drinks. That's gonna be one sour cocktail.' We burst out laughing, trying to keep it quiet.

'Come on, bitch, piss on my cock—it's rock-hard for you.'

I rolled my eyes, thinking, *If this was real, he'd be drenched head to toe as I worked my way from his mouth to his balls.* Talk about a wet mess. Go figure.

Fifteen minutes in, I threw in the towel. This was dragging on for-freaking-ever. Frustrated, I turned to Sandra. 'How much longer is this guy going to take? Why can't he just blow already?' I was itching to nudge him along before I died of sheer boredom.

Trying to sound nice and sexy—though I really couldn't give a flying shit—I said, 'All right, sexy man, my girlfriend and I want to piss on you together, but we need to go have a few more drinks first. Would you mind taking a break and waiting for us?' I fully expected him to hang up, but nope. To our surprise, the horny bastard told me he understood. Not only that, but he didn't want to lose the momentum and asked if I'd mind if he kept yanking himself while we grabbed more drinks.

Honestly, this wasn't at all what I expected, especially considering how the call started. He almost apologetically asked for permission to keep pleasuring himself—guess he was really in the zone. Five more minutes dragged by, and with only ten left to hit a bonus, I thought *Screw it, might as well go for it.*

I grabbed the phone and moaned, 'Oh, baby, my girlfriend and I are so horny—we both want to have you before we piss on you.' His moans hit a new level, leaving Sandra and I staring at each other, wide-eyed.

Sandra told him she'd sit on his face while I rode him. Setting the cups down on the desk, she cranked up the theatrics, moaning and rocking back and forth like she was grinding his face, hands in the air for added flair. Meanwhile, I sat in the chair, pretending to ride him. At five in the morning, we were beyond exhausted and delirious, mind you, we were getting the job done.

It felt surreal, and honestly, I was glad I hadn't thrown in the towel earlier. This crazy act turned out to be my best idea of the night, snapping me out of my loser mentality.

Mid-performance, Sandra accidentally knocked over a cup of water onto my lap. 'Oh, fuck me, I'm all wet!' I yelped, the icy water a harsh reminder it was the middle of winter.

My client perked up instantly. 'What's happening?'

Thinking quickly, I cooed, 'Oh, sorry, your cock's just so huge I can't help but piss on it while I ride you.'

Sandra hit the floor, laughing so hard she could barely breathe.

A loud yell erupted from the client, followed by a thud and heavy breathing. Sounded like he'd collapsed in satisfaction and forgotten to hang up. Without much effort, I hit my bonus—what a win!

Sandra and I decided we'd earned a trip to Macca's for proper coffee on the drive home. Just as we were heading out, the supervisor zipped past us, yelling, 'Sorry, gotta piss!' as she bolted to the toilet. That set us off again, laughing hysterically as we walked out.

A few months later, I found another couple eager to jump onto the same wild ride. Using my past chat as a playbook, I kept them hooked. Working in this crazy industry completely flipped how I saw things, especially when it came to personal preferences. It made me wonder: had I been too quick to judge things I didn't understand, or had outside opinions just messed with my head?

Lesson: Sometimes, pushing through when you want to quit is the secret to hitting the jackpot.

CHAPTER 28

Operation schmuck: Tales from the client list

Nights, when the world had settled, marked the start of my journey. Driving into the city with empty lanes, surrounded by the beauty of moonlit silhouettes, felt surreal. Thoughts swirled about the secrets awaiting revelation by the men who would call me that evening.

Dealing with a mix of callers was absurd, but it was all part of the chaotic world of my job. I juggled a colourful client list, each person bringing a unique experience, ranging from genuinely intriguing to downright bizarre. While some clients were logical and straightforward, others thrived on confusion, as if their mission was to make my life harder with the most nonsensical requests imaginable. Every illogical caller added a twist to my day, turning what could have been a routine task into a hilarious adventure. Navigating this wild mix taught me to expect the unexpected, and I learned to find humour in the pandemonium.

How many lonely men did I talk to, all craving either a chat or a little satisfaction? There were times I could've used a friendly ear myself, but mostly, I kept my thoughts on lock. Thank God for the women I worked with—they were my real lifeline. Work was the one place that gave me a break from my very own personal ball and chain, Chris.

Stepping into the phone room was like slipping into something familiar—a second skin. The hum of the lights, the buzz of voices coming from the other side of the curtain; it was a world that wasn't quite mine but was exactly what I needed. Behind that curtain of secrecy, we all shared the same twisted little bond. We were either the objects of desire or the butt of their jokes, and let me tell you, some of these jokers were real pieces of work.

Some of them were awful—like, I'm talking full-on head-scratching requests that made me wonder if they were calling from another planet. There were the ones who just wanted to hear their own voice, rambling about nothing, making me regret every second. Others thought it was a stand-up comedy show, cracking lame jokes like they'd discovered a new punchline in the middle of their monologue. And then there were the few who really thought I could solve all their problems with a couple of well-timed 'mmm-hmms' and a comforting tone.

As frustrating as it was, there was something darkly amusing about the chaos. The absurdity of it all made me laugh more than I'd like to admit. I didn't want to be there, but some days, it was the only thing that made sense.

The endless parade of quirky clients kept me on my toes. Each one left a mark, pushing me to dig deeper into a well of determination I didn't know I had. The job was all about handling every kind of personality that came my way, forcing me to toughen up while surviving late-night hours for barely any pay, all at the expense of my sanity. I had my regulars, sure, but you never knew what was coming next. Then one night, a surprise hit me.

A woman called in, and I instantly assumed she wanted the usual: sex talk. But nope. Lesson learned: never assume anything in this job.

'Whore, do you know who I am?' she spat, her words dripping with hostility.

'Um, I'm sorry, you must have the wrong number.'

'No, you cheap-arse fucking prostitute, I don't—'

I yanked the phone away from my ear, momentarily stunned by her aggression. As she unleashed her fury, I found myself pleading my case as if I were on trial. No matter how I defended myself, her insults kept coming, striking a nerve and dredging up memories of past family violence and my husband's outbursts.

Before I worked in the sex industry, I was blissfully ignorant of the job's realities. My understanding came straight from my husband, who crudely claimed that prostitutes earned easy money just by lying there—totally clueless about the challenges women actually faced. I was just as much in the dark, relying on him for my opinions about everyone else.

That call threw me right back to my nineteen-year-old self, just two years into a marriage, suffocating under his expectations. I was his cook, maid, breadwinner and object of desire all at once, leaving my brain in a constant state of disorder. Then there was the staunch Catholic family friend preaching about a woman's place: obey your husband. To her, women were sinners—like prostitutes—just for thinking about another man. It twisted my brain into knots.

The word 'prostitute' carried so much baggage, thanks to people with their misinformed, holier-than-thou opinions. But here's the thing: I knew the truth. Life in the sex industry was tough, but there was almost always a damn good reason behind it—just like me.

When the caller tossed the word 'whore' my way, it cut deep. I couldn't help but think… maybe I was exactly that. Chris was my pimp, and I was his working girl. No, not the glamorous kind—you wouldn't catch me walking the streets in heels—but I was certainly working the phones, making sure he stayed comfy at home. I tried to shove that thought out of my head, but it wasn't exactly a 'throw it in a drawer and forget it' situation. I couldn't let it take me down—not when there were bills to pay and my sanity was hanging by a thread.

Once the shock wore off, I realised something: if they were calling to abuse me, they were paying for it, and they damn well deserved to get their money's worth. I couldn't let it break me. I toughened up, transformed, and became a hard motherfucker on those phone lines.

I would let these delightful callers rant as long as they wanted, letting the clock tick closer to the dollar sign while their agitation grew. I embraced the challenge of dealing with curious and insulting clients, leaving nothing off-limits. And if a conversation bothered me too much? I found ways to make them hang up.

At times, women would call, complaining about explicit TV ads late at night, insisting their partners were 'compelled' to call. They'd rather blame a faceless voice on the other end than admit their partners willingly picked up the handset. I mean, I didn't exactly have a gun to their heads, did I?

I quickly became the scapegoat for people's problems. The harassment became overwhelming. My mind felt ready to explode from the verbal abuse. How was that fair? I didn't control the ads, and I sure as hell didn't control the actions of those who saw them!

One night a concerned parent called in. I sympathised, explaining how hard it was to tell the caller's age, but I still engaged with anyone who rang—unless their voice screamed underage. In that case, I'd just hang up. I suggested parents contact their service provider to block the number. I could only imagine the showdown those boys would have with their parents!

Then there was this one guy who called to complain about his son racking up a bill. Surprisingly, we ended up having a good chat. I would've loved to see the look on his wife's face when she discovered that bill—ah, the good old days of paper bills!

Sometimes, parents or partners would throw insults at me, as if I was running a hostage situation to get their family members to call. I figured those curious boys were better off talking to us than diving into some risky relationship out there.

When wives called, I'd explain that their husbands were just looking for advice on spicing things up in the bedroom. Not always the answer they wanted to hear. More often than not, it was something like, 'So you know what they need better than I do? Fuck off, slut!' before the phone was slammed down.

Every now and then, though, a curious caller would ask what info I'd share with their partner—a nice change of pace. But the toughest nights were filled with an endless stream of angry callers, making it feel like a personal attack while I was just trying to do my job.

Thinking back on all the men I spoke to, I couldn't help but wonder, *Was I really influencing their perspectives and sexual behaviour?* I needed to find a way to separate work from my personal thoughts or risk spiralling into a world of pain.

Some clients I met in person left a lasting impact, forcing me to face hard truths about myself and reshape my self-perception. I didn't want to be just an object of sexual pleasure anymore; I wanted to be seen as an intelligent human being.

Unfortunately, some men wanted perfection, expecting the women they spoke to to fit their ideal fantasy. I was guilty of leading them to believe I was that woman. Others tried to transfer their problems onto me, unable to cope with life's challenges. Newsflash: I wasn't responsible for their shit!

I had to shake off the impact those clients had on my mind and learn to draw a line. I couldn't carry everyone's guilt. This became crucial two decades later, shaping my inner voice.

The air-conditioning was on the fritz, and I was only halfway through my shift, already fed up. It was one of those nights. Life felt pointless, and jumping out the window was tempting—if only the damn thing wasn't locked on the eleventh floor. Things back home were getting worse, and while some nights at work offered a sweet escape, others just dragged me deeper into a crevasse.

I wasn't one to give up easily, so I shoved those dark thoughts aside and refocused on the present, cursing the ringing phone before picking it up. Fifteen painful minutes later, boredom crept in, and just as I sensed the client was about to hang up, I realised he was frying my brain without even bothering to give me his name. So, I dubbed him Sir Dick—because, well, dickhead.

True to his name, Sir Dick went on and on about how the world revolved around him. The more he talked, the more his peanut brain screamed, *I can't handle a real conversation.*

Then came that sound. The familiar one that meant *I'm not satisfied.* I shrieked internally. Suddenly, staring out at the apartment across the street, a movement caught my eye. An opportunity? Hell yes. I seized it.

'Oh, there's a woman undressing a man in an apartment across the street. He's got great arms.'

He perked up. 'What's he doing to her?'

I decided to tease him, coyly taking my time to respond, relishing the power shift. His curiosity was palpable.

'He's taking her bra off.'

'Does she have big tits?' Typical question from a dumb-arse.

'Yeah, they're huge. You could go mountain climbing on them for a whole day and still not reach the peak.'

He didn't get the humour. 'So, what's he doing with them?'

My God, he was irritating. 'What's he doing with what?' I couldn't help but ask, all innocence.

'Her tits! For fuck's sake, what else?'

Sir Dick's arrogance stirred something in me—too bad I hadn't had this fight in me years ago. I painted a vivid picture of the woman's breasts, and he was pleased. 'She's unzipping his trousers,' I said, wondering if they could see me watching them. *Am I a pervert, or are they exhibitionists? Doesn't matter. I'm reaching my goal.*

Two other women nearby were taking advantage of the situation, too. 'She's on her knees, cradling his cock between her breasts,' I continued. Sir Dick gasped.

'Wow, he's bent her over the bed, looks like he's in a hurry. Oops, he tripped, guess he forgot his trousers around his ankles!' At this point, the scene was straight-up comedy—the man's cock was going limp, and I watched him desperately yank on it.

Like I'd always said, men couldn't multitask for shit. Women, on the other hand, could juggle it all and still look flawless.

Too bad I couldn't say that to Sir Dick. I focused on my bonus instead. 'Oh, man, now he's pounding her over the end of the bed.' And that's when Sir Dick was done. Taking a few breaths, he said, 'That was great, love. I'll be calling again.'

'Can't wait,' I replied. I really couldn't care less, but hey, bonus in hand, it made my night a little better.

Last call of the night. 'Hi, babe, looking for some fun?'

'No, bitch! Who the hell are you sending my husband a picture of yourself with your tits out?' an agitated female voice shot back.

'What? I don't know what you're talking about.'

'Yes, you do, you little fucker!' she yelled, her voice echoing in my ear. She'd somehow found this number on the back of a picture in her husband's coat pocket—one of those company promos with scantily clad models. I tried to calm her down, but it made no difference. She unleashed a storm of obscenities.

I could've hung up, but instead I let her vent. Ka-ching—just like that, a bonus. Sweet, right?

But after a while this potty-mouthed drama queen was draining me. I'd had enough. 'You do realise this is a phone sex line, right?' Silence. I sighed. 'Who's your husband?' When she said his name, I immediately recognised one of my regulars.

'Well, by the way, your husband's been professing his love to me.'

After a moment, her voice settled and she quietly asked, 'What's he doing calling you?'

'Your husband told me he was divorced and looking for a relationship.'

That only set her off on a tirade of F words—some I'd never even heard before. I interrupted, reminding her that her anger wouldn't change a thing; if she wanted the truth, she needed to catch him in the act.

I'd strung her husband along for as long as I could. I'd probably lose him after this, so why not have a little fun? She was almost in disbelief, but eventually calmed down and wanted to confront him about his indiscretion.

As it happened, he'd been trying to set up a face-to-face meeting. So, I suggested that the next time he called, I'd arrange for us to meet somewhere she could catch him in the act.

We set the plan in motion: I would give him the name of a hotel she'd picked. She would check in with me weekly until she had the exact time and date.

I shared the details with Sandra, and we dubbed it Operation Schmuck. It didn't take long for the guy to call and Operation Schmuck to begin.

A week later, the wife got in touch to let me know it went off without a hitch. Apparently, he told her he had a business dinner with overseas clients and needed to stay in the city. She gleefully described how she caught him at the hotel with roses and chocolates—things he'd never bought her.

Curious, I asked for a description of him. Turned out, he was nothing like he'd portrayed himself to be. A bloated man with a receding hairline. The moment felt golden—his karmic payback, served up fresh. The cheating husband never called again. His wife had him right where she wanted him—firmly tethered to her side.

It was always a mystery how intoxicated men managed to dial the sex phone line, let alone hold an intelligible conversation. Most responses were a mix of belches, slurred words and incoherent sentences. It was baffling, but it happened—especially during major sports events.

There were times when groups of men would try to talk to me at once. As funny as it was, it was also annoying. I couldn't make out a word they were saying and my responses usually ended up sounding ridiculous.

Once one guy tried to hold a conversation while another yelled, 'Show us your tits!' followed by a burst of laughter. The absurdity was off the charts—especially since they couldn't see anything. Their drunken rambling jumped from topic to topic, asking questions and answering them before I could even blink. It was chaos that would've given a stand-up comedian a whole new routine.

Then there was the time a very drunk client went totally quiet during a call, leaving awkward pauses between ramblings. I soon realised he was drifting in and out of sleep. After about ten minutes I decided to make use of my time and read a few chapters from a book out loud. Surprisingly, it worked—whenever he came back to his senses, he repeated the last few words I'd said. It was so hilarious I ended up earning a double bonus for it!

Honestly, I'd say anything to these tipsy men just to get a laugh. They'd fire off long-winded responses that didn't matter to me, as long as they stayed on the line. I kept them hooked with a mix of playful banter and risqué chatter.

Of course, there were also the abusive calls—from both men and women—starting with gems like, 'Hey, slut, spreading your legs again for the blokes?' These calls were pointless and just there to annoy me.

My reaction depended on my mood. If I was having a good night and wanted to stay on a high, I'd challenge myself to make a bonus from these troublemakers. I'd switch into money-making mode, deliberately provoking them to keep them on the line for at least thirty minutes.

The calls followed a pattern. They'd start with insults: 'You're a motherfucking slut.' My response? 'At least I have a talent.' This would get them riled up. 'Your mother's an even bigger slut.' And I'd fire back, 'Yep, all thanks to your mother teaching her how to slut around.'

Mentioning their mother always set them off, ensuring the minutes kept ticking by. It wasn't about targeting a specific nationality, but most of the abusive callers were young men from the same cultural background, all using the same slang.

Sometimes, the women were worse than the men, chiming in with ridiculous comments. I played along—if I was getting paid to keep them on the phone, I could be just as offensive. Their vulgar language flowed like water, making them sound like uneducated thugs. I couldn't fathom how belittling a woman on the other end of the line made them feel powerful. Maybe it was their only way to grab attention. I taunted them back with things like, 'Oh! Blah, blah, blah! Where'd you go to school, the Fuckwit Academy?' That's when I knew I had them locked in for the thirty-minute bonus round—it was like a boxing match to see who could outlast whom.

As soon as the clock hit thirty minutes, I hung up. Without fail, they called back. My responses might have stemmed from my own frustrations, since I couldn't express what I wanted to say to my husband. Unfortunately, I projected that onto callers who provoked me, even though they weren't really the cause. But once those words came out, they became an onslaught aimed at whoever was unlucky enough to be on the receiving end.

In a way, I felt like I was serving them their just desserts, considering they were willingly shelling out money to showcase their stupidity. Credit to them for mastering the art of doing two things at once. But there were nights when I just couldn't endure the barrage of abuse.

One such night was during a graveyard shift that kicked off at midnight. Exhausted and annoyed by my responsibilities at home, I found it especially tough. The early hours brought a call from a man with a clear agenda. Unfortunately for the little dickwad, he picked the wrong night to objectify me. Determined not to give him the satisfaction of a reaction, I decided to pull out my secret weapon: reverse psychology. It was a tactic I'd learned from a fellow phone operator, often used with kids to encourage good behaviour.

I responded to his insults with a pleasantness that only seemed to fuel his frustration. I even thanked him for his backhanded compliments, one after another. I kept up the charade until I hit my bonus, then slammed the phone down on him.

Clients who wanted to insult me thrived on provoking a reaction. Their love for verbal abuse became my motivation to rack up the cash. I countered their rudeness by doing the exact opposite of what they expected. I guess being a pretend shrink came in handy at times.

Lesson: Don't get stuck in the overthinking trap.
Ditch the mental clutter. Keep the good stuff, toss the rest.
Turn that anger into fuel and own it like the boss you are!

CHAPTER 29

An Englishman's fantasy

One of the call centre's sideline businesses tapped into the overseas market, and my next call came from England. Ayden was fixated on fantasy, and I was all in to entertain his desires. I had initially lured him with the promise of meeting, but after half a dozen calls it was clear he knew it would never happen. Still, he was more than happy to indulge in his fantasies with me.

That night he greeted me with a formal, 'Captain Bryce at your service, ma'am.' His impeccable English accent was a little too prim for my liking, but who was I to judge? During our first encounter, Ayden spilled his passion for role-playing, lamenting that his wife didn't share his enthusiasm. So naturally he turned to me to bring his wild scenarios to life. While his preferences weren't exactly my idea of fun, I had to admire his honesty—and creativity.

As soon as I answered, he dived in headfirst. Ayden cast me as an Italian woman on his yacht, sailing with my much older husband from Greece to Spain, while he played the role of my secret lover. I'd never travelled, but Ayden's vivid descriptions of each location made it feel like I had. His weakness was elegant women with seductive flair, so I went all out describing my outfit, knowing it would hook him every time.

He requested I go without underwear—no surprise there—and I could almost hear his brain exploding with graphic thoughts. His aristocratic accent might've been as fake as his yacht, but I played along.

'Ma'am, may I say you look enchanting tonight?'

'Yes, Captain Bryce,' I purred. Then, with a mischievous giggle, I added, 'I'd like your thoughts on my underwear. Take a quick look but be careful—my husband will join us for dinner soon.'

'But ma'am,' he replied, 'you haven't any underwear on.'

I sighed. 'Oh dear, I must've forgotten.'

The story unfolded like a bad romance novel. We were 'eating dinner' when I 'accidentally' dropped my napkin. Captain Bryce, being the gentleman he was, crawled under the table to retrieve it. According to Ayden, my partially deaf and blind husband remained oblivious while the captain lingered between my legs, discovering other 'delights'. Then came the unmistakable sound of pleasure as Ayden, bless his heart, started stroking his cock.

'My goodness, Captain,' I murmured, 'this feels incredible, but please come up—the food is being served, and it looks like my husband has fallen asleep.'

Ayden upped the ante, dismissing the waitstaff for the night and leaving us alone. I played along, moaning and simulating all sorts of enthusiasm, while my imaginary husband snored away in a deep slumber beside us. Totally believable, right?

As his breathing quickened, I slowed things down—gotta aim for that bonus. I asked him to blindfold me and do it to me again, and he practically squealed with delight. Ayden mimicked the most over-the-top noises and I joined in with a carefully timed moan. Glancing at my watch, I saw I was sixty seconds away from that sweet bonus, then—bam!—Ayden let out an almighty, prim-and-proper grunt.

Halle-fucken-lujah! I stayed in character to the end and secured my bonus. Ever the gentleman, Ayden lingered on the line to thank me before hanging up.

*Lesson: Unleash your inner wildness
and let your imagination shine!*

CHAPTER 30

A sense of wonder

Sex with women was a topic that would've made me blush years ago, but working on the phone lines gave my confidence a serious glow-up. Once I got past the initial shock, I dived headfirst into conversations that would've left past me hiding under a blanket.

These calls sparked something unexpected; not a sexual awakening, although I could fully appreciate women's beauty, but a connection to my own vulnerabilities and needs. I started pondering the what-ifs in my own life, seeing things with fresh eyes.

Among the endless callers, one stood out: Liz, a forty-six-year-old from the quaint town of Sawtell. A second-generation banana farmer, she'd spent her life running the family plantation. The moment she mentioned Sawtell, I was transported back to my honeymoon twenty years earlier, wandering through that picturesque coastal village. Funny how life ties little strings between strangers.

Back then, as a seventeen-year-old bride, I thought I was all grown up—married and having sex like a rabbit on heat. My naive little brain thought marriage meant adulthood, that I was suddenly a life expert. Well, newsflash: I sure as hell wasn't. I mean, who is at that age?

It's wild how a young mind twists the world into whatever shape fits their version of reality. Most teens are wrapped up in their own bubble, convinced the world is all about fun and freedom. Then there was me, ditching school to chase independence, working my butt off and quickly realising laundry didn't fold itself and bills didn't magically get paid. Still, I was young. Why stress about the hard stuff when I could pretend to have it all figured out, right? Sure, teens might seem self-absorbed, but throw them a challenge and they'll hit you with depth and empathy. They're not selfish, they're just winging it, one awkward step at a time, praying life doesn't knock them off course.

Liz had been stuck in a rut since losing her husband four years earlier. Their marriage had been ... let's just say uninspiring, especially in the bedroom. A week-long trip to Sydney to visit her cousin flipped a switch for Liz. Her cousin lived a vibrant life, confidently navigating life solo, unfazed and genuinely happy. It hit Liz hard. It was the kind of joy she had never known, and suddenly, she was hungry for it.

She bombarded me with questions. While I wasn't a certified sex therapist, my phone line experience felt like enough to be able to help. Her sex life had been limited to Sunday-night missionary—a routine so predictable she could set her banana plantation clock by it.

I encouraged her to explore her own body and told her about the lesbian couple who once called just to have me listen in. Her breathless little moans gave away what she was up to, and I couldn't help but feel proud—my star student was taking notes and doing homework.

When she told me she'd never felt that wet before, it was time to up the ante. Like any good mentor, I introduced her to the world of sex toys. With my experience making sensual body ticklers for a sex shop, I had just the right recommendations. Liz couldn't believe how much she'd come along in just that one call. And I was as proud as a teacher watching their student go from clueless to fully informed.

Lesson: Keep that curiosity alive—you never know what wild, amazing things you'll uncover about yourself. Who knows, you might just blow your own mind!

CHAPTER 31

Bankroller, saviour and friend: The PI

The growing hunger in my stomach drove me to make a 4 a.m. Maccas run. Returning to my booth, I inhaled the greasy burger and salt-saturated fries, gazing out the window at the fading night just before the morning sun stretched its arms and embraced the new day. In that moment, I longed for the comfort of my bed, aching to soothe my weary mind and exhausted body.

My thoughts were interrupted by the phone. TJ's raspy voice came through, a welcome distraction. We'd shared an interesting chat a week ago, but I had no idea he'd end up as my personal bankroll, saviour, and (somewhat unexpected) friend.

'How's your burger?' he asked.

I blinked, confused. 'How could you possibly know?'

His voice dropped a little. 'So, it's true then—that *was* you.'

A knot twisted in my stomach. *Did I say something I shouldn't have?* My memory was a blur, and I had no clue what I might've blurted out last time we spoke.

He rattled off the building and floor I was on, but I shot him down with a laugh. Then he casually dropped that he'd been standing right behind me just now, describing the ribbon in my hair, where I'd stood in line with the other woman, and what we'd ordered.

What the fuck? Alarmed, I threatened to report him as a stalker.

Laughing, he assured me there was no need—he was just having some fun. He reminded me I had mentioned working near Macca's in the city, and he was in the area. His light tone put me at ease, saving me from having to confess my carelessness to my supervisor.

He asked me to look out the window. Leaving the phone off the hook, I wandered into the chill-out room. True to his word, he was standing on the opposite side of Young Street, waving and blowing kisses my way.

What audacity! And yet, there I was, grinning like an idiot and waving back. He was a solidly built figure with dark hair—maybe glasses, too, from what I could see. He waved and blew kisses again, and I found myself scratching my head, wondering how the hell he knew my floor. Then it hit me—our floor was the only one lit up like a damn Christmas tree.

Back on the phone, TJ assured me he knew exactly how these calls worked and offered to stay on the line for hours next time. Perfect arrangement. That's when he officially became my personal bankroll.

It was a welcome relief, cutting down on the usual small talk. As I got to know him, his wit shone through. At twenty-nine, he was single and Lebanese—a combo I'd always associated with generosity and warmth, from my Granville days. TJ lived up to it; he felt familiar, like someone from the neighbourhood where I spent my teenage years.

TJ was a well-known, valuable guy to know. If you wanted something, he was your guy. A bit of a bad boy, he knew how to get things done without the drama.

He assured me he wasn't a criminal or into hard drugs, describing himself as a 'skilled businessman'. He owned multiple mobile phones that would occasionally ring during our talks. Surprisingly, this worked to my advantage, as he'd leave the line open, letting me catch snippets of muffled conversations.

Sometimes, he'd return to the phone, explaining he had things to handle; other times, he'd forget I was still on the line after shoving the phone in his pocket. When I asked about the cost of the calls, he assured me it wasn't a problem for him. I accepted that explanation without a second thought.

TJ told me he owned a private investigation and accounting firm, among other side ventures. One of his gigs involved referring people with expiring travel visas to an immigration lawyer in the city, earning him a small finder's fee for each introduction.

He invited me to send people his way, offering me a two-hundred-dollar finder's fee for each referral. As I mulled over the money he was willing to dish out, I couldn't help but wonder just how much he was raking in from these side deals.

He seemed like a jack of all trades and master of none. But when he mentioned he could get fake IDs, I started to think he might have connections most people would rather avoid. Then again, he could've just been bullshitting. Still, he was an interesting guy—harmless enough, at least.

Our talks knew no boundaries. He told me about an encounter where things got hot and heavy with a woman against a wall near the Parramatta River, right by a department store. I recognised the spot—it was completely exposed to anyone walking by, but he didn't care. His mantra, *I never miss out on an opportunity*, quickly became mine.

I admired his honesty. Once, he mentioned that being a big guy made sex tiring for him and that he preferred women to take charge. At first, I was irked, but then I realised he wasn't trying to be disparaging towards women; it was just his blunt way of putting things.

He wanted to lose weight, and joked, 'I can't see my dick anymore, not sure if it's even still there.'

That made me laugh. And it got me thinking how with each pregnancy, I lost sight of my own vagina, so why wouldn't it be the same for a guy?

I joked that his dick had shrunk inside his body, not realising I'd said it out loud. Instead of being offended, he laughed, and I appreciated his good-naturedness. I tended to blurt things out, but thankfully, TJ didn't mind.

I looked forward to speaking with him. Despite his unconventional business ideas, TJ was a good guy. He treated me with respect and never resorted to verbal abuse. Our chats were light-hearted, no explicit content, and whether he had those kinds of talks with other girls was none of my business.

He did try to get me to talk seductively a few times, but I skilfully avoided it, and we always ended up laughing.

'Come on, talk dirty to me; I'll give you hours on the phone,' he'd say.

I'd playfully respond, 'You're too cute for dirty talk; it'd be weird now that I've gotten to know you.' Which, let's be honest, was true—I was starting to like him as a person. He was goofy, sweet, a little vulnerable, and intelligent. Maybe I was seeing more in him than I'd originally thought.

And then it happened.

TJ called one night. I was feeling unusually vulnerable. I spilled the beans about something embarrassing that had happened just a week earlier. Maybe it was because I hadn't met him in person yet; he was just a voice at the end of the phone. I confessed that I'd committed an offence—nothing too serious, but I had broken the law and needed help. Caught up in a moment of madness, I'd been busted for shoplifting.

I'll never forget being taken to the police station and fingerprinted twice—because I mixed up my left and right hands. Rookie mistake. The officer didn't even notice when I offered my hands, and I awkwardly apologised for the mix-up. I was humiliated, crying my eyes out, but the officer was surprisingly nice about it. One of the older constables noticed my shaking hands and showed some real kindness.

He comforted me by placing his hand on my shoulder, saying, 'We all make mistakes. It'll be all right. Just don't do it again.' But then he dropped the bomb—I'd have to appear in court. I wished the earth would open up and swallow me whole. The thought of a permanent bad reputation haunted me.

So now, I was a crim. How the hell was I going to live with that label?

Enter TJ, my unexpected saviour. A few nights later, he called with some info about a connection he had, and set me up with a specialist lawyer. He reassured me that I wasn't a bad person, just emotionally screwed up. That was a relief.

After I shared my story, the lawyer told me about a young man who'd done nearly the same thing, but on a larger scale. Now that young man was helping others. Yep, he was talking about himself.

The universe was on my side that day, because this kind-hearted lawyer didn't charge me a fee. I sensed his genuine compassion, reaffirming my belief that TJ was indeed a decent guy.

In the office of this professional lawyer, I burst into tears. He was the second man I'd met who wanted to extend a helping hand without expecting anything in return. It was a shock—a wonderful one—because I had never experienced such kindness before. I'll always remember him and TJ for their non-judgemental attitude towards me.

Those events turned out to be a blessing in disguise, sparking a process of reflection on the effects of my actions. Though I didn't recognise it at the time, I was suffering from depression. I was stuck between a rock and a hard place, barely hanging on. Money was tight, and sleepless nights for work had pushed me to swipe No-Doz tablets. It wasn't for kicks; it was survival.

After lengthy phone conversations with TJ, I felt like I knew him well enough to trust him, so I admitted that I was married with kids.

Surprisingly, that didn't scare him off. Honestly, it was exhilarating. He had seen me at Macca's in the line-up and knew what I looked like, so I was eager to meet him face-to-face. Still, I wanted to make it a surprise—I was curious to see if he was telling the truth about himself.

I was a bit apprehensive about meeting another client, especially considering my track record with men wasn't exactly stellar. But maybe this time would be different; after all, he had helped me when he wasn't obligated to. At no point did I think he wanted to use me. I liked him, but not romantically—there was no heat, no spark.

Surrendering to my inner snoop and my talent for being delightfully reckless, I decided to pay a visit to his office in Parramatta. It was risky, but I couldn't resist—I knew exactly where in the business district he worked.

Feeling like an undercover agent, I approached the door. The sign read: 'Private Investigator, Accounting and Financial Adviser'. So he *had* been telling the truth. I was relieved.

Peering through the glass door, I spotted the usual office equipment. When I walked in, a pretty woman in her early twenties greeted me. I couldn't help but wonder why TJ would want to meet with me when he had someone like her around. I guess that said more about how I viewed myself than it did about him.

At that point, my plan to catch him off guard—or worse, lying—now seemed childish. After I introduced myself, the office assistant led me through to TJ. His surprised look said it all.

The receptionist left, closing the door behind her. TJ stood up from behind his enormous desk, wearing a grin as wide as the one at Luna Park. In a single stride, he approached me, extended both arms and lifted me off the ground, hugging me like an old friend. I was in shock—unsure if it was because he could lift me or the unexpected attempt at a kiss. I quickly turned my face, and his lips landed on my cheek instead.

Looking into my eyes, he complimented me, saying I was even more beautiful than he remembered. Then, with a playful glint in his eye, he asked, 'How about a real kiss?' I smiled and shook my head.

Despite his obvious disappointment, he grinned and declared he'd kiss me before the end of the day. I laughed and shook my head in jest.

He graciously accepted that small defeat, which was refreshing. Then he put his hands to his face, expressing admiration for my stunning blue eyes. Once again, I was taken aback and flushed with embarrassment.

Glancing at his luxurious gold Rolex watch, he reached over to the intercom and informed his secretary that he was going out for a meeting, cancelling the rest of his appointments for the day.

I apologised for taking up his time and got ready to walk out. I didn't want my whim to put him out. But then he shuffled around in his top drawer, pulled out a card, and scribbled something on it. He rummaged some more before sliding something into his pocket. I was curious but thought it would be rude to pester him about it.

Before I could think it any longer, he leaned over, grabbed my hand, and asked where I thought I was going. I frowned, and he laughed, saying, 'Come on, let's do brunch. I know a great little place just around the corner.' And off we went!

After placing our orders, TJ handed me a small box. I hesitated to open it, unsure what could fit in such a tiny container. It was his business card. Baffled, I looked at him, shaking my head while laughing. 'Why?'

'Turn it over.'

On the back were the letters *IOU*. TJ explained that I could contact him whenever I needed assistance, and he would be there for me.

Perplexed, I remarked, 'I don't understand. I'm the one who owes you.'

He made a waving gesture with his hand. 'It's all good. I've got your back.'

I couldn't help but shed a tear as I smiled, thanking him. Leaning in to kiss his cheek, he brazenly turned and our lips met instead.

'Told you I'd kiss you by the end of the day.'

TJ wasn't someone I would typically find attractive, yet his confidence was magnetic—an attribute I wished I possessed. Towering at about a hundred ninety-eight centimetres compared to my petite hundred and fifty, he had a pale olive complexion, short black wavy hair and a moustache, almost resembling a Mafiosi boss.

He sported a pair of heavy-set, black-framed glasses that continuously slid down the bridge of his prominent nose. Dressed sharply in a suit and tie, his little tummy pouch was discreetly tucked behind his vest. Though he might have been a bit overweight, he carried himself with confidence.

I observed a cute habit of his—after every sentence, he would scrunch up his nose and then use his finger to push his glasses back up.

He broadened my perspective—I began to understand that attraction extended far beyond surface appearances. It encompassed countless elements that made a connection between two people meaningful and surprisingly, it was the unexpected things that caught my attention.

Throughout our brunch, which turned into a drawn-out lunch, TJ repeatedly expressed that I was sexy, unable to look away from my eyes. Despite working on a sex line, I remained quietly modest, dismissing his words as a man's attempt to get into my pants. Naive as I might have been, my experiences so far had taught me that men often expected something in return, even if I tried to convince myself otherwise.

But secretly, those words elevated my self-confidence, leading me to reconsider the way I perceived myself. We engaged in conversation for hours, and I was pleasantly surprised by his genuine friendship and generosity.

Afterwards, we strolled back to his office, where he showcased the multifaceted organisation he had set up for himself. I was in awe of his audacity to go it alone. Rows of fake IDs and licences caught my eye. With a smile, he said, 'See these? I get two hundred dollars apiece. Not bad, hey.'

'Not bad at all.'

On a shelf was a display of brand-new mobile phones. 'These are already promised to people, but if you need one, it's free for you.'

My eyebrows shot up, then I laughed, saying, 'Sure, a new mobile phone would be great.' I was joking, but I did genuinely need one.

A week later, we met up for a quick catch-up, and there in a box was a shiny, brand-new Samsung flip phone.

That same night, he called me at work and gave me two bonuses. He then asked me out to lunch again, which I happily agreed to. Despite my initial reservations about his motives, I thought, *what harm is there*? After all, I had already been out with him.

Deep down, I questioned whether he might expect compensation for the gifts and help he had given me. Yet, I wanted to believe he was not like that. When we met this time, he brought a box of cherry liqueur chocolates, remembering that they were one of my favourites. Receiving all this attention and gifts was something I was not used to from my husband, and I enjoyed it.

Chris and I started having occasional meet-ups at the Park Royal in Parramatta for drinks. These outings gave TJ the chance to introduce his builder buddies to Chris, which led to a ton of electrical work coming Chris's way, and he couldn't have been happier. He wasn't exactly a magnet for work since he'd ventured into self-employment, and when he did land a job, collecting the money owed was a whole other story.

All the while I kept the true nature of my friendship with TJ under wraps. To Chris, TJ was just a friend of a work colleague, and as long as he was getting those recommendations, he was all smiles.

During Chris's business discussions with TJ's friends, I found solace in TJ's company. Chris, engrossed in financial matters, remained oblivious to TJ's interest in me. But at that stage, I didn't care what he thought; I was just biding my time and waiting for the right moment to escape. Despite my persistent push for a divorce, Chris always managed to talk me out of it. And even though I didn't desire TJ, I found myself making comparisons between him and Chris.

TJ, a self-made entrepreneur, managed his business finances with a humility that starkly contrasted with Chris's grandiose delusions. Being with TJ was refreshing; he brought some fun into my life, temporarily overshadowing my husband's flaws. For a few months, TJ continued to call me at work, offering bonuses and engaging in private conversations after hours.

Feeling a sense of indebtedness for the kindness he showed me, I eventually agreed to a romantic rendezvous with him.

He arranged everything, chilled champagne, my favourite cherry liqueur chocolates, and a trail of rose petals leading to the bed. While I appreciated the romantic gestures, I sensed this wasn't just a date—he had expectations for sex. Despite my hesitation and the plain truth that our chemistry was about as exciting as a lukewarm cup of tea, I found myself behind that locked door, contemplating a pity fuck just to wrap things up.

I was standing by the hotel window when suddenly TJ's body pressed against mine. His arms encircled my shoulders, and he began kissing my neck. It was a pleasant sensation, I suppose, but I wasn't turned on and didn't desire him that way. When he spun me around, locking his hands around my face and kissing me on the lips, I pushed him away. 'No, you're not what I want; I need a real man.'

As soon as those words escaped my lips, regret washed over me. I hadn't meant to insult him; I was just frustrated at finding myself in such an uncomfortable situation.

Despite his attempt to mask it with a laugh, his hurt expression was unmistakable. I recognised that look—the same one I'd often hidden when my husband mocked me.

I sat on the bed as tears of shame streamed down my face. I berated myself for being unkind to such a sweet guy. TJ approached me and offered a heartfelt apology for making me cry. I looked up at him, shaking my head, confessing that he was too nice and too good for me. Tenderly, he wiped away my tears, assuring me that we didn't have to proceed with anything. With a look of compassion, he suggested we could just talk and hang out. I agreed to stay a little longer. He playfully remarked that he had that effect on women.

Engrossed in conversation, we found ourselves lying on the bed, facing each other, when unexpectedly, our lips met in a lingering kiss. Although I would have preferred otherwise, the impending school pick-up time prompted me to apologise and ask for a ride back to my car. During the drive back, my thoughts raced: *What the hell just happened? Why did I go to a hotel room with him, knowing what might transpire?*

Morality struck me—how weird was that? I couldn't ignore it. Why? I had no idea. But I was married to an arsehole and still that didn't excuse my actions. I grappled with these questions repeatedly; clearly, I had a lot to learn about how to break free from the sense of obligation to men.

As it turned out, TJ and I remained friends for a long time, even after I left the phone lines, but our relationship never evolved beyond a platonic friendship.

It took me some time to finally accept that I needed help for all the confusion in my head, which only drove me to make decisions that worked against me. At first, it felt like admitting defeat, like I'd failed at life. Eventually, I realised that asking for help wasn't giving up—it was the first step towards taking back control.

Lesson: Never give a damn about your reputation or what anyone thinks — just keep moving forward and grab the help when it comes, no strings attached.

CHAPTER 32

Knock, knock, who's there?

A woman spoke when I answered the phone. Nothing unusual there—I'd spoken to women before. But there was something about her voice, like she was trying hard to sound formal, enunciating each word. Then she hit me with, 'Are you there, madam?'

'Yes, yes, I'm here.'

Her tone had this weird, purposeful edge. 'I'm from a national relay service, and I have John on the line. He wants to speak with you. Are you available?'

Confused but curious, I said, 'Of course, tell John I'm all ears.' There was a muffled exchange, then some weird clicking in the background.

Wait, what? Is this some bizarre three-way call? I was so not in the mood for that tonight. My mind raced—was John in the background, doing … God only knew, while this woman—who sounded like she had a plum up her arse—was putting on airs to make it sound fancy?

After what felt like an eternity, she came back on the line. 'John's ready, but he can't speak.'

My response was a slow, 'Um, sure.'

'He can't speak. Do you understand that?'

'Oh, most men get like that once they've experienced sex with me,' I stupidly responded.

'No, you don't understand. John cannot talk. Do you grasp what that means?'

'Is he shy?' I asked, genuinely confused.

Sounding frustrated, she said, 'No, please listen.' Meanwhile, light knocking sounded in the background. 'I'm from a national relay service, conveying what your caller wants to say. John, your caller, cannot speak. He's mute. He'll listen to you and respond with one knock for yes, two for no, and three for more. Do you understand now?'

'Wow! Sure, can I write that down before I forget?'

She sounded exasperated. 'Yes, go ahead.'

Oh, boy, did I get that all wrong! I jotted it down, assuring her I understood—though I was thinking, *I have no idea how this is going to play out.*

After a few more minutes of introductions between the woman, John and me, I felt like I was ready for this new adventure. I'd never interacted with a mute person before, which made me realise how clueless I'd been about it. After all, how could I know without ever having the experience?

Working the phone lines definitely made me more aware of things, but this moment had me laser-focused—like a cat chasing a laser pointer, except I had no idea where the hell it was going.

Holy shit! How is this going to work? I thought, letting her do the talking for a few seconds, hoping for more clarity.

She explained that John wanted the full experience. She could've stayed on the line without me knowing and honestly, it didn't bother me. But getting it right? Now that mattered. No inhibitions here—I wanted a five-star rating from him, even if I had no clue what I was doing.

Though I hesitated to turn this into some 'knock, knock, who's there' scenario, I convinced myself that his imagination and my voice would have to do the trick. It wouldn't be much different from the usual calls ... right?

'Okay, here goes. Hi, John, I'm Dominique. Can I share a bit about myself?' One knock.

Good start.

I gave him the full-on visual: me, all dressed up and ready to wow, painting a picture so vivid I could practically hear him drooling. But ... no response. I wasn't about to let that stop the show, though, so I switched gears. Decided to give him the juicy details—how hot and bothered I was, all alone in my bed. I mean, I was practically roasting, so why not share the heat?

Suddenly, three sharp knocks echoed—*more*. He was into it. Smiling to myself, I conveyed how pleased I was that he was there with me, then playfully asked if he could imagine joining me. Another knock followed, signalling his approval.

I slowed down, laying it on thick, talking about how I imagined touching his body and getting him to do the same. I dragged out every word like I had all the time in the world, creating this vibe between us. To really get into it, I closed my eyes and lost myself in the scene I was painting for him. It felt real, like our connection was tangible. It was a total shift from my usual game. Damn, it was working.

I kept going, describing stuff I'd never done, pushing the limits, and honestly, I was kinda impressed with myself. Well done, me!

He only knocked twice when I suggested sliding my finger in his arse. I mean, I figured most guys were into that, but clearly, I hit a nerve—or not. Lesson learned. Honestly, I was just relieved he didn't hang up on me then and there.

Surprisingly, I enjoyed the call. The lack of trash talk was a refreshing change from the usual parade of losers. It made me wonder if those guys thought throwing around nasty words somehow boosted their power and superiority. The way guys got their kicks from calling me names and bragging about the size of their cocks was downright ridiculous. Surely it was just wishful thinking? I'd imagined a few of them were micro-sized … and guess what? Less than a year later, my new job taught me I wasn't wrong. Those little guys *definitely* existed.

My chat with John lasted about twenty minutes. The knocking became rapid-fire, and his breathing became heavy, I figured he was about to finish, then—boom—silence. The phone went dead.

That call turned my lack of confidence upside down. John called me back once, but then requested someone else. At first, I took it personally, thinking he was over me, but he probably just wanted to try a new flavour. Yeah, that stung a little, because I wanted to be his go-to girl. Guess you can't win 'em all.

Lesson: Assumptions? Total trap. Don't fall for it.
Just roll with the punches and embrace what new experiences
teach you—there's always something you don't know.

CHAPTER 33

The noose around her neck

Little did I know, my next caller would drop a truth bomb that would later echo in my own life.

'What would you do if you suspected your husband was lying?' a woman's voice, thick with sadness, cut through the line. 'Do you meet up with men? Has my husband been with you?'

'I'm sorry, but this is a sex line, not an escort agency.' 'Figures. That's what I get,' she snapped.

'Look, just tell me what's going on, and maybe I'll have something for you.' 'Typical answer. Should've known better.' She was pissed.

'If you don't like what I'm saying, you know where the hang-up button is.'

It was either going to end in disaster or somehow work out in my favour. Surprisingly, she stuck around, her tone softening. She told me of her suspicions about her husband, a man who travelled frequently for work, making her feel insecure in their marriage.

Years of trouble had piled up, with separations and reunions whenever it suited him. A man who could leave and return like he was changing seasons was a big red flag.

And yeah, that was my future, too—my oh-shit moment was fast approaching.

Lydia had put her husband, Judas, on a pedestal. She was drawn to his so-called intelligence, all starry-eyed, thinking he was the ultimate catch. The more she put him up there, the less she seemed to value herself.

He had this way of cutting her off in every conversation, just to prove he was right. Lydia found herself caught in an endless loop, needing his approval before making any decisions. I didn't even need to say it—she was too busy thinking she was the one in control, while Judas had his hand on the puppet strings, making her believe otherwise.

But of course, I couldn't keep my mouth shut. 'He's controlling you, can't you see that?' I blurted out. A heavy silence followed. Had I crossed the line, or was I just saying what needed to be said?

Finally, she spoke. 'I can never win an argument; he confuses me so much. I'm an idiot,' she said, her voice shaking.

'No, Lydia. You're not an idiot. He's making you feel like you are.' My voice was a little sharper than I meant it to be. Honestly, it hit me deep because I knew what it felt like. Guys like Judas loved having the power to make you doubt yourself.

Another pause. Then came the sobs.

I felt like a jerk for making her cry, but I wasn't backing down. 'He's not worth the tears.'

After a beat, Lydia finally quieted. 'You're right. He's not worth it. But … he does take care of us.'

And there it was. The trap. That twisted empathy women felt for the ones who tore them down. It's a vicious cycle. Breaking free from that mental grip was harder than it seemed.

Lydia couldn't ignore it anymore. Even though she had all the financial perks, the misery was slowly suffocating her. She'd kept her struggles to herself, not trusting family or friends with the truth.

Why? Because in their eyes, Judas was the golden husband—perfect, amazing. So Lydia felt guilty for even thinking the way she did.

Judas was a master manipulator. He had that classic move where he shifted all the blame onto her, like some petulant child trying to avoid getting in trouble. It was as if he was playing a game where he never lost.

The thing was Lydia's gut was telling her something that made her skin crawl. Judas wasn't just sneaking around with women; she had a hunch he was enjoying himself with men, too.

'So is he secretly gay, or maybe bi?' I asked.

'What? No!' she stumbled over her words, seemingly thrown off.

'But you said men and women. He was spending time away with both, right? Those were your words, Lydia,' I pressed, feeling the tension rise. I wasn't about to let this go.

She paused, then her voice broke through the silence. Judas had been playing this game for so long, she'd known all along he'd deny it. But now, finally, Lydia admitted it: her husband wasn't just lying to her, he was living a lie. He had a thing for men, and she'd been the one left in the dark.

Lydia always had this nagging feeling that something was off whenever they had sex. Judas would bury his face in the pillow, refusing to look at her. And if he wasn't doing that, he'd insist she get on her knees and give him oral until he came in her mouth. Same old, same old. It pissed her off that he wouldn't even look at her. It felt like he was somewhere else, thinking about someone else.

I told her the best way to handle it was to catch him in the act. Do some sleuthing—check his flight details, dig into his bank statements, call the hotel. It'd give her the truth she was craving. She seemed up for it and promised she'd give it a shot. 'Can I call you back if I need to?' she asked. Of course, I said yes.

A month later, Lydia called. She was furious, her voice shaking. She'd caught him in a lie, and after a nasty argument, he'd stormed off, blaming her for being late for his flight.

Lydia was a mess. Her sobs were punctuated by ragged breaths. She felt guilty, like the fight was somehow her fault. In a desperate attempt to fix things, she called him. First call, no answer. Second call, he picked up.

'Why are you calling?' he asked.

Lydia pulled the classic move: apologised, claimed she missed him, and said she just wanted to say goodbye. Judas, of course, made some lame excuse to hang up fast.

'I'm boarding the plane, gotta go.'

But here's the kicker—just a week before, she had overheard him booking a hotel near Sydney Airport. So how was he now supposedly on a plane?

At first, the hotel booking didn't set off alarm bells. But the next message from him was the punch to the gut. 'Taxiing, about to take off. Will call when I get to my destination.'

That's when everything fell into place.

I couldn't help but admire Lydia for her plan to expose Judas. She wasn't just sitting around waiting for the truth to slap her in the face.

Lydia wasn't stupid. She knew exactly what was going on. So after a short pause to let her blood boil, she dialled the hotel where Judas was supposedly staying. She got connected to the room. Guess who picked up? You got it. Judas.

At that moment, Lydia wasn't just relieved—she was fuming. Her suspicions were confirmed. Judas wasn't even flying out until eleven the next morning, and here he was at the hotel. Lydia had him. Real, undeniable proof. She was ready to shove it right in his face.

Judas's voice was shaky. 'My plane was delayed,' he mumbled. 'I'm just catching up with the boys from work for a few drinks.'

Right. Lydia didn't buy it for a second. She suspected it was about something more intimate, but she couldn't pinpoint who the lucky person was. He dodged her questions, threw in a couple of his own, and tried to make her feel dumb for even asking. But for the first time, she wasn't the one who was clueless here.

By this point in our conversation Lydia was hyperventilating, her words spitting out like fire: 'The damn bastard, the damn hypocrite.' She had wanted to take a cab and confront him at the hotel, show him just how pissed off she was. But she knew it would make her look unhinged.

Then Judas actually claimed that Lydia wouldn't understand; that she was stopping him from having fun. I was floored. Those words would stick with me later—years down the road, when I had my own struggles with trust in relationships.

'Stop, Lydia, please!' I couldn't help myself. 'Do you seriously believe him? Your husband's a dick, and that's the bottom line!'

Lydia said she had wrapped up their conversation by telling him to enjoy his time with the boys before hanging up. But she'd hoped for more. She wanted him to come home so they could spend time together. Instead, the jerk—scratch that, the big jerk—stayed cosy in his hotel room, knowing full well his wife was a mess.

That night, he texted Lydia, claiming he'd just returned after a couple of drinks with the guys and telling her how miserable it had all been. And, of course, he added that it wasn't her fault he hadn't had a good time.

It wasn't her fault! Seriously, what the hell is wrong with this guy? I was fuming. I could have punched him right in the balls.

Judas kept pushing the same tired line, assuring Lydia that it was all just him goofing off with the boys. He didn't want her thinking he was having a good time, which he claimed was hard to share with her because she made him feel guilty for wanting a life.

My blood was boiling. 'Lydia, he's a piece of shit—like the kind of crap that sticks to the toilet bowl. For God's sake, flush him away!'

I could see it clear as day: Judas was playing her, twisting everything to make her feel guilty while he took no responsibility for his lies. He was a cunning manipulator. I reminded her how he always made her feel insignificant, like she wasn't worth the truth.

'Don't let him have that power over you anymore, Lydia. Remove the noose around your neck before Judas squeezes the life out of you.'

There I was, spewing powerful words that I should've taken on board myself. Funny how it's easier to dish out advice than actually take it.

Clearly rattled, Lydia went on about all the times she'd tried to get Judas to show her a scrap of affection. He never did.

She was stuck at home, juggling kids, the never-ending mountain of chores and her job, all while Judas claimed to be on one of his 'work trips'.

And despite it all, Lydia still thought she loved him.

'If he truly loved you, Lydia, he wouldn't lie. He would move mountains to keep you. You should be the centre of his world. Ask yourself: is he worth this misery?'

Lydia's story wasn't unique. I'd heard it all before. Women in this situation, women I knew personally. The lies? They could have gotten away with murder.

I didn't hold back. I told her to get whatever proof she could in case she needed it for the inevitable battle with a manipulative man. Trust me, if you end up in a divorce, having a paper trail will save your arse. Men may promise they'll play nice in court, say, 'I'll be fair.'

Don't buy it. When money's on the line, they'll go straight for the jugular and bleed you dry.

As for Lydia? She never called back. I hope she found peace, found her strength. Honestly, I felt proud to dish out the advice, even though I wasn't brave enough to take it myself—at least, not yet.

***Lesson:** Don't be an option. If you are, you'll be stuck waiting forever to become a priority.
Put yourself first and take charge of your own happiness.*

CHAPTER 34

Londoners and ingenious scams

The business partners had a knack for getting rich off the sex phone lines, and during my time there I saw three ways they managed to milk money out of these poor sods. Who knew how many other scams they cooked up over the years?

It baffled me how easily men fell for it—like moths to a flame. But I guess when you're lonely and desperate, a little false hope goes a long way. These lines didn't care what the men were after—fetishes, companionship, or just a quick thrill, they got it all.

One of the better business ideas was convincing Londoners they could chat with a free-spirited Aussie girl. Ads in English papers had guys calling in, thinking they'd be chatting with real Australian women backpacking through London with a bunch of girlfriends, just waiting for someone to call.

My job? Make them believe it. We had a map of the Buckingham Palace area and Victoria Coach Station—great for looking official, but no one bothered to give us the rest of the damn city.

I hadn't travelled myself, so when men mentioned meeting at a cafe or pub, I had no clue where they were talking about. But then, about two weeks later, we got a new night manager—Sydney. And she was bloody English. Jackpot!

Without hesitation, Sydney told me how her hippie parents had embraced the whole free love vibe in Sydney during the 1960s. A few months after they landed back in Putney, London, they found out they were expecting. They decided to name her Sydney in honour of her city of conception. Her parents split up before she was born, but her mum quickly met someone else, who Sydney still calls Daddy to this day.

Her biological father? Well, that was anyone's guess, thanks to her mother's revolving door of relationships. Her mum wasn't shy about the fact that she didn't stick around with anyone long enough to make it official. Honestly, I kind of admired the woman's frankness.

Sydney, however, was unfazed. She'd received a lot of love from the men in her mum's life, which I thought was strange but somehow sweet. *Lots of love from men.* I couldn't help but feel a pang of longing, though I often went about getting affection in all the wrong ways.

Her words stuck with me, though: 'From a tough start, something good came. I'm grateful for all the love that went into me getting here.' It took me a while to get that, but years later I'd realise how right she was. All the mess, all the hard times—sometimes they were leading you to something better.

Sydney always ended her calls with a perky 'Cool bananas!' At first it seemed odd, but by the end of the day I found myself grinning like an idiot every time she said it. The girl was an absolute dynamo—helping callers left and right, bouncing from one to the next, then back to her desk.

One night, I found myself chatting with an Englishman who asked me where I'd like to go out. Completely clueless, I called Sydney over for backup. True to form, she snatched the phone, introduced herself as my friend, and casually mentioned it was my first time in London.

She suggested a bunch of things I'd probably like and convinced him I'd meet him at The Ten Bells. She handed the phone back to me and I finished the call, still blissfully unaware of the pub's shady past. Thanks to the charming caller, I learned all about it soon after.

My client spent the next fifteen minutes chatting about the history of the pub. Turns out it was linked to the infamous Jack the Ripper, and his last victim had a drink there the very night she was killed. Not exactly the cheeriest topic, still, it earned me a bonus!

As planned, my caller showed up at the pub but I, of course, was a no-show. He called back, wondering where I was. I whipped up a quick story and we set up another meeting. When I flaked a second time, he gave up and never called back.

This was the usual drill. Once they realised I wasn't the real deal, they cut their losses. But there were always those persistent ones, the ones who kept coming back. As Sydney would say, 'They aren't the full quid.'

Englishmen and my Aussie regulars had something in common: they were all a bit sex-starved.

The big difference?

Their tone.

Englishmen had that posh, almost reverent vibe. It was like being wooed by a character straight out of a Victorian romance. At times, their politeness was more annoying than charming. I never knew if they were being sarcastic or if they were just … nice? It was a weird feeling.

And then there was the scheme where we convinced men to buy our underwear. I'd drop a line like, 'I wish you could see how wet you're making me; it's all over my undies.' That little nugget usually did the trick—wallets were whipped out faster than you could say 'panties'.

Sometimes they'd call back, complaining the underwear wasn't smelly or stained. I'd quickly divert their attention by diving into some spicy sex talk, shifting their focus from my undies to their, well, dicks. Men were funny like that; once the blood rushed elsewhere, they forgot about everything else.

I had one married client who wanted my underwear. I suggested he have them sent to a friend's address, which turned out to be profitable since his friend was single, so I gained him as a client, too. The regular caller stayed blissfully unaware that his friend was chatting with me behind his back.

Another hustle was a stack of generic black-and-white photocopies of girls in various positions and stages of undress. Each woman I worked with picked one photo to send to clients. There were only about twenty different women in these photos, but with more than twenty women working the phones, the whole thing got confusing, fast.

Honestly, the photo gig was a bit unrealistic. At the very least there should've been a unique photo for each operator, with a register to keep track of who had which one, so no one ended up with double-ups.

My photo? Forever etched in my mind. It featured a curvy, topless woman in her twenties, leaning back slightly, long hair cascading over her shoulders.

She had that sweet, sultry vibe—definitely the best photo. The rest were far too raunchy for my taste.

One young woman I worked with kept clients' addresses to herself instead of reporting them to the supervisor. She figured out which men were willing to pay more for things, and she built a side hustle. She used a post office box to cover her tracks and, to make it even more tempting, she'd wear the underwear before sending it off. You bet the guys kept calling her.

By the time she shared her hustle with me, the underwear gig had ended at work. I couldn't help but admire her for taking the opportunity and running with it. A little entrepreneurial spirit never hurt anyone.

Lesson: Life throws opportunities at you, grab them and make them work for you.

CHAPTER 35

Every dog has its day

The night crawled by agonisingly slowly. Watching the hands of my watch move at a pace that could only be described as glacial, exhaustion settled in like a heavy blanket, threatening to keep my eyes shut for good. Before I knew it, I'd given in to sleep. Not even half an hour later the phone rang, yanking me out of my peaceful state like a bucketful of cold water. Struggling to lift my head, I reached for the receiver, took a deep breath and tried to shake off the drowsiness. 'So what's your name, handsome?' I rasped.

'Yeah, hi, I'm Geoff.'

The moment I heard his voice, my brain lit up like a Christmas tree. That distinct lisp. Surely he wouldn't be foolish enough to introduce himself by his real name. But there it was: Geoff. A man I detested, and for good reason. He was my husband's closest friend, the one who introduced him to the Masons. This was the guy who slapped one of my daughters across the face because she sat in his car to escape the rain. He was worried she might wet the interior.

At just eleven, Katya often helped her father on weekend jobs. When she told me what had happened, I went ballistic. A heated argument with Chris escalated into him hitting *me* across the face and giving me a stern warning. He claimed Katya probably deserved it. I couldn't believe he sided with that jerk instead of supporting our daughter. I wanted to rip both Chris's and Geoff's heads off their shoulders with my bare teeth.

The next time I saw Geoff—whom I'd fittingly dubbed Devil Man—I let my fury fly. Arrogance and dismissal spread across his face as he laughed me off and sauntered away without a care. In that moment, I realised he wasn't worth another ounce of my energy.

Not long after, Geoff got a taste of karma. He was mistakenly arrested, confused with a guy who'd robbed a petrol station at gunpoint. That was just the beginning of his payback and tonight I was serving him another course. Every dog has its day, and that scruffy wimp was getting his.

Luckily, Geoff didn't have a clue I worked here. With the advantage firmly in my hands, I decided to have some fun, roping in another woman to help. Geoff was thrilled about the idea of two for the price of one. A spineless sponger in his early forties, he still lived at home with his mother—seventy-something and happy to indulge his every whim, including letting him bring his sixty-something girlfriend over for sleepovers.

I met his girlfriend once—shy, softly spoken, way too nice for him. At the time, I was judgemental. The age gap? Ridiculous. It felt more like a mother–child relationship. And I knew Devil Man didn't love her. The way he spoke about her to my husband was full of disrespect. He was using her, taking advantage of her kindness. Her lack of confidence made her an easy target for jerks like him. Years later, I realised those insecurities were mine, too.

Devil Man had it made—two women cooking for him, two places to stay for free and sex without commitment. Meanwhile, here I was, sitting at the end of the phone, holding all the cards. It was my duty to string him along for as long as possible. The goal? A fat bonus.

He surprised me by waiting while I went to grab my girlfriend to talk to him. Luckily, Ellen—the one-armed bandit—was the supervisor that night. After I told her who this jerk was, she was all in. She knew exactly how to keep him on the line.

First, she got him worked up. The way he blew his load … hilarious. It wasn't the most pleasant thing to hear, but now I knew what Devil Man sounded like during sex—imagine a donkey's hee-haw and you've got it.

I described his physical features to Ellen—red hair, bushy beard. She got it. Being a strawberry blonde herself, Ellen had experienced the mockery redheads got—she'd been called a 'ranga' more than once. And Geoff was the type to argue for the sake of it, even when he was dead wrong, always needing the last word. Armed with that knowledge, she knew exactly how to push his buttons.

Looking me in the eye, Ellen winked and whispered, 'This buzzing in my ears is giving me a headache. Let's get some compensation from this guy.' Couldn't have put it better myself.

An hour later, I was grinning from ear to ear, counting my bonus. When it came to getting the last word, Ellen handed me the phone and I got to ask him one final question.

'So, you think you know everything, Geoff? Here's one for you: can you go fuck yourself?' I slammed the phone down, satisfaction swelling in my chest.

In that moment, I felt like I'd gotten some small piece of justice for what he'd done to my daughter. Not that I'd been seeking revenge—he brought it on himself by reaching out. I'd done my job, and oh, it felt sweet.

He was the only man, aside from my husband, who I truly despised. Before that night, revenge wasn't even on my radar. Funny how life works, though. Sometimes, it hands you exactly what you need, just when you least expect it.

From then on, whenever Geoff came around I couldn't help but flash him a knowing smirk.

Little did he know I had a secret—and it was a good one.

Lesson: Don't waste time planning revenge. Sit back, relax, and watch those who've crossed you dig their own graves.

CHAPTER 36

Break free

Some people had natural charisma, the kind that turned heads without trying. Anna, a woman in her forties, was one of them. She worked alongside me on the phone lines and, despite her knockout looks and sharp wit, kept things refreshingly honest with her clients. We bonded quickly, our lives intertwining over shared struggles.

One evening, I found her at her desk, her usual spark replaced by a shadow of something heavy. She stared at the phone like it had personally offended her.

'What's up, babe? Difficult client?'

She glanced at me, lips pursed, and shook her head. 'Nope. Just my husband being a self-absorbed prick. Again. Honestly, I'm starting to think he's allergic to honesty.'

The phones were quiet that night, so we got deep—real deep. It was a conversation we'd revisit many times over the next few months, peeling back layers of Anna's life like an onion that kept stinging your eyes.

'My husband's a predator,' she said one night, her voice flat. 'He targets women he sees as weak. I should've known better—third wife and all.'

I blinked. 'Third? Babe, you deserve a medal—or maybe a stiff drink.'

She smirked but quickly sobered. 'Jimmy swept in during my first divorce, all knight-in-shining-armour vibes. Turns out the armour was tin foil.'

Anna unravelled the reality of life with Jimmy, a man whose charm had worn thin to reveal a controlling, manipulative underside. 'He made me feel like I owed him everything,' she said.

'Like breathing his air was a privilege.'

She told me how he'd twist every argument to make himself the victim. If she caught him lying, he'd flip the script so fast it left her dizzy. 'And the worst part? He knew I was scared—scared of being alone, scared of starting over. He used that fear like a weapon.'

I listened, horrified but riveted, as Anna painted a picture of a man who saw her vulnerabilities and pounced. He'd make her feel small, incapable, like she was the problem. Even intimacy was on his terms, his needs front and centre, hers barely an afterthought.

'I'd ask for love, companionship, a conversation,' she said. 'He'd act like I was asking for the moon. But God forbid someone else even smiled at me—then I'd get the emotional cold shoulder for days.'

Therapy gave Anna the clarity she needed. She taught me that therapy was a good thing, nothing to be ashamed of. She learned to see through Jimmy's tactics—the gaslighting, the ultimatums, the endless guilt trips. It wasn't easy, but she began piecing herself back together.

'I started to realise something,' she said one night, her eyes burning with determination. 'Jimmy's biggest fear wasn't losing me—it was losing control of me.'

That realisation lit a fire in her. Slowly but surely, Anna rebuilt her confidence. And one day, she made her move.

She described it to me later, her voice steady and full of pride. 'He was in the middle of one of his rants, going on about how I'd never survive without him. I looked him dead in the eye and said, "You're right. I won't survive—I'll thrive. Without you." Then I packed my suitcase and left. The look on his face? Worth every ounce of fear I'd carried for years.'

As Anna recounted her story, I couldn't help but admire her. She hadn't just walked away from Jimmy, she'd reclaimed herself, her worth, her power.

Her courage planted a seed in me, though I didn't fully grasp it back then. I'd already crossed paths with my own Jimmy—maybe I wasn't ready to admit it, but deep down, I knew the truth. And as life would have it, I'd meet another one down the road. Anna's story would be my guiding light when I needed it most.

Lesson: Never let self-absorbed arseholes appoint themselves as the centre of your universe.
Take back your power and make them irrelevant.

CHAPTER 37

What's old is new again

My misconception about intimacy among older couples got flipped upside down during my next call. William and Lily, a sprightly couple in their eighties, shared a love story that felt like it had time-travelled from a golden era. They met at the Anthony Hordern Emporium, which once held the crown as the world's largest department store—now, that was a meet-cute straight out of a black-and-white film.

The place was torn down in 1987 to make room for the World Square development. The store's motto, 'While I live, I'll grow', stuck with me for years—something I'd come to believe in, even though it took decades for it to sink in.

Back in its prime, this wasn't just a shopping destination, it was an experience. Tea-rooms, a post office, restrooms, public phone booths and even a bank branch. Plus, there was a library, a surgery, and it was even used by the NSW Institute of Technology. It was practically a mini city. I could only imagine how fancy it must have felt to visit back in Lily and William's time.

Hearing about the Emporium always hit me right in the nostalgia feels. I used to walk by it all the time when I worked in the city, so when it was gone it was almost like losing an old friend. A few years later, when the opportunity came up, I bought furniture made from the floorboards of that once-grand building—treasured possessions and memories from a bygone era.

During our chat, I learned that William and Lily had tied the knot in 1938 after a whirlwind twelve-month courtship. A whole year of stolen glances and sweet nothings! At first, I couldn't figure out why an elderly couple like that would be calling a sex line. Catching my parents at it in my teens was bad enough, but a couple old enough to be my grandparents was unfathomable—I was starting to think not having grandparents growing up was a blessing in disguise. But, of course, it didn't take long to find out.

This couple, once as young as I was, was still looking for excitement in their relationship. Lily boldly told me she wanted a little more spark in the bedroom, and William thought maybe a third person could help spice things up. I figured at their age, the biggest thrill was getting a recliner that didn't require a crane to get out of.

What I thought would be a chill conversation with an older couple quickly turned into one of the weirdest role-play scenarios I'd ever been part of. Lily wanted me to pretend I was a lesbian artist, desperate to make love to her, with her husband secretly watching us.

Lily's imagination painted a wild scene where I supposedly made advances on her after being led to the bedroom. Apparently, I was supposed to 'inspect' the ceiling to justify being there, while William stood in the doorway. At this point, I wasn't sure if I was on a phone call or stuck in a low-budget porn film with a script no one had bothered to read.

I played along, lying on the bed to inspect the ceiling while twirling her hair. As the scene progressed, my mind was fighting my mouth—my brain screamed, *This is weird*, while I narrated my pleasure with Lily.

The sounds coming through the phone ... Well, let's just say they were louder than I ever needed to hear. It sounded awful and not sexual at all—almost turned me off sex for life. I imagined William, poor guy, wheezing like he'd just climbed Mount Everest, only to collapse at the top.

And then, after about twenty seconds of heavy breathing and one last grunt, it was over.

At the time, I didn't get it, but as I matured, I finally understood why Lily wanted more. It wasn't about age or pleasure—hell, it was about needing to feel wanted, cherished and yes, even desired by another. In the end, we all craved excitement, no matter how many candles were on the cake. Instead of judging, I should've been giving Lily a standing ovation for still chasing the fun.

Lesson: Old age doesn't mean trading passion for a good book. Turns out, love and desire don't come with an expiration date —if anything, they just get more creative.

CHAPTER 38

Hook, line, and sinker

Saturday night and there I was, sitting at my desk, squinting at my watch like it was some kind of cruel joke. Two-thirty a.m. 'Oh, come on. Seriously?' I muttered under my breath, as if the universe would somehow feel bad for me. Three more hours of this godforsaken shift left. My brain was running on empty and I'd forgotten my No-Doz tablets. Staying alert? Yeah, right. It was more of a survival instinct at this point.

Then, the phone rang. That all-too-familiar sound I was way too tired to deal with. I could feel my eyelids begging for mercy, but I let the phone ring on. What was the point in picking it up? Not like I could fake enthusiasm at this point.

'Operator fifty-six, pick up!' the night supervisor's voice echoed across the room, her tone somewhere between 'I'm losing patience' and 'I'm about to snap'.

'Sorry!' I yelled back, grabbing the phone.

'Hey, Dominique! Missed my sexy babe. Got something rock-hard just for you,' Richard, one of my regulars, chimed in.

Why are these guys always so damn horny at this hour? Is there some secret 'horny o'clock' I don't know about?

I forced myself to focus. 'Hey, I've been waiting for you.' What I really wanted to say was, 'Go fuck yourself,' but instead, I begged him to pound me hard. His language was as explicit as you'd expect from a guy who clearly wasn't interested in anything other than getting off.

'Yes, do it to me like that,' I pleaded. His groans deepened, his breath came faster, and then—click. Just like that, he was gone. Impolite moron. No goodbye. Five minutes of my time cost him $14.75. Guess he wasn't raking in the cash like some of the other callers who stuck around longer.

Before long, the phone rang again.

I reluctantly lifted my head from the table, flicked back my hair, and answered with a cheerful, 'Hello, gorgeous.'

Fraser's story hooked me. He'd met a young Brazilian performer at a nightclub. Her voice was hypnotic and her features were a striking mix of masculine and feminine. I could practically see her dark complexion and those haunting green eyes as he left the club alone that night. The next evening, curiosity had him back, introducing himself.

Fraser was captivated by Alexandrea, not just her presence but her brains, too. After one night of getting to know her, they were sharing a bed.

Running his hands over her perky breasts, touching, sucking—it was exciting. But when his hand slid down into her underwear, he felt something unexpected. Her clitoris was more like a penis.

What started as just another phone chat turned into an unexpected lesson on awareness. Naturally, I asked all the questions. Fraser laughed and answered every single one without hesitation. I learned Alexandrea had both male and female genitalia. Did that stop Fraser?

Nope. They kept seeing each other for a while.

His story taught me one thing: assumptions would mess you up.

I realised my ideas about men weren't always spot-on. I'd been living under the assumption that most guys were too macho to admit that a real connection was better than a quick romp. They acted like feelings were for the weak, like getting off was all that mattered. Boy, was I wrong.

After that, I stopped letting other people's opinions guide me and started forming my own. I even asked Fraser to call me back, and he did.

Next up was Marty, a fifty-year-old geologist and university lecturer. He'd never been married, living a life entirely dedicated to himself and his research in Egypt and Italy. At first, his commitment-free lifestyle felt foreign to me, but our conversations had me rethinking everything.

Marty told me about his time as a lecturer in the 1980s, and especially about Genevieve, a French colleague with a wild side. She'd stroll into class during breaks wearing nothing but a trench coat, teasing him with a flash of her breasts and bush—totally *au naturel*, clearly before the world became obsessed with waxing. I mean, it was the eighties! Who needed grooming when you could make a statement?

Genevieve was bold. She'd slide her fingers inside herself, making Marty lick them like it was just another Tuesday. She'd even park herself on a stool and have him pleasure her orally, then leave right before his next class. The teasing drove him wild all day, knowing she'd be his again that night.

Her appetite for sex was insatiable, and Marty often found her with younger lovers—both male and female. She'd invite him to join or just watch. Sometimes, she'd bring out a vibrator and convince Marty to let her use it on him.

From Marty, I picked up a vital lesson: own your desires, no shame. That realisation hit me like a slap in the face—I had to start standing up for my own needs, too.

Lesson: Embrace your desires without shame or judgement, because, like us, our needs are all unique.

CHAPTER 39

Bittersweet Bambi

She was a rare breed, both on and off the phones, commanding attention the second she stepped into the office. The way she strutted—arms loose at her sides, hands angled outwards—made her look like a peacock working a runway.

Bambi's high-pitched voice—grating to some, oddly captivating to others—made her sound way younger than she was. And when she spoke she had this habit of bobbing her head like one of those dashboard figurines. Her whole vibe was sweet and airheaded, like she was one deep breath away from forgetting her own name. But underneath all that? She wasn't stupid. Hell no. She was so damn sharp, she would use those traits to pull in men without breaking a sweat.

With clients, Bambi was a chameleon, like a method actor who never broke character. As much as I wanted to roll my eyes at her over-the-top antics, I had to give her credit. Every time she answered a call, she'd tilt her chin down and peek up through fluttering lashes, as though the guy was right in front of her. The commitment was next level. Honestly, I wondered if she'd missed her calling as an actress.

She played the role of a statuesque eighteen-year-old Scandinavian model—platinum blonde, hypnotic blue eyes, a body to die for, always ready for action.

Reality check: She was in her late thirties, barely five feet tall, with a deep complexion and shoulder-length black hair. The one thing she didn't have to fake? Her boobs. Nothing like the rail-thin runway models, but damn, she made it work. And somehow, she kept the illusion going strong over the phone.

Even though her snootiness got under my skin, I couldn't deny the lesson she unknowingly drilled into me: self-assurance was everything. Confidence wasn't just her armour, it was her damn superpower. She sailed through life like she had VIP status, never letting anyone dim her shine.

She was full of surprises, too. Her fashion choices were unpredictable at best. One night, she strutted into work wearing pyjamas—full-on bedtime attire—paired with sky-high stilettos, a studded handbag and tiny silk flowers scattered through her hair like a 1960s flower child.

Her moods shifted as unpredictably as the weather. Some nights, she'd waltz in like royalty, announcing her arrival as if the party couldn't start without her. Other nights she'd drag herself through the door with a yawn, mumbling about being kept up by construction noise. Honestly, I had no idea if she ever actually slept. She worked like a machine, clocking in way more than the usual six-hour shift, like she was trying to squeeze forty-eight hours out of a single day.

Heaven help you if you ever stole one of her regular clients; she'd make damn sure you never made that mistake twice. Yet she had no problem luring clients away from other women. And when it came to profanity, she was fluent. Every curse word rolled off her tongue like it belonged there.

Her talents didn't stop there—she was also a master of bullshit, and men fell for it every time. Bambi was undeniably a genius, which, unfortunately for the rest of us, meant she reeled in more repeat clients than anyone.

She had a way of stretching conversations like they were some grand performance, each word drawn out with precision. Her quirky charm and air of mystery kept men hooked, giving her the ultimate edge. That was her golden ticket—a skill as natural to her as breathing.

One of her regulars was a young guy, possibly the most gullible man I'd ever come across. Somehow, she had him convinced she'd meet him in person. The catch? He had to call her every night she worked until she felt safe enough to see him.

For weeks he stayed loyal, racking up hours on the phone. Then— poof. He vanished. Most likely after realising she'd been stringing him along just to drain his wallet.

Sure, our job was to keep callers on the line, but I couldn't shake the feeling she was being especially cruel to this poor guy—someone I assumed was innocently searching for love. But was I being unfair? Let's be real: I was doing the same thing. The goal was to keep men hooked for as long as possible.

Bambi's ability to keep men talking for hours was impressive, but what really floored me was how these guys racked up phone bills in the hundreds, sometimes thousands.

Her appetite for earning was insatiable, and she wasn't shy about swooping in on other women's clients. The prime time to strike? Those busy nights when the rest of us were already tied up on calls.

Sometimes, Bambi barely said a word to her clients. Instead, she'd have them paint vivid pictures of what they wanted to do to her, while she sat back, relaxed, and casually threw in soft moans every now and then.

I learned a lot from Bambi—she didn't just talk the talk, she walked it. She made it clear: don't think you're better than anyone unless you can prove it. That chapter of my life pushed me out of my comfort zone and opened doors I didn't even know existed.

Our paths didn't just cross on the phone lines, though. Not long after I hung up my phone sex hat, I bumped into Bambi again—this time she went by a different name, playing a different role. Let me tell you, it was like seeing a whole new side of her, and I got more than I bargained for—maybe a little too much for my senses!

I kept plugging away on the phones until late 1999, when I started questioning everything. My marriage was up shit creek without a paddle, and motherhood? Yeah, that was a lesson I should've learned before I even thought about having kids.

Honestly, parenting's a crash course only those in the trenches truly understand—no judgement! You can't learn it from a textbook; it's a hands-on process. We only hear about the cute parts, but no one tells you about the stuff that really tests your patience.

Don't get me wrong, I loved my kids—but parenting? It had been a grind. School costs, keeping up with their activities, and trying to keep up with the Joneses. It wasn't about luxury, it was about surviving and making sure our daughters thrived. And that meant money management. Sticking around in my marriage was a daily uphill battle, especially with our finances in turmoil.

One of my daughters had her heart set on a performing arts school, and I knew it would do wonders for her. But since Chris flat-out refused to cough up the money for the fees, it fell on me. I couldn't let her down—I knew how that felt. And that was the fire under my arse to start earning more.

To add more stress to our already chaotic situation, my brilliant husband had big plans for a multistorey home and refinanced to get it built. But all I wanted was a couple of extra rooms. I never dreamed of a luxurious home—hell, with six of us crammed into a two-bedroomed granny flat, more space sounded pretty damn good. But Chris? Oh, he thought it'd be a genius move to refinance for the Taj Mahal, which—surprise, surprise—meant a bigger mortgage.

And now we were behind on loan repayments. Why? Your guess is as good as mine. I didn't quite get the refinancing game, but it sure tied me to Chris in ways I didn't want. With the bank breathing down our necks and threatening to take our home, I had to find another way to make more money.

Working as a floor receptionist in brothels wasn't my dream job, but the thought of cash in hand sounded a hell of a lot better than losing everything. My transition to floor receptionist gave me a whole lot of skills I never anticipated. And it definitely gave my résumé extra flair!

Lesson: Never underestimate what you can learn from someone else's complete lack of consideration.

CHAPTER 40

My not-so-glorious brothel debut

It was towards the end of 1999 when I graduated from phone sex operator to working in brothels. The first one was in Chatswood, where I earned myself a legendary title as the most scolded, forgetful and accident-prone floor receptionist around. My badge of dishonour. Yet, I still managed to smile through it all.

I worked four to five shifts a week—weeknights, and day or evening shifts on the weekend as required. Leanna, the madam, wasn't one to shy away from promoting her businesses. I had spotted an ad in the paper, showed up for an interview that morning, and started that very night.

She ran two brothels in Chatswood—one in the upper part of town, and the other a little down the road, making sure to capture all of Chatswood's business. One of them was a 1950s-style two-storey red-brick building across from the train station. From the layout, it seemed like it had once been a boarding house.

Contrary to the Chatswood building's once grand vision, the interior was a disappointment; a shock to the senses—with leopard-print carpet throughout, metal pedestal ashtrays straight out of a bad retro movie and disgusting, clashing maroon crushed-velvet curtains sectioning off the tiny waiting cubicles, reminiscent of a magician's curtain hiding a disappearing box.

Those cubicles were about the size of a shower, enough for one man, or two at a squeeze. Two men would be lucky to fit without stepping on each other. High on the wall a bulky black TV played a constant loop of porn—classy, right? This left men craning their necks to get a view.

Even the music streaming down the halls barely covered the noises coming from the rooms. And the rooms' tiny 'window rattlers'—so-called air-conditioning—proved useless during those extended sessions of heated activity. It wasn't glamorous, but it was one hell of an entry into the business.

The other establishment down the road was also an old two-storey brick building that might once have been a storefront with apartments above—an awkward setup, to say the least. The bottom level had an entire wall-to-floor window, now serving as a storage area, while the top level housed what were likely boarding-style apartments, similar to the other place in the upper end of Chatswood.

One good thing was the large side-entrance car park. Men could easily park and take a few steps up the staircase to reach the brothel's entrance, saving their energy for the main event. At the top, there was an alfresco-style balcony exclusively for the working women and staff, accessible from the women's quarters' lounge area. The receptionists and working women who smoked used it frequently, and I hated cleaning out the filthy ashtrays that left cigarette stink lingering on my clothes.

During significant renovations to the smaller Chatswood brothel on the upper level, a temporary area was established on the ground floor to keep operations running smoothly. This makeshift space comprised about six partitioned areas, each surrounded by curtains, much like those around hospital beds. In a way, you could say sex was a form of healing. But the curtains did little to muffle the sounds of people shagging their butts off.

As the front wall was entirely glass, large sheets of newspaper shielded the inside from view, ensuring the workers' privacy and making the entire space resemble a squatter's zone. And while portable showers were set up near the screened-off compartments for clients, the overall appearance still screamed substandard.

The setup seemed inadequate for paid sex, but apparently, men didn't mind as long as they left with a smile. Dressed as a scullery maid—always in black slacks, sneakers and a white tank top or shirt—I diligently performed my duties while the working women donned femme fatale attire to lure clients to their den. On rare occasions, clients propositioned me, but I dismissed their advances, writing them off as dickheads playing mind games—except for a handful of them.

I admired the working women for handling countless men and their ridiculous personalities—it was like they were offering free therapy. Some men would chat with me, and from what they spilled, it was clear some were after both emotional comfort and physical satisfaction. Navigating that mess must've been a challenge, yet the women handled it like pros, with one clear goal in mind—money. And that's what kept them hustling.

The lengths women went to in order to fulfil their needs, no matter the personal cost, was nothing short of admirable. While I didn't have the demanding job of servicing men, I understood sacrifice all too well—pain could be a hell of a thing, but it could also fuel you to conquer just about anything.

Despite our differences, there was this connection with the women I worked with—like a weird kind of friendship. I got to know a few more personally, and they opened up about their plans for the future. Most were realistic, fully aware they couldn't do this job forever, so they made the most of it while they could. They had a timeline for when they'd exit the industry, and they taught me a valuable lesson: always set goals.

Of course there were rare exceptions, such as Jasmine, whose actions were enough to make me want to pull my hair out. One night, after she and her client had used a room, another woman and her client were booked into the same one. To their horror, as they stepped inside, the foul stench of raw sewage smacked them in the face—only, there wasn't a toilet in sight, just a shower cubicle. It didn't take long to figure out that Jasmine's client had taken a dump in the shower. Upon closer inspection, half of it was still stuck in the drain.

Luckily, one of the owner's daughters—who actually had a shred of empathy—was at the desk that night and kindly helped me shove it down the drain with a fork. I scrubbed the shower floor with bleach until it was squeaky clean, but the smell … that lingered like a fart in an elevator. Even with the window wide open and a whole can of air freshener blasted into the room, the repulsive odour refused to go anywhere, making the room off-limits for the rest of the night.

When I questioned Jasmine, she played the I-don't-know-a-thing card. Later, it came out that the client had paid her extra to let him literally shit on her. That was enough to make me want to return the favour—only I'd do it for free. If he ever showed his face at the brothel again, I'd shit on him big time.

My tasks were physically and mentally draining. Booking women at the brothels wasn't as simple as it sounded. Challenges cropped up when there weren't enough women on shift, or when a popular woman was in high demand but not working.

In those moments I had to get creative. Once the men were through the door, I worked my persuasion skills to book someone else. It was a real art form, selling something we didn't have. When describing the women, I didn't hold back. I'd often stretch the truth or flat-out lie, claiming we had women as young as eighteen, even though every woman working that night was well over thirty, with a few pushing fifty. If there were only five girls working, I'd somehow manage to describe ten, rattling off names, ages, body types and specialties. But since my memory wasn't exactly reliable, I did my best to stick to the script—though, knowing me, I always managed to veer off course, making up specialties that probably only existed in late-night porno plots, not real life. Of course, that backfired when the clients walked in. Even so, credit to me for trying.

The most agonising times were when only a few women were working and for whatever reason, men turned into complete arseholes, getting impatient and lashing out at me for the inconvenience they thought I caused. No joke, I was like a punching bag, taking each blow one at a time. But I figured that deep down their bad behaviour was probably due to the blood meant for their dicks getting all stuck in their brain cells, triggering an explosion of vulgarity towards me, like some sort of aneurysm.

The larger of the Chatswood brothels had several waiting rooms, including a courtyard for larger groups of men. I had to walk past these groups all night while doing laundry or restocking. It quickly became clear that men in groups turned into complete pricks. They jeered at me as I raced past, balancing baskets of laundry or trays of whiskey-filled glasses. They demanded attention I didn't have to spare.

Sometimes, their words cut deep, reducing me to nothing more than their personal indentured servant. Those wounds never fully healed—they would reopen every time Chris pulled the same shit. I couldn't shake the crushing realisation of how little men valued me—at the brothel, at home, everywhere.

In those moments, I didn't care if my life ended. The depression clung to me, lingering far too long. I wish I'd understood what I was going through; wish that I'd reached out for help. But being a mum meant snapping that shit out of my head the second it crept in—except it never truly left. It just hid, waiting to resurface.

Adding to my distress was the constant annoyance of endless requests for the most popular women, which stirred jealousy among the others. Some women were booked repeatedly throughout the night, going home with over a thousand dollars, while others had only one job, leaving with just eighty dollars.

As if I didn't have enough shit to deal with, I also got blamed—sometimes outright confronted—by pissed-off working girls when their bookings were slow. Apparently, I didn't advertise them enough, didn't hype up their specialties, didn't do this, didn't do that. It was always on me. Never mind that maybe, just maybe, these men wanted something different. After all, they were the ones paying. But taking responsibility? Owning their own damn appeal?

Nah, easier to dump it on me.

Sometimes, I even had to hide the fact that a popular woman was on shift when she was rebooked, just to make sure the others got some work. Funny how I was somehow the villain, yet I was the one making sure everyone got a damn booking.

Guess I could bullshit like the best of them when needed.

Lesson: Give yourself credit where it's due,
and don't carry blame that isn't yours—other people's
baggage is their problem, not yours.

CHAPTER 41

Not on my watch

Sometimes, fabricating the truth wasn't just necessary, it was the right thing to do. Like the time it saved an eighteen-year-old girl from a nightmare.

She didn't want to have sex with this man, and the second I walked into that room, I saw why. There, illuminated in the shadows, was a tubby little man sitting on the edge of the bed. On closer inspection, he appeared breathless, looking as if he had one foot in the grave. He must have been well over seventy and obviously in bad health. The lamp shining on his balding head revealed age spots as big as thumbprints, and his hairy body did nothing to disguise his swollen beer belly resting on his lap.

I stood there for only a second, watching in disgust as he furiously yanked his cock. Immediately, I ordered him to stop. I certainly wasn't getting paid to watch an old man masturbate in front of me.

It was a blistering hot evening, and the air-conditioner in that room was broken. The pedestal fan rattled as it spun around, hardly making a breeze in the stuffy room. Beads of sweat dripped from his brow and puddled on the top of his enormous stomach, which made me want to throw up in my own mouth. All I could think of at the time was how disgusting it would be to be fucked by this blob of a man. My words echoed prejudice, but the thought of him with such a young girl repulsed and infuriated me. Maybe it was the fact I had daughters that brought out my protective mother-bear side.

Possibly as a form of reprieve, this young woman, notably anxious, insisted I check him for crabs. With that, I undertook the role of crab inspector. Taking a deep breath, I bent over, my face literally centimetres away from his irregular-shaped penis, looking for signs of infection. I saw nothing, so decided to speak to her outside the room.

She pleaded with me not to make her have sex with him. That was my moment to shine. With my maternal instincts kicking in, I told her to go back to the women's quarters, making her promise not to say a thing to the other women when they came out of their bookings. It was a busy evening, and all the women were occupied. The supervisor in charge of the desk that evening was sweet Amy, who gladly held the secret. Fortunately, this occurred just before the owner of the brothel installed cameras, so no one except the three of us was any the wiser.

On entering the room, this man was once again jerking at his pathetic excuse of a penis as if to revive it. I swear I could have detached it from his body quiet easily, but instead I yelled at him to stop, get dressed and leave. I gnashed my teeth and growled at him like a possessed banshee, causing his cock to go limp almost at once. I was truly gifted to have that effect on men when called for.

In his fury, he told me he was going to complain to the owner. I told him he should be ashamed of himself and would be banned if he didn't leave immediately.

I looked down at the remnants of what was once a semi-hard-on and gave him an unsympathetic smile, telling him he was useless to anyone anyway. Still filled with rage, I stood there, staring him down as I ordered him to hurry up or I would have him taken out in a body bag.

He looked at me, almost choking on his own breath. He must have been stunned as he said nothing in response. I then fetched the supervisor, who joined me to refund the man and escort him out before any of the other girls emerged from their rooms. The young woman quickly found another job as the cubicles were full of waiting men.

For some reason, it made me feel powerful to have the ability to help another woman, even if no one else knew. I recognised it in myself, and that was a significant achievement for me to acknowledge.

Lesson: Power isn't in recognition—it's in knowing you made a difference, even if no one else sees it.

CHAPTER 42

Working hard for the money

At times, men would leave without booking anyone, causing a real problem with the madam. Walkouts were frowned upon, and I would receive a dressing-down for my perceived incompetence. It made me anxious and wanting to leave. But I couldn't, as I needed the money.

Late one afternoon, I opened the door to find a professionally dressed woman. She requested an hour appointment, and Renata was the only one on that shift willing to take the booking. I swear, I would have seen her myself if Renata didn't. She had a captivating look of intelligence and elegance. Although stunning, I would've needed a box to reach her lips, but I don't think she intended for anyone to reach the lips on her face.

Once the booking was made, I was given two dental dams by the front desk receptionist to give to Renata to perform oral sex on her client. With neither Renata nor her client wanting to use them, I placed them in my pocket and forgot about it until I found them after putting those particular pants through the washer and dryer.

Curious, I decided to taste the dental dam. I stretched it and ran my tongue over it; it was unpleasant, like a rubber balloon. When

I mentioned this to Sasha, she laughed and explained that they were flavoured, though the flavour disappeared when washed.

Sasha, a popular and striking young woman of about twenty-two, had the allure of a swimsuit model. Her tousled, beach-blonde hair and flawless physique were accentuated by freckles delicately scattered across her nose and cheeks. Her piercing blue eyes seemed to penetrate deep into a man's soul, or groin, depending on what captured their attention first.

Sasha was envied by her fellow workers and desired by clients, effortlessly earning well over a thousand dollars a night, leaving little time for showers or meals between clients.

Sometimes it worked against me; when a man saw Sasha leaving her booking while paying at the desk for another woman, he would cancel and rebook with Sasha instead. This led to resentment among the other girls, as one woman monopolised all the jobs.

Sasha confided in me about her desperate need to work as much as possible—she was paying for her university tuition fees. I knew she was a student; she would arrive at work during the week carrying a bag full of books and notepads. I admired women like her who worked in the industry to better themselves, but those who squandered their earnings on drugs disappointed me.

Working double shifts wasn't uncommon. I often worked from eight to seventeen hours straight, which left me utterly exhausted. The long shifts wreaked havoc with my hair, leaving it frizzy, as if I'd been electrocuted.

Part of the job included changing bedsheets and collecting used towels, then laundering them in the laundry room. Some women didn't clean thoroughly, and the odours would linger, leaving a kind of haze in the rooms, especially those with spicy food odours from clients. It often took an entire can of air freshener to clear it. The receptionist would do a final check and if anything was amiss,

I would clean again, ensuring ashtrays were emptied, glasses cleared, and the room was perfect for the next client.

Floor receptionists travelled from all over for the cash-in-hand job and its flexibility. I knew one who commuted from Newcastle, arriving on Fridays for the weekend shift, and heading home on Monday mornings. Some of the working women from coastal suburbs followed the same routine.

Then there was the couple in their twenties, both working in the industry—she in the brothels, he as a male escort. I couldn't even wrap my head around how that dynamic worked, but apparently it did. Curious, I once asked her if they ever felt jealous about each other sleeping with other people. Her response was simple, almost too simple: 'This is work. Once we walk away from our jobs, we don't talk about it.'

I had to respect that. They were obviously secure in their relationship and mature enough to manage it. Jealousy killed everything good, and they had figured out how to make sure it didn't kill theirs. I wished more people had that level of honesty—including some of the women I worked with.

Take Leanna, for instance. Not just the woman with the gift of persuasion, she ran the whole damn show. If things weren't running smoothly, she'd be the first to tell you to fuck off.

In her late fifties, she had these striking green eyes and was downright pretty. Tall, too—always a bonus, in my opinion. I was as close to the ground as humanly possible with my short stature.

She had short, wavy strawberry-blonde hair and always looked polished—full make-up, red lippy, the whole deal. She was so well-spoken, I swore she was posh. And her outfits? Always on-trend, hugging her incredible figure like they were custom-made. For unknown reasons, her eyes were constantly glazed over, perhaps due to lack of sleep. She typically appeared to be in a state of agitation if things weren't as she expected, though it was hard to tell at times. Sometimes, when I walked past her at the reception desk, she appeared zonked out, just staring ahead. But I kept my head down and arse up, working the floor.

Her temperament was unpredictable, swinging from yelling out profanities to showing genuine empathy towards others. I was constantly anxious when she staffed the desk. I got so paranoid that I carried a dust cloth around to appear busy wiping things down, even when there was no need. Anything to minimise the chances of her berating me—I already had enough of that from Chris back home.

I will admit, although I feared her, I was also entertained by her at times. You see, there were moments when Leanna would suddenly swear at a client for leaving without booking a woman, only to turn around and blame me for their departure. Letting a man leave without parting with his money was the ultimate cardinal sin; it was my job to convince them to stay.

Leanna's fiery disposition when dealing with unruly clients was quite the spectacle. She would shout at men, forcefully ejecting them from her establishment and slamming the door behind them, jesting, 'Who do they think they are, the King of England?'

Of course, some men would yell back, 'You're a fucking crazy lady!'

Several months into my job, Leanna had surveillance cameras installed for security purposes. The place had been robbed before, and even though security guards were often around, the cameras acted like a shiny deterrent against any future robberies. But for us floor receptionists, they were the ultimate nightmare. While they did their job of capturing every move, it felt like we were under a microscope, with Leanna keeping a hawkish eye on all our activities.

On nights when Leanna wasn't around we waited for her call, especially during the slow periods. It was unnerving knowing we were under constant watch, only to get blamed later for the lack of walk-ins.

The job drained me—physically, mentally, emotionally. Hopelessness hit hard. Some nights I'd drive home half-hoping to crash and end the misery. I used to think the phone lines were tough, but at least they didn't leave my whole body feeling like I'd been run over by a steamroller. Silly of me to think that was the hardest gig I'd ever had. Turns out, brothel life was worse, probably because the business owners were always lurking, judging, their expectations hanging over me. The exhaustion was not just real, it was multiplied a hundredfold. On the plus side, though, I sweated so much from running up and down hallways and stairs that I was almost back to my pre-baby weight. I guess there's always a silver lining … if you squint really hard.

In between cleaning and restocking, I served drinks to waiting clients—sometimes right in the middle of their sessions with a woman. These men were completely naked, with no shame whatsoever. I guess they thought I wouldn't notice them shelling out extra cash to extend their time. Spoiler alert: I did. Even with my 'warning knock', it didn't make a difference.

At first, their nakedness made me want to disappear, so I'd quickly avert my eyes, pretending the air didn't smell like sex and sweat. But eventually, I couldn't care less—just another day at the office. Men had the audacity to lie there, exposed and proud, like I should be impressed by their glorious erections the moment I walked in. Honestly, none of them were worth a second glance. Out of the countless penises I saw, only a handful ever earned an eyebrow lift of approval.

As for Leanna, despite her flaws, she was unstoppable. Both of her businesses thrived—one catering to the younger crowd, ages eighteen to thirty, and the other drawing in a more mature clientele, featuring ladies over forty.

Leanna also dabbled in other ventures, raking in even more cash. She kept tight control over the women's appearance in her establishments, making sure they always looked top-notch to guarantee higher bookings, which I assumed only added to her ever-growing bank account.

Working at Leanna's establishments was limited to women who possessed a specific and expensive aesthetic—a sense of luxury. Those who lacked it were obligated to acquire it from her before starting their shifts.

The extravagant French lingerie she sold played into the inherent allure of the women; a characteristic the men appreciated. Though I sensed a form of exploitation of women's roles in the workforce. Despite this, I could also perceive that, in a way, Leanna was assisting the women in showcasing their best assets to maximise their opportunities for work.

Women found themselves compelled to take on at least one job just to cover the cost of a G-string, and perhaps two or three jobs to afford a full set of the exquisite lingerie. Yet, Leanna's entrepreneurial spirit didn't stop there; she seized every available opportunity to generate income.

Leanna purchased lubricant and condoms in bulk, and the receptionist would then repackage them: five condoms—two large, two medium, and one small—along with a tube of lubricant, all neatly packaged in a brown-paper lunch bag. Women would buy these packages when their own supply ran out. It proved to be a lucrative side hustle.

Leanna went a step further by offering shoe rentals to the women. An entire wall adorned with stiletto heels—red patent, black leather, silver glitter, an extensive variety—was securely displayed behind a locked glass sliding door. I fondly dubbed this section 'the wall of fuck-me shoes.'

For a fee, women could rent these killer heels for the night, each pair possessing the potential for near-fatal danger to the wearer. I demonstrated this one evening, attempting to balance in a pair just for fun, nearly breaking my ankle in the process. Despite my shorter stature, I failed to comprehend the appeal of high heels for women.

In addition, there were transient women who might have sought employment in between their regular jobs or for brief periods while in Sydney. During that time, I witnessed Leanna's compassion as she provided lodging for women travelling a long distance to work—a genuinely kind gesture that also helped her keep her workforce in check.

However, when I tried to show a little care by bringing in homemade cookies for the working women, Leanna didn't exactly appreciate it. She was worried they'd lead to weight gain. Despite my good intentions, this act earned me a reprimand. On the bright side, Amy, a senior receptionist, affectionately nicknamed me Cookie Girl, which I found endearing.

Though the madam wasn't keen on seeing the girls eat too much, her adult daughters and son-in-law were a different story. Whenever they ran the desk, the atmosphere lightened, and eating during the quiet periods became our guilty pleasure. We'd order food and sneak bites in between the chaos of busy and slow spells.

Then came the unfortunate incident when I tripped down half a flight of stairs while eating on the go, sending my Lebanese falafel wrap flying everywhere. It was a mess, and left me with hunger pangs that stalked me for the rest of the night. Fortunately, no one saw my culinary disaster. My bruised backside and twisted ankle didn't help, but with only two floor receptionists on duty, leaving wasn't an option. So, I hobbled around as best I could for several more hours, enduring pain with every step.

Sure, my role was haphazard at times, but I was grateful for the chance the madams gave me to earn money. Looking back, I saw how female business owners were true pioneers, paving the way for women across industries. Their boldness in taking risks created safe spaces for women to work. The madam held real sway over men, setting the price for a woman's time. Back then, I didn't fully get the challenges they faced, but I soon realised these women were unstoppable.

Lesson: *True power isn't just about making money—it's about creating opportunities and proving women don't just play the game, they own it.*

CHAPTER 43

How to toughen up

Working at the brothel gave me a deeper understanding of the challenges sex workers encountered, and trust me, it's a world that most people would rather ignore. My perception? Unchanged. But there are still plenty of people who don't view it as a real job. If they take a second to step into the shoes of someone living it day-to-day, maybe they'll get it.

Picture trying to chat with someone at a dinner party—except the person across from you is a sex worker. Now, imagine you ask them, 'So, what do you do for work?' The answer's not gonna be like, 'Oh, I'm a teacher,' or 'I'm in marketing.' No. It's gonna make people squirm in their seats and they won't know what the hell to say next. You can't exactly unload your frustrations about your boss or your clients in that environment.

Or perhaps you're sitting in a mothers' group, where every other sentence is about little Johnny's latest tantrum or his super-picky eating habits. You're half-listening, sleep-deprived, when someone pipes up, recounting a session where their client was so determined to 'eat pussy' that he kept at it for the entire damn hour, leaving her legs cramping up. It's a conversation shift that would make most people choke on their coffee, but for sex workers, it's just another Tuesday.

And that right there is the heart of it—people don't realise the mental gymnastics sex workers do just to survive in an environment where any mention of their work can feel like a ticking time bomb.

There had been moments when I so badly wanted to share my experiences—just needing someone to acknowledge the grind and the bullshit—but I kept my mouth shut, too damn scared of the judgement that would inevitably come. I mean, let's be real, I thought the women in the industry were total bad-arses. They faced down man after man, night after night, and I could barely wrap my head around it. My views on men shifted, often depending on the day and the kind of crap I was dealing with. But it wasn't until those long, soul-sucking nights in the brothels that I really started seeing the difference between the ones who could handle themselves and the ones who were just plain not worth my time.

Like those groups of three or more men throwing around trash talk and vulgarities while they waited for their turn with someone. That's when the disgust really set in. I wanted to knock their heads together and shake some sense into them—but then I remembered: no brains, no pain.

When men pushed me to my limits, demanding those goddamn details about the services women offered, I'd be ready to rip them a new one. It always took me back to Chris—the arsehole I was still stuck with. He'd demand kinky sex, but after a whole night dealing with men like this, I had nothing left to give. Working there only made me hate him more, if that was even possible. I really did hate him some nights.

And then there were the men who took things way too far, thinking they had a free pass to grab at me like I was some kind of plaything. I'd walk by and they'd reach out to grab my breasts or my arse, throwing out the usual, 'Come on, you want some of this?' like it was cute or something. I had to bite my tongue, fight every urge not to kick them square in the balls. I swear, it took every ounce of self-control I had not to show them exactly what happened when you screwed with me.

In the early weeks I tried to play nice. I thought being polite would make them stop mocking me, but it didn't. Eventually, I got the hang of it and started firing back like I had a damn bazooka.

'You'd have to rob a bank to afford the experience.' Yeah, there was a no-negative-talk rule, but these guys were disrespectful as hell. The boss was the only one with the power to boot them out, but when she wasn't around—especially on those soul-sucking nights—I took matters into my own hands. I'd tell the unruly bastards to 'calm the fuck down or else.' That little dose of assertiveness became my lifeline when I felt like I was drowning. The anger behind it? Well, that was the result of all the shit I was dealing with and, honestly, all the moral chaos swirling in my head.

Sure, brothels had their compassionate side, with some guys just looking for a connection. Some were lonely, others had partners dealing with health stuff, or intimacy issues—they were all sorts of screwed up. It wasn't all jerks. There were the shy ones, too, the ones who couldn't even look me in the eye because their confidence was as fragile as an overcooked noodle.

Men of various ages with special needs also sought female attention. I witnessed an innovative approach that tailored services to meet the unique needs of these individuals. Several rooms on the lower level of one particular brothel were transformed to create larger spaces, allowing men in wheelchairs to manoeuvre comfortably. The madam at this establishment was ingenious, offering a much-needed service that proved to be financially advantageous for her.

Men like Kenny found a safe space to express their needs freely, with a woman who made them feel special. Kenny faced the challenge of muscular dystrophy, which caused progressive weakness and degeneration of his skeletal muscles. This affected his speech and upper body strength, leading him to rely on a wheelchair equipped with a small tabletop and a keypad. He used a pointer controlled by his mouth to operate a text-to-voice synthesiser—kind of like the one Stephen Hawking famously used—to communicate his thoughts and desires.

Despite his body not co-operating, Kenny's sense of humour was impeccable. There were times when pushing him up the ramp became a real challenge, and he was all too aware of it. I often found myself rolling back several times before finally getting him onto the verandah area. The slight tilt of his head and his half-grin spoke volumes. I could've been mistaken—maybe he was just angry at me—but despite the physical challenges he faced, Kenny couldn't hide his inherent cuteness. The twinkle in his eyes always managed to bring a smile to my face.

As a standard practice before the arrival of any wheelchair-bound client, we set up a wooden ramp over the steps to ensure easy access to the brothel entrance. While there were two entrances at the front, we typically used only one, reserving the other for wheelchair access. Specifically, the double doors closest to the disabled rooms were the go-to when accommodating clients in wheelchairs.

What I admired most about Leanna was her lack of discrimination. Despite her flaws and all the chaos swirling in her personality, she had a good heart. At least, that's what I told myself. I wanted to believe she was good deep down. Sadly, some of the women wouldn't even look at men in wheelchairs, but there were always exceptions—those rare ones who showed patience and understanding, putting a smile on these men's faces.

As for the word 'discriminate', it should be tossed out the window. Our differences and quirks are what make us interesting, and they deserve to be celebrated, not hidden. I was stoked that this brothel had at least a few cracks of inclusivity peeking through.

As much as I wanted to brush it all off, the physical strain of dealing with clients like Kenny wore me thin. The ramps, the awkward positioning, the strain on my back—it was a daily battle. But then there was that damn twinkle in Kenny's eyes. No matter how bad I felt about everything going on in that place, Kenny somehow reminded me that there was still room for kindness, even in the darkest corners.

Although not all the working women I encountered were nice, I still regarded them as extraordinary. They were diverse in age, size, abilities, educational backgrounds and ethnicities. Their ability to provide a safe and welcoming space for men from all walks of life was truly remarkable.

I saw how brothels could be a kind of refuge for men with tangled sexual or emotional baggage. It was like a safe space where the average guy could find whatever kind of comfort he was after. It wasn't just about the physical; it was a place where men could feel heard and understood, no judgement, no eyerolls, while spending time with whichever lady caught their eye. Sure, they paid for the privilege, but it was a learning experience on all kinds of intimate levels.

Of course, the industry came with its own set of challenges, like the glaring shortage of services for women. Help for mistreatment was as rare as finding a needle in a haystack. It seemed like just another ugly truth that came with the territory.

I often felt frustration bubbling inside me when clients insisted on waiting to see all the available women, fearing they might miss out on a perceived 'real' beauty. Even with the ladies occupied for hours, these men annoyingly sipped drink after drink while they waited. I wished I could've urged them to take a good, hard look in the mirror—many were no oil painting themselves! They were lucky to have the company of such lovely women.

Many of the sex workers had the potential to earn anywhere from a couple of hundred dollars to over a thousand in a single night, but it was demanding work, literally having to work their arses off.

I noticed men walking through the doors of the brothels, some well past fifty, looking for more than a quick hook-up—they were after intimacy. Clara, a woman in her fifties who worked alongside me really stood out. She had this warm, beautiful nature about her. When she finished with a client she'd walk them to the door, kiss and hug them goodbye—something that was rare among the other women. Clara became almost a therapist for older men, reassuring them that they were still human, still wanted.

You see, I didn't hate men all the time; I actually had compassion within me when it was earned.

This was a wake-up call—not all men were just after sex. Some were craving someone who could listen and help sort out their mess of emotions. Like Clara, I often found myself playing therapist to these guys, whether it was on the phone lines or in the brothels. And let me tell you, it wasn't all sunshine and rainbows. Some men dropped bombshells, like their sick desire for young girls. That hit me hard, and I didn't hesitate to shut them down fast.

One middle-aged guy couldn't take a hint. The dude chased me down like his life depended on it, showing up at the brothel for months, despite my repeated rejections. I couldn't get rid of him. Eventually, he backed off—probably when he realised I wasn't going to play his game—but it was clear as day what he was after: not my company, but a damn power trip. He was getting off on the idea that he could wear me down. And trust me, he was delusional if he thought I was ever gonna let that happen.

Before diving into adult services, I had no clue how women were treated in the sex industry. But, let me tell you, I learned more than I ever bargained for. It threw me face-first into the ugly truths about my husband's views—like how he wanted me to keep my job a secret, shutting me down at every chance he got. And yeah, I regretted giving in to him. I should've been loud and proud about doing what I had to do to support my family.

The longer I stuck around in the industry, the more pissed I got at myself. I started questioning why I just went along with everything without saying a damn word. I'd hear all these shitty comments about women from my husband and his idiot friends, and there I was, silent as hell, too scared of being judged. If society could just pull its head out of its arse, maybe women in this line of work would get some damn respect and be seen for what we were—providing a service that people actually needed.

Lesson: Your hardest times will break you, shape you, and teach you—because the toughest roads make the strongest souls.

CHAPTER 44

Duty calls, chaos follows

I understood the many reasons women entered the industry, often driven by need. For me, it was all about financial obligations and a craving for independence. I dreamed of breaking free from my husband's control and starting fresh.

Some people love to say women have other job options—yeah, sure, a lot of the women I knew worked multiple gigs. But for some, there wasn't much of a choice. Life threw punches, and the flexibility of the industry meant better pay than most regular jobs. It wasn't glamorous, but it worked when nothing else did.

Angel was one of those women who just shone. Married to an Aussie and with a kid here, she worked her tits off to send money back home to her extended family in the Philippines, supporting them every chance she got. When I'd visit her at her house, I'd bring toys and clothes for her community back home—just a little something to help out. She was always pitching in with local projects, lending a hand however she could.

Then there was Channel—single mum, left behind by her husband, juggling two jobs to take care of her child with special needs. Her mum helped out during the night shifts, and Channel did whatever it took to make sure her kid was all right. Meanwhile, some men just avoided their responsibilities, taking the easy way out. I got that lesson myself a few years later.

Women should own their story—no shame, no apologies. They're out here slaying, showing up when no one else will. And yeah, it might take a minute to realise it, but once you do?

Damn, it feels good. So here's to all the bad-arse women—let's raise a glass to the ones who kicked obstacles to the curb and kept on moving!

As for me, I became an expert in pouring endless amounts of booze to keep the guys entertained, especially when the selection of ladies was running low. My mission was to make sure they spent big. My least favourite duty? Inspecting the girls like they were headed to a beauty pageant—every hair and bit of make-up had to be perfect. And, of course, if anything was off, the madam would come for me with her wagging finger. Apparently, it was my fault if even one single lash was out of place. How that was fair was beyond me, I guess, that was the price I paid for being the floor receptionist.

After showing clients the women, I'd return to ask about their preferences. If a man left without choosing, it was deemed my fault. Criticism didn't just come from the madam; the working girls chimed in, too. Smooth operations and bookings were my responsibility and blame often fell on me during my shifts.

For each booking, we provided two towels, two top sheets, and sometimes an extra drink. After every session, towels and sheets needed replacing, and it was up to me to restock everything for the ladies.

Before getting down to business, the women checked clients for visible conditions like open wounds or crabs, and clients showered before and after their sessions, leading to a constant influx of laundry for receptionists to manage.

Despite a laundry service providing a good number of towels, most of the washing was still done in-house. The sheets, often frayed at the edges, barely covered three-quarters of the bed and were draped over a fitted sheet. I tried my best to arrange the two spare towels on the bed like an elegant swan, but they often ended up looking more like a strangled duck.

Occasionally, I'd forget which rooms were waiting areas and accidentally walk in on clients with the working girls. I was also notorious for mixing up bookings and sending girls into the wrong rooms, leading to disgruntled clients demanding changes. 'Numbskull' was a term thrown my way more often than I liked.

One evening, Brooke, one of the most popular girls, had back-to-back bookings all night. I mistakenly told a client over the phone that she was available when she wasn't. When the client showed up, I had to improvise, claiming she'd gone home ill, which didn't sit well with him. Unfortunately, luck wasn't on my side when the client later spotted Brooke in the hallway as he was leaving.

I hurriedly escorted him out the back door and returned to my tasks, only to spot him on the monitor heading back towards the front. Realising I needed backup, I dispatched a security guard to handle him, knowing he wouldn't dare argue with someone as imposing as the guard.

Another chaotic evening, we faced a shortage of working women and a steady stream of men. To my dismay, the boss-lady was present, forbidding me from turning anyone away. I scrambled to find space for them anywhere I could—bathroom stalls, the kitchen, corners of the hallway, vacant rooms and even the backyard. It was madness.

Running on empty, I rushed around serving drinks and appeasing the men to keep them happy. The fear of facing the boss's wrath pushed me to satisfy every client. In my haste to answer the front door, I collided with a waiting client who had popped his head out of the bedroom. Embarrassed, I shoved him back into the room, scolding him like a schoolteacher. In my frenzy, I completely forgot about him, leaving him waiting for over an hour without seeing any women while I attended to other clients who arrived after him.

Luckily, he didn't complain, and I managed to convince him to accept the next available woman without even seeing her, assuring him she was one of the most sought-after workers that evening.

Among the countless tasks a floor receptionist juggled one stood out as particularly loathsome: inspecting men for crabs. This duty, reserved for times when there weren't enough women for double screenings, was a task I dreaded even more than checking the women's presentation.

The first time I was beckoned by a working woman named Tina, who had a reputation for being as subtle as a sledgehammer, I thought I was heading in to chat with a client. Oh no, I was in for a surprise. I walked into the room and found a rather grotesque man standing next to a floor lamp in the corner, the light shining directly on his hard dick like a spotlight at a talent show. Tina casually told me to check him to make sure he was clean. Because, you know, that's how we roll in this business!

I was so naive, asking him if he had showered while grabbing the lamp and shining it up and down over his body. Both he and the working woman looked at me rather strangely. As she seized the lamp from my grip, she shone it onto his pubic hair and said, 'For fuck's sake, get on your knees and check him for crabs! Look, there they are!'

I was dumbfounded and told the client to excuse us. I stepped outside for a quick debrief with her to figure out what the heck I was supposed to be looking for.

Once back inside, I reluctantly got down on my knees, my face only inches away from his penis. Straining to see, I took a pen from behind my ear and pointed it at his grey, wiry pubic hair.

Sneering, I muttered, 'Yes, definitely crabs—big ones, too.'

Tina shook her head disapprovingly. 'He needs to leave. I won't see him. Tell the receptionist to refund his money; no one will see him.'

The man remained silent, seemingly in disbelief at being turned away. As he dressed, I waited outside the door and then escorted him to the receptionist's desk, where he received a refund. In a heated exchange, he was bluntly told, 'You and your crabs need to fuck off.' And just like that, he was gone.

I soon learned these so-called crabs were tiny parasites that actually looked like miniature crabs.

Later that evening, the same woman approached me and handed over a small book. 'This is your fucking bible. Now, study the damn thing,' she said, her gaze intimidating.

I nodded in acknowledgment, muttering under my breath, 'Rough night, huh?' She shot me a death stare.

Armed with knowledge from a book filled with graphic images of skin infections on genitals, I confidently walked the brothel halls, feeling like I held a doctorate and viewing men as walking venereal laboratories. Despite the book's explicit content, it was easier to digest than the reality of older men with erections—a phenomenon I hadn't imagined possible at their age.

Besides my usual duties, I played unofficial chauffeur, driving the women between brothels at all hours. Once, I had to take Celeste—the only lady available—to a smaller brothel in downtown Chatswood, even though her so-called 'ladylike' charm left a lot to be desired.

Celeste sat beside me, mumbling to herself. Ignoring her didn't do much, and at a red light, she suddenly slumped onto my shoulder. I panicked and shoved her back, accidentally bumping the gear stick into neutral just as the light turned green. With one hand on the wheel, I fought to keep her upright and get the car moving.

Finally, I dropped her off and returned to the main brothel, only to be told to go fetch her back immediately. Turns out she'd been banned from the place for drug use, and I got a scolding for not catching on to her state earlier.

Feeling unfairly blamed, my self-doubt grew. Despite the madam and head receptionists' mistreatment, I feared losing my job and had to tough it out. My duties included running to the bottle shop when booze ran low and hitting the chemist near the train station for lube, condoms, and sea sponges for women on their periods. Numbing cream was also a regular pick-up, helping the women keep working if things got a bit tender.

Sometimes I'd come back with extra-large condoms, which the women hated—especially when their clients had, let's say, less-than-impressive equipment. This meant more trips, hassling other women for condoms, or buying a whole new batch.

Laundry duty? A total nightmare. Some women, too lazy to toss their used tissues or condoms in the trash, left them tangled up in towels and sheets. I'd be folding, and next thing I knew, a shrivelled-up condom would go flying across the room like a clay pigeon. And if I was lucky, I'd find one stuck to me—usually pointed out by a client or receptionist. Not only was it risky, but it was humiliating—everyone knew when I got stuck with laundry duty.

When I wasn't dodging condoms, I was handing out free whiskey shots to clients, restocking shelves, scrubbing kitchens and bathrooms, and juggling parking spots for the next shift. What really got under my skin were the men asking for schoolgirl costumes. I swear, I'd have shoved that dress down their throats if I could've and made them shit it out whole.

Then, one night, my attempt to be helpful backfired big time. With all the women busy, I thought I'd tidy up their rooms, even though they were technically supposed to do it. Trying to speed things up, I vacuumed everything—even the ashtrays. Naturally, disaster struck when an ashtray tipped over and the vacuum nozzle jammed between a chair and a bag, sucking up a G-string and who knew what else.

Panicking, I opened the vacuum to get the G-string out, but tore the bag open, sending dust and junk flying everywhere. With no G-string in sight, I just shoved everything back together and left the room worse than I found it. Little did I know, the next receptionist found a syringe poking out of the vacuum. I couldn't exactly admit to my little cleaning mishap—not with my stellar reputation already hanging by a thread.

Lesson: Never doubt your strength—chaos hits, and it's there, ready to save your arse.

CHAPTER 45

Lipstick Olympics

During the 2000 Sydney Olympics, the Chatswood brothel, always a busy spot, was absolutely buzzing. One night, while working with Suzie, another receptionist, I opened the door to four sharply dressed men, all in their forties or fifties. The youngest, who looked like he was plucked straight from a box of fancy chocolates, really stood out. With his silky Italian accent—something I was all too familiar with—he definitely had charm.

I led them to one of the larger rooms, explaining our fine selection of services. Carlo, the younger man, claimed they were part of the International Olympic Committee, though I wasn't completely buying it. Still, they looked the part, and more importantly, they seemed like big spenders. I sweetened the deal with free drinks, hoping to loosen their wallets even more.

As I returned from the office, carefully balancing a tray of Scotch and ice, I did a double take. Suzie had undergone a full-on transformation. Her once loosely pinned-up hair now draped over one shoulder, and her white shirt, formerly buttoned to the neck, was now tied at the waist, showing off a black bra and a teasing flash of midriff. She'd even thrown on some lipstick.

My head spun. What the hell was she doing?

Before I could say a word, she bolted over, nearly knocking the tray out of my hands. 'I'm better equipped to look after them,' she declared, her eyes twinkling. 'You look much too scruffy to entertain men of this calibre.'

I blinked. *Scruffy? Me?*

I tried to push back. 'I can handle it.'

But she wasn't having it. 'You need a break,' she insisted, giving me a once-over. 'You look completely exhausted.'

Oh, sure. Because playing cocktail waitress for high-rolling imposters was so draining.

Feeling small and put in my place, I caught my reflection in the hallway mirror. Dishevelled, sweaty, like a Victorian chambermaid who'd just lost a battle with a coal stove. Maybe Suzie had a point. With a sigh I handed over the tray, but a nagging thought crept in— was she about to proposition the men herself? I shoved it aside and got back to business, rallying the ladies to prepare for clients.

Lined up and ready, they waited for Suzie to guide them in. But the reception desk buzzed, asking what the holdup was.

'She's handling it,' I explained.

Apparently, that wasn't good enough. The receptionist snapped, telling me to quit dawdling and get the women into the rooms before the men changed their minds. Great. So despite this being Suzie's grand show, I was the one getting chewed out. Feeling like a glorified errand girl, I swallowed my resentment and did her job for her—again.

As angry as I felt, there was nothing I could do, so I carried on and hustled the women to follow me into the room.

Opening the door to the waiting room, I was surprised to find Suzie chatting with the men as if they were old friends. These men were clients, here to spend time with the sex workers, not sit around swapping life stories with Suzie. In this line of work every second counted, and her little ego trip was costing us money.

Startled, Suzie shot to her feet the second she saw me. She slipped out of the room, and I followed, making sure she actually left. Just before disappearing, she threw me a smirk and mouthed, 'That Italian stallion should be mine.'

The air around her reeked of scheming. I had a feeling this wasn't over. Annoyed but biting my tongue, I figured I'd let her have her fun—sooner or later, the tables would turn.

The desk receptionist told me to take charge, so I did. After the men made their picks, I hurried downstairs to assign the women their clients and rooms. Handling all four bookings like a well-oiled machine, I made sure each woman took her client to pay up before heading off. The men wanted to leave together, so once their time was up, the ladies corralled them into a waiting room. With them all gathered, I stepped back in to finish the job.

Just as I was about to lead them out, I caught sight of Suzie near the front entrance, pretending to wipe the doorknob like she was the Queen of Sanitation. Yeah, right. As I got closer, she shifted, planting herself right between me and the door, flashing her best I-got-this act.

Rude. I held my ground, not budging an inch.

Then, with a glare sharp enough to slice steel, Suzie inched her way towards the Italian stallion and oh-so-casually slipped him a folded note before vanishing like a cheap magician.

Right on cue, another client strolled out of a nearby room and I just knew—Suzie's little stunt wasn't over yet.

As he reached for his pocket—probably to stash the note—I 'accidentally' bumped into him. Hard. Sending the note flying. Before he could react, I snatched it mid-air and quipped, 'I'll take care of your rubbish.' With that, I shoved it in my pocket, shut the door behind him, and got back to work.

At home hours later, I reached into my pocket and pulled out the crumpled paper. Unfolding it, I found Suzie's signature move—her lipstick imprint, name, phone number, and a desperate little 'Call me.'

What a sneaky bitch. The boss wouldn't have been pleased if she'd known. Receptionists were hired to manage the women and the floor, not to poach clients. But there was Suzie, diverting business. Word spread fast among the working ladies, and from then on, she was known as the Lipstick Olympics Trash.

Working women didn't take kindly to others snatching their opportunities—or so I'd heard. That incident taught me never to underestimate myself or my intelligence. Sure, I'd stumbled, let people get under my skin and even doubted myself. But when it really mattered, I stood my ground and reminded the world I wasn't someone to mess with.

Lesson: Don't underestimate yourself.
Use your strengths to the best of your ability.

CHAPTER 46

Bambi's return

As fate would have it, I crossed paths with Bambi again. There she was, standing in a line-up of about six women, dressed in nothing but a full-body black netted stocking. Everything was on display—including her bulbous clit, boldly peeking out from its hiding place. I knew she saw me, but she gave me the poker face, which I guess was code for *Fuck off and don't talk to me.*

Bambi's distinct silhouette and that unmistakable high-pitched voice—still as grating as ever—echoed from my phone sex days. Yep, it was definitely her.

She seemed to have lost her magical powers with men—not like on the phone lines, where she was in high demand. Most guys who walked through those doors had their sights set on something else—maybe it was the whole package, or maybe she just wasn't as enchanting without a phone between them.

At the brothel, it was obvious Bambi rubbed the other women up the wrong way, just like she did on the phone lines. Some things never changed. One of the workers filled me in on Bambi's less-than-charming traits. She mostly kept to herself, but the second she thought her opinion was needed, she was all in. She probably thought her arrogance was confidence, but no one was buying it.

During their downtime, the women gathered in the lounge area, which doubled as their prep zone. That's when I 'accidentally' bumped into Bambi—now going by Trixie. Of course, she was annoyed by my total lack of spatial awareness. While I pretended to tidy up, I greeted her with, 'Hey, can you believe we're back working together? It's been ages since the phone lines!'

She rolled her eyes and waved me off like I was a pesky fly. That was my cue to not give two shits about being nice to her again. I believe in treating everyone with respect, but I also know when it's not appreciated. Honestly, watching her stomp around like she owned the place taught me more about self-awareness than any self-help book ever could. I mean, if she didn't notice how utterly obnoxious, she was, who would? But I digress.

Although the receptionist and sex worker roles were totally different, the key to success, for both management and the women, was teamwork for our shared goal: keeping the men around. A lot of that fell on the floor receptionist—that'd be me. We were the ones convincing men to stay, especially when they weren't exactly thrilled with the women they'd seen. The men acted like they were being offered leftovers and trust me, some of those dickheads used that word more than once.

Selling them on the remaining options was like convincing a drunk guy he needed more booze: pointless and exhausting. But I kept at it like a bulldozer taking down a building, and nine times out of ten, I got them to pick someone they hadn't even considered. I guess when the blood rushes to their dick, decision-making takes a backseat.

It dawned on me that Trixie was too busy with her own agenda to care about mine. Typical.

One evening, a sex worker let me in on Trixie's not-so-savoury tricks for snagging bookings. Initially I brushed it off, but my suspicions heightened when I overheard her making promises to a client outside the waiting room that went beyond what others offered. Men often asked who would do anal, who would let them go down on them without a dental dam, and things like that. *Did I hear that right? Did she just break brothel girl code? Oh, hell yes, she did.*

That left a bad taste in my mouth—like expired milk, but worse. She wasn't that sweet, sultry voice from the phone lines anymore. Nope, she'd curdled into something bitter and toxic.

She completely disregarded the boundaries. What were those? If you got in Trixie's way, she'd flatten you like a steamroller and then walk over you in her stilettos. She appeared to lack emotional maturity, making it difficult for her to relate to others with compassion. During her short stint at the brothel, she managed to alienate everyone, which only made my job as the floor receptionist tougher.

Whenever the women were dissatisfied, I could feel it in their attitude towards me. If Trixie snagged a booking instead of them, I became the scapegoat. In their eyes, it was my fault clients requested services or activities that other women wouldn't entertain. I was always to blame, no matter what. I'd become a pro at playing that role. The difference now? I wasn't even mad about it. *Yeah, throw me under the bus, I've survived worse.*

My job? A total grind, and then some. It was physically and mentally draining, teetering on straight-up miserable. Between pushy clients, condescending madams, and a few catty co-workers, it felt like everyone had me in their crosshairs. And let's not forget my husband, who was just another name on the list of people making my life harder. Honestly, I still don't know how I made it through without snapping—or setting something on fire.

It was now late-2000, and I figured I'd be working for Leanna a few more years, but something unexpected happened that changed all that.

The receptionist that night was Amy, and she was late. The madam blasted her, and Amy broke down in tears. Her car had broken down, and she lived over an hour away from Chatswood. Oh, and it just happened to be Christmas Eve. I did what any decent work wife would do and stood up for Amy, calling out the boss for treating her like crap. Good deed for the day done.

After a seventeen-hour shift, right as I was about to leave, the madam handed me a Burberry bag, then snatched it back with a few choice words, telling me to get out and never come back.

The madam was clever, waiting until I was dead-tired to chew me out. Needed to remember that one for future reference.

No fancy bag, no 'thank you for your service.' But that's okay. I rolled my eyes, smiled, and said, 'Thanks anyway, but that bag wouldn't go with anything in my wardrobe, before heading out. I didn't know the first thing about how expensive a Burberry bag was until later. All my bags were cheap and practical—luxury items meant nothing to me.

By the weekend, the boss's son-in-law showed up at Amy's place with a plastic shopping bag stuffed with $20,000 in hundred-dollar bills—a 'gift' for a new car. Guess the boss felt guilty for going off on her! As for me? I got shown the door. No big deal. I was used to landing in the gutter, and somehow, I always managed to crawl out unscathed.

Then came a card from Amy. It read, *My dearest Cookie Girl, this card says it all. I know the way you left work wasn't what you deserved, but hopefully I can make that up to you. What you did for me was above and beyond the call of duty, and I want you to know I will never forget. Hoping to catch up soon. Miss you heaps. Keep baking, Cookie Girl.*

We stayed in touch for a while. I still have that handwritten card, and it's one of the few things I treasure. It was a reminder that, sure, I walked out without the designer bag or thanks from the boss, but at least I walked out with my dignity. And that was worth more than all the fucking designer crap in the world.

Lesson: *Never undervalue yourself.*
You're worth more than you know.

CHAPTER 47

Brothel catastrophes and more

It didn't take me long to land another brothel job after being unceremoniously booted from the fine Chatswood establishment. One minute, I was out on my arse. The next, I had a whole new hustle lined up.

This one was a whole different world from Leanna's. More responsibility, sure, but way more chill—probably because I was the only receptionist on duty. No one breathing down my neck.

Just how I liked it.

Enter Lavinia, my new madam, a striking European beauty who looked to be in her late thirties. Tall, poised, and rocking a body that could stop traffic. Her long, wavy blonde hair screamed young Ivana Trump, and she never stepped out without her signature red lipstick and frosted eye make-up. And those legs! She could've been a swimsuit model, easy.

She even had that polished, calculating air of a politician—with the brains to go with it. I mean, you didn't set up and run four high-end brothels by accident. Whenever she walked in to check on things I'd freeze mid-task, watching as she scanned the room like a queen surveying her kingdom. She had that kind of presence—sharp, deliberate, always one step ahead.

Unknowingly, she taught me to do the same. The only problem? My brain and my mouth had never been on speaking terms. Whereas she mastered the art of assessing a situation before saying a word, my thoughts tended to bypass the whole thinking step and launch straight out of my mouth. It took me another decade to grasp that whole *pause before speaking* concept. Even then, it was a work in progress.

And her style? Immaculate. She had that effortless elegance that made it look like she'd just stepped out of a fashion editorial. Flowing dresses that draped perfectly over her sleek silhouette and those iconic double-breasted jackets with that slightly oversized padded shoulder power vibe. She nailed that early-2000s mix of structured sophistication and laid-back confidence, the kind of look that said 'I own the damn place'—because, well, she did.

Her establishments, sorry, massage parlours, were spread out across Parramatta, Harris Park, Eastwood, and Chatswood. We all know, the services went well beyond a relaxing rubdown. As for her husband, I assumed way too much about him. He looked a solid fifteen years older than Lavinia and always seemed to have a tool belt on—plunger, hammer, you name it. He was the handyman, or at least that's what I thought until I realised, he was also some kind of singer.

Whenever he came in he'd break into song—totally weird. I mean, it wasn't the Opera House, it was a damn sex house. Still, the guy had pipes, I'd give him that. He could belt out a tune, no doubt, but I never knew where to look. And, let's be honest, the men in the rooms getting their rocks off probably weren't exactly vibing with his impromptu concerts.

I had to give him credit, though—he was head over heels for Lavinia. The way he spoke to her … all respect, no questions asked. He didn't even bat an eye at the women strolling around in their underwear. Not a glance. His gaze was always locked on his stunning Lavinia.

Their love story was straight out of a romance novel. At least, that's what Betty, one of the more mature sex workers, told me. She had worked for Lavinia for years and spilled the details: Lavinia had once been a sex worker and was rescued from the industry by a regular client—her husband. They'd married and opened their own brothel. It sounded like something you'd read in a book, but I couldn't help but wonder if it was too perfect to be true.

I worked in three of her establishments, each with about four service rooms—way smaller than Leanna's, but a definite upgrade. The linen was pristine, not a frayed edge in sight. Every room had a clean, pleasant scent, and little touches for the men, like massage oils, extra towels, a splash of cologne, because, you know, ambience. Two of the rooms even had a massage table with two headrests: one for the man's head, and the other for, well, his other head.

The walls were white, keeping things simple and clean, and the floors timber, with a few rugs scattered around to make it feel cosy. There was a large mirror and a separate shower cubicle in each room, normal by modern standards.

Surprisingly, the working environment was pretty chill—who knew brothels could have such good vibes? The decor was modern, tastefully done, and the furniture was comfy. The downside? Only one receptionist per night, so I was left juggling a circus of chaos on my own.

On busy nights, keeping everything under control was a challenge, especially with having to wrap up before my shift ended. But when the women were occupied, I got a breather. Downtime meant I could sit at my desk, cleaning supplies at the ready, sipping on whatever was left from the break room stash. Otherwise, it was a full-on hustle to restock, handle phone inquiries, and manage walk-ins.

It never crossed my mind—nope, not even once, while working in the brothels just how capable I was. Here I was, managing the whole operation like a pro, making sure everything ran smoothly, yet I never bothered to give myself a pat on the back. Isn't it funny how women always downplay their strengths? Seriously, we need to stop that!

When Lavinia popped in unannounced, she was usually pleasant—except for one night when she decided to unleash her inner critic on my appearance. 'You could try putting a brush through your hair once in a while, and a little make-up wouldn't hurt either.' Maybe she had a point; my hair was a wild mess of waves and frizz that swelled the second I broke a sweat. But who had time for that? Between running the show and trying to keep the place from falling apart, personal grooming was far down on my priority list!

Looking back, I get it—she was the picture of elegance, always impeccably dressed, with every hair perfectly in place. Meanwhile, there I was in my modest black pants, white button-up shirt, sneakers, and hair half-tied back. But, she was the boss, so she didn't have to roll up her sleeves and wrestle with the cleaning like I did.

But the night she decided to critique my appearance left me feeling like a poor street urchin. I wished I could've told her it wasn't my job to impress men—I wasn't for sale! I didn't have the guts to speak up, so I absorbed her insults like a machine gun unloading bullets—each one landing harder than the last and draining whatever was left of my self-confidence.

My life consisted of tackling challenge after challenge. A family to care for, hardly any sleep and people's constant condemnations left me shattered. I should've let those words bounce off me and reminded myself that I was doing a damn good job. But, instead, I let it get to me.

It didn't help that the entire operation rested solely on my shoulders the nights I worked, from the moment I showed up to the second I locked that place down at night. And let me tell you, that was no small feat. By the end of a shift, I was drained, and a little freaked out, especially when everyone else had already split and the security guard was nowhere to be found.

The possibility of being mugged weighed heavily on my mind. The idea of being left for dead while hauling cash around in the middle of the night was enough to make anyone's skin crawl. The Eastwood brothel was tucked away at the end of a dark, sketchy alley with zero streetlights. At the back there was this tall, rusty metal gate.

During daylight hours the gate stayed open, allowing the women to park their vehicles and giving clients a discreet way in, because apparently, no one wanted to be seen entering a brothel. But come nightfall that gate had to be locked, which I did without fail. Once I shut the place down, I'd unlock the gate, drive my car out to the other side of it, then get out again to lock it back up before I could drive away. So much for a quick exit.

But despite the heart-racing anxiety that came with working solo at night, I never complained. I sucked it up and did what needed to be done.

Of course, calamity was always trailing behind me. One memorable incident happened when a regular client visited the Eastwood brothel. This guy had a fetish for getting his whole body lathered and shaved before sex. He'd lie on a pile of towels on the floor, masturbate while being shaved, then shower and have sex. By the time he was done showering, there were at least half a dozen towels to toss in the laundry.

On this particular night, halfway through the shave, the sex worker frantically called out for help. I found him on the floor, bleeding all over the towels. She had accidentally cut his balls. I immediately went into first aid mode and told him to pinch the wound together, but he didn't seem too impressed, especially when I suggested putting plasters on his testicles. His erection? Vanished—it just disappeared.

Shit almighty, really? How the hell was I going to get blood stains out of the towels? I refunded his money, and, as expected, I never saw him again.

There were times when men were scheming, self-centred idiots, treating women like objects.

They'd go doggy style, then rip off their condoms, thinking the women wouldn't notice. Yeah, right. They always knew when it happened—women would roll out of their rooms, wrapped in nothing but a towel, quickly escorting their client out the door, clothes in hand. And let's not forget the ones trying to sneak it in the back door, thinking the women wouldn't catch on. Please. There was always that one guy who thought he could get away with it.

Being the sole receptionist had its perks: peace of mind, less drama behind the scenes. But it wasn't all sunshine and rainbows. Sometimes the men's waiting area, where my desk sat, felt like an open invitation for them to spill their guts. I was their unofficial shrink. They'd lay bare their secrets and sometimes, I could've done without the emotional baggage. But, of course, compulsion was one of my character flaws, and it led me straight into life's temptations—like Kyle.

The moment I swung open the door and laid eyes on Kyle, I was a goner. He was a dashing, refined client from the Eastwood brothel, who always parked his car on the adjacent street. I couldn't help but notice his routine: he'd step out, adjust his belt buckle with the precision of a secret agent, straighten his trousers like he was prepping for a photo shoot, and run his hand over his crisp white shirt to smooth out any rogue creases. Then he'd polish his shoes against his trouser leg, the final touch to his look, before raking both hands through his luscious blond hair. And that smile! It lit up the street like a Roman candle, making everything seem possible, as though Thor himself had just stepped out of a cloud.

While he waited, we'd chat to pass the time. As strange as it sounds, a twinge of jealousy hit me every time he strolled off with one of the working women. I couldn't help but imagine it was me with him behind that closed door, sharing all kinds of pleasures. What started as polite small talk quickly morphed into something juicier, our conversations peeling back the layers of our lives like an onion, revealing all the messy, tear-inducing bits beneath.

Unbeknown to me, my true personality began to shine brighter than it ever had on the sex phone lines. Kyle made me feel like I was on top of the world, hanging on my every word, treating me like I was the smartest person in the room. Our platonic relationship blossomed on a higher mental level—something I hadn't realised was missing from my life until he walked through that door.

One afternoon, with all the women busy entertaining clients, Kyle lounged opposite my desk, explaining the theory of energy generation. Meanwhile, I couldn't help but envision us making love, our passion igniting like a brand-new energy source. As my thirst for both water and Kyle consumed my senses, I rose to get a drink from the water fountain. That's when the atmosphere shifted. As I strolled past him, he reached for my hand, pulling me closer.

My senses exploded. The sexual chemistry between us was electric; the heat was rising. My mind raced—I calculated that no one would be emerging from their rooms for at least half an hour, giving us a bit of privacy in the charged atmosphere. And if anyone decided to show up at the entrance, they'd have to ring the doorbell first—a little warning in the enticing, dangerous game we were playing.

Kyle stood up, wrapping his hands around my waist and drawing me into his body. A warm sensation surged through me, intensifying with every second. The firmness of his chest matched the hardness of his cock as he pressed it against me. Leaning down slightly, he kissed me, guiding my hand down the front of his trousers to explore what was hiding inside.

Suddenly, there came the unmistakable sound of footsteps coming up the stairs. In a moment of panic, I shoved him away, realising the downstairs door was locked. Only one possibility remained: my boss.

Composing myself, I darted behind the desk just in time. To my relief, Kyle had strategically placed a cushion on his lap, concealing any evidence of our intimate moment.

My boss was none the wiser. It was a narrow escape, one I never dared to repeat. After that incident, whenever Kyle returned to the brothel, we maintained a strictly professional demeanour, despite the lingering awkwardness in our exchanged glances. Each time he came in for his booking the tension between us simmered beneath the surface.

And then it happened.

One night, while he was busy with his booking, I focused on wrapping up my shift for the handover to the next receptionist. Knowing Kyle would be leaving soon, I rushed to finish my duties and discreetly slip out the back door to my car.

Halfway down the lane, I stopped when I noticed Kyle leaning against the fence. Apparently, I hadn't slipped away quickly enough.

To my surprise, he suggested we grab a drink. I mean, who could resist the mix of my stupid crush and the chance for some excitement in my otherwise boring routine? So, I agreed. I called my husband, spinning some bullshit about needing to stay late at work. I jumped into his car, and we took off for Parramatta.

At a cosy cafe by the river, we settled in, diving into intimate conversations about our lives and desires. The attraction between us was indisputable, and the connection grew stronger with every laugh and shared secret. Afterwards, we made our way back to the parking station.

At the car, just as my hand touched the door handle, Kyle reached across, stopping me. He pressed his body against mine, pulled my hair over my shoulder, and trailed his lips up my neck. And that's when I knew I was in deep trouble. He leaned in and whispered in my ear, 'Can you feel how badly I want you?'

Oh, I could feel it all right—his cock was begging for attention against my back.

He spun me around, pulling me into him with a kiss so intense I swear I almost lost consciousness. His hands slid up my skirt, squeezing my arse as he dragged me even closer. 'I want you,' he murmured, and that's when it hit me—this wasn't just some random attraction for him. It was torture, seeing me behind that desk every time he came in, knowing he couldn't have me.

My head was spinning, caught between wanting to give in to the flood of desire and the cold reality that everything would explode into chaos if I did. My life was already a tangled mess and the last thing I needed was to drag him into it. I'd be playing a game of tag if I jumped into something with him now. Sure, the idea of a potentially amazing relationship was tempting, but the weight of not knowing if it could last had me second-guessing everything. Too many unknowns, and no matter how hard I tried to shove them away, I knew that what we had could easily be mistaken for nothing more than lust.

With all that swirling around, taking a break from the Eastwood brothel seemed like the only sensible move. A clean break. No more ties with him. I shuffled my shifts around, spending more time at the Harris Park and Chatswood brothels instead, trying to put some space between me and that mess.

Kyle was one of those rare types, the kind I'd met before, on the phone sex lines, no less. He made me take a good, hard look at my marriage, and it didn't take long to realise there was zero chemistry between me and Chris. What *was* there, then? A case of co-dependence I never should've had, plus the fact that we were both from ethnic families so toxic they could give a cauldron of drama a run for its money. I started wondering if there'd ever been anything between us besides plain habit.

Thinking back to my teenage self, married at seventeen—what the hell was I thinking? The only thing I'd figured out back then was what was trendy. So why had I stuck around in a relationship that lacked any real connection? It wasn't just about the physical stuff, it was the whole damn package. Where the hell was my spark? I was determined to find that connection, the real deal, somewhere in this hot mess of a life.

In the meantime, I kept my nose to the grindstone, making a few friends along the way. Funnily enough, they weren't the receptionists. Nope, I bonded with the working women instead. One of the best was Betty, a seasoned pro in her fifties who'd seen it all. We got close quickly. She trusted me with stories from her past, like how she'd started out as a floor receptionist for Lavinia—the same madam I worked for. Full circle, right?

One day, Lavinia convinced her to work on the other side of the desk. I suspected she might've taken advantage of Betty, knowing about her financial situation after her divorce. I admired Betty, though; she was thoughtful and kind of motherly towards me.

After Betty stopped working for Lavinia, she invited me to her apartment by the water in Hunters Hill, which was way closer to my place than I'd expected. We went to a cafe nearby for coffee, and being the thoughtful one I am, I made her some traditional Italian sugared almonds—wrapped in white organza, of course, and tied with ribbon—for her daughter's wedding. A little homemade sweetness to balance out the brothel chaos. In return, Betty loaned me some high-quality timber chairs for a function I was hosting at home.

When Betty switched to a brothel above a computer shop in West Ryde, I'd drop by to hang out. You know, just the usual casual visits to check on the world of brothel life.

Some brothels were like sparkling palaces—if you ignored the lack of actual sparkle—where the women were all about cleanliness. Others? Let's just say they were like that one cousin who never learned how to clean up after themselves. They looked like a garbage dump had a love affair with an ashtray and lipstick. I would walk in and have to mentally adjust to the shock.

One time, I opened the door and saw a woman in a lacy bra and five-inch lace-up boots with one leg up on a chair, while another woman kneeled on the floor in front of her, head buried between her legs. Turns out she was helping pull out a sea sponge that had gotten lodged inside. The women used them during their periods to keep working without creating a bloody mess. Not what I was expecting to walk in on, yet, all part of the job, right?

At first, seeing stuff like that was a shock, but after a while it became normal. I'd walk into rooms to collect payments and there'd be men frantically jerking off, trying to stay hard while the girls just sat there waiting for the money to clear. Some of them were real arseholes about it. Kinda reminded me of my time at Leanna's brothels.

The women, like Stella—this tiny Italian dynamo I nicknamed Little Pocket Rocket—shared their industry wisdom and gave me the lowdown on its dangers. At twenty-six, with five years of brothel life under her belt, she was plotting her escape. Her big plan? Buy a second property within the year. Smart move. She was all about setting goals, a lesson I'd later find pretty damn useful when I had to start living within my means.

Stella's family had no clue what she did for a living. She wasn't exactly winning beauty pageants, but, she had this magic touch with men. She made them feel special, like they were the only one in the world. She knew how to keep 'em coming back—literally and figuratively. I even got a front-row seat to one of her 'talent showcases' one night.

As luck would have it, I barged in on Stella with one of her clients. Yeah, big surprise—walking into rooms unannounced was my thing. There she was, on her knees, doing her thing with a client sitting on the edge of the bed, looking like he was having some kind of episode. I swear, his eyes were rolling back so far, I thought he might need an electric shock to revive him.

Stella? Unfazed. She glanced up at me, not missing a beat, then got right back to business. The way she had that guy down her throat, I didn't know how she managed to breathe. It was so impressive I couldn't help but ask her about it later. And, being Stella, she didn't hesitate to give me a live demo—using a cucumber, of course.

Emerging from the booking, Stella rubbed her jawline, complaining about lockjaw with her usual sense of humour. She had a knack for making challenging situations look easy. She explained that her client wanted her to perform oral for the entire half-hour since he never got it at home.

Stella's dedication and hustle turned her dreams into reality. She taught me that goals weren't just wishful thinking—they required hard work, even if it meant stepping out of your comfort zone. Something I'd been doing my whole life without even realising it. Go figure, right?

Then there was Jodie, another woman with an amazing talent for giving great oral, who had a reputation for stirring the pot. I was at the desk one night when she plopped down opposite me in the office area, clearly deciding I was her target for the night. 'Do you want to see something beautiful?' she asked. Upon looking at her, she spread her legs wide apart.

Rolling my eyes, I caught her smiling at me as she asked, 'Want a nibble for free?'

'Really,' I mumbled, shaking my head as I reached into my desk drawer and pulled out a vibrator. 'See this, Jodie? This is what I can offer you if you're feeling horny.'

She laughed. 'How did you know I was horny?'

'When are you not?'

It was often like that at the brothel.

Beth, a seasoned woman in her sixties, stood out with her long, wavy blonde hair, busty figure and a husky voice from a lifetime of cigarettes and scotch. We clicked instantly outside the brothel when I decided to check out her place, and that's when I witnessed her entrepreneurial genius in action.

The first time I visited her home in Balmain, I was sold on the area—those terrace-style homes had charm—but it was Beth's setup that really got me. Once a month she'd host a get-together for mature singles, charging sixty bucks a head, offering wine and some light snacks and letting them mingle for about three hours. Simple, safe, and surprisingly lucrative, especially with only eight people showing up.

Watching older people flirt and chat opened my eyes. Who said love and life stopped when you hit a certain age? Beth was living proof that independence had nothing to do with age, and it hit me—this was the kind of woman I wanted to be confident, financially stable and calling the shots.

But I was still too scared to follow in her footsteps. My dream of breaking free from the chains of my own life wasn't happening just yet—it would take a hell of a lot more than daydreams to get me there. For now, I threw myself into figuring out what made men tick, especially the ones who kept showing up at the brothel. Maybe if I cracked that code, I'd finally understand where I was going wrong.

Lesson: Impulsive decisions are like stepping on a rake—sometimes you smack yourself in the face, but hey, it might be life's way of stopping you from stepping off a cliff.

CHAPTER 48

The haunted bordello

In a typical Sydney suburb, a respectable federation-style brick house in Harris Park was hiding more than just its age. Masquerading as a massage centre, it was really a discreet brothel. Appointments were the norm, but if a walk-in showed up, they weren't turned away. With a maximum of five women per shift it was rather relaxed, more so than the other parlours I'd worked at.

A low brick fence outlined the tiny lawn, with a rusty wrought-iron gate welcoming clients along a narrow side passage to the wooden front door. They'd ring an old-fashioned mechanical doorbell, which probably had more personality than many of the people who walked through it. Inside, a narrow hallway opened into a salon that looked deceptively classy—lounges lined both walls, and the receptionist's desk—my desk—was tucked in the corner, because, apparently, I was the last person you wanted to see unless you were booking or paying.

Every step on those creaky timber floors seemed to scream *We've seen some things*, and the worn Persian rugs scattered around didn't know if they were there to decorate or to trip me up—I'd done my fair share of both. Winters inside were brutally icy. The only warmth was from those plug-in oil heaters. Summer wasn't much better, just a few pedestal fans fighting the air like they had something to prove. But the spa room up front? That was the VIP suite, complete with air conditioning—a small mercy for anyone lucky enough to book an extended appointment.

The rooms were arranged from the front of the house to middle, four working rooms in total, with the women's quarters tucked in the back. It had a basic lounge, a small TV, and was cluttered with the women's belongings. At times, it looked like a bomb had hit it—though, of course, that all depended on which women were working that day. Just off the main salon was a cramped bathroom with a stained-glass window that cracked open just enough to let in the distant sounds of kids playing next door—a reminder that normal life existed elsewhere.

Beside the women's quarters, the galley kitchen buzzed with activity. It was our hangout spot, where the working women and I would grab a quick bite. Across the hall sat the laundry room, the rhythm of the washing machine providing a near-constant hum.

When I needed food or had to swap cash, I'd make a run to the corner shop almost directly across the street. The young guy behind the counter always had something to say about 'the business', shooting me that knowing look as he watched the clients and women coming and going. Something about his stare made my skin crawl, like he was judging me—though maybe I was projecting. Either way, every encounter left me feeling like I'd walked through a spiderweb.

One Sunday evening, with only four women on shift and two already occupied, two men strolled in off the street. I didn't have many choices to offer, but I did my best to make it work, showing them the two available ladies.

When I asked about their preferences, they laughed and said they'd been promised six women when they called—hinting that I might be one of them. I shrugged it off, though part of me wanted to fire back. As the receptionist, I often had to take the heat, especially when I had to inflate the number of women on shift. They weren't thrilled, but I didn't waste any time letting them know they were lucky to have the two most popular girls on shift, with bookings filling up fast.

They were barely in their twenties, dripping booze and sweat in the summer heat. 'Big night for you boys, huh?' I said. 'Choosing from these lovely ladies isn't easy, but don't hang around too long, someone else might snatch them up.' Without waiting for their reply, I added, 'Let's get you both settled in your rooms, and I'll grab you a drink. How's that sound, boys?'

To my surprise, they got up without a word, handed over their cash, and followed me into their rooms. *Damn, that was easy. Maybe I've got the Midas touch?*

I handed each woman a Scotch and Coke, along with towels and a bedsheet, before they headed off to the young men. Soon after, another client came by, happy with his pick of the two women who'd just wrapped up. With time, I learned to spot the types who were just there to window shop, and I made it my mission to get them to part with their cash before they left.

And every time I did, it felt like a small victory.

This unassuming establishment also held a chilling rumour: a ghostly presence haunted its halls, lingering, particularly in the bathtub. As the clock struck seven each evening, an ominous stillness enveloped the place, except for the eerie sounds of water swishing in the bathtub. It would echo through the silent corridors, even with the lights off and the bathroom door firmly shut. When anyone dared to enter the bathroom, the unnerving sounds would abruptly cease, leaving a palpable sense of unease behind.

And it didn't end there. As midnight drew closer, the spirit's tricks seemed to ramp up. In the middle of routine cleaning, no matter how securely I propped up the mop or leaned the vacuum against the wall, they'd clatter to the floor as if unseen hands had given them a shove.

Doors creaked shut on their own, shadows appeared out of nowhere and a chill drifted through the rooms, even with every window sealed tight.

At the end of the night, after logging every last transaction, I faced one final task that I hated: handling the cash. Divvying up the women's earnings was one thing, but taking the night's full earnings home was my least favourite responsibility, one that left me exposed to robbery every time I left.

As I locked the door behind me, plunging everything into darkness, a chilling feeling crept over me, like eyes were on me in the shadows. Maybe it was just my nerves, or maybe my imagination was in overdrive after a long night. But I couldn't shake the feeling, like someone was waiting for me to crack, waiting for me to break under all the weight I was carrying.

I'd come home, exhausted, and Chris would barely look up from the TV. No 'How was your day?' No acknowledgment of the grind. I was stuck in a loop of doing everything for everyone—food on the table, clothes washed, kids tucked in—then I'd slip away to work like some crusader fighting a battle no one could see.

Even though I wished Chris would step up and take on more responsibility, deep down, all I really wanted was for him to show that he saw me. That he cared about me and appreciated what I was doing. Instead, I felt like an invisible slave in my own home.

Lesson: Own your struggles, even if no one else gets it. You don't need their applause—you're already crushing it.

CHAPTER 49

A legacy of dysfunction

In some twisted way, staying in a messy relationship like mine almost felt … cosy. Like I'd inherited a family heirloom of dysfunction. If that didn't scream 'I'm insecure and too numb to care' then I didn't know what did. Maybe if I'd seen what a healthy relationship looked like as a kid I might have spotted the red flags sooner. Instead I stayed, repeated the same mistakes and had zero idea how to set boundaries. 'Enough' wasn't in my vocabulary. Instead, I dived headfirst into one bad decision after another.

What did a fifteen-year-old know? I was a kid when I met Chris. So, it wasn't that strange that I stuck around for a torturous twenty-five years. The cycle never changed: his charm, his mind games, and me feeling like I was the last person in the room. I'd wonder why no one ever spoke up. Family, friends—people saw it, so why was everyone so damn silent? Were they all blind, or was this just the norm of the time? Why was it so okay for women to be treated like crap, hit, or verbally torn down? That silence ate at me, gnawing away at the edges of my sanity, as if everyone just shrugged and left me to clean up the mess alone.

Chris had his on-again, off-again charm routine down to an art. One minute, he was a jerk, the next Mr Sweet-as-Sugar, thinking he could wipe the slate clean with one nice gesture.

Predictable as clockwork.

Most nights, after long hours on the phone lines or at the brothels, I'd drag myself home, barely keeping my eyes open. All I wanted was sleep, but nope, Chris wanted sex. I'd give in, going through the motions like a trained circus animal, counting the seconds until it was over.

My disgust for him only grew, and I'm sure that fuelled my affairs. Maybe it was revenge, maybe it was my messed-up attempt at normalcy, a little payback for his twisted mind games.

There were times I'd sit on the doorstep, head in my knees, waiting for the kids to wake up. When they did, I'd open the door, walk in, and feel safe—at least for a moment. Work drained me, but Chris was like a slow death. I'd rather run on empty all day than crawl into bed to face his endless demands.

He hurt me—physically, verbally, mentally. No wonder I often felt like I was losing my mind. And when he'd try to make up for it, he'd show up with flowers and some half-hearted apology: *I am deeply sorry for the hurt that I have given you over and during our marriage together, I hope that one day you will realise that most of the hurt was done unknowingly, I am sorry, Chris.*

Most of the hurt? What did that mean? Did he intend to hurt me sometimes? What went through a man's mind when he berated and attacked a woman? If I had known it was all wrong, maybe I wouldn't have stayed. But I did. I just stayed.

His words were a mess of love and possession, like I was something he owned. And that warped idea that a man was entitled to a woman just because he was a man? That needed to die already.

I'd get pissed, toss the flowers aside, and he'd just come along and pick them up, broken stems and all, and stick them back in the vase. For more than two decades, I stayed, scared of being shunned by family and friends if I left. Most didn't know the real him—why would they? The ones who did turned a blind eye. I feared ending up with nowhere to go, alone with my daughters. I let all these ridiculous reasons pile up in my head and just accepted it.

One letter he wrote me was a confusing mix of praise and horror. He called me beautiful, sexy, the envy of his friends. Then in the same breath he justified holding me down with a knife at my throat while violating me. Somehow, I got through that incident, but he crossed a line that couldn't be uncrossed. I guess it's called rape.

I didn't report it. Fear for my children, fear for myself, and honestly, I worried about looking ridiculous—imagine telling the police my husband did that. I'd have been a joke. I had actually blocked that memory until it resurfaced while writing this book. The pain of that night still lingers, but I smile because I will never let him steal my hope. Because, at times, hope is all we have to hold on to.

Chris viewed our marriage certificate as a licence to treat me however he pleased, oblivious to the fact that a piece of paper was not permission for spousal abuse. No man has the right to control his wife, ever.

But, yes, I tolerated his abuse, trying to keep it quiet, especially in our bedroom, so my children wouldn't overhear an argument—or worse.

Late one night, somewhere between a sane conversation and the light switch turning off in his mind, Chris pinned me against a brick wall in the hallway, hands around my neck, my feet dangling. It was horrific. Worse than the rape, even, because a family member witnessed it and chose to pretend it never happened. I called the cops. When the police asked the family member what happened, they said, 'I didn't see a thing.'

In the meantime, I did what I did best: ignored the situation and consumed myself in the belief of true love. So along came Ted. Yes! I began a relationship with another man before the ink even touched my divorce decree. That was one decision that turned against me big time—but at least my reputation for screwing up stayed intact.

Lesson: Everyone messes up—hell, I've got a PhD in screwing up. But those screw-ups? They're the lessons that teach you. Don't waste time regretting them—use them to level up your next move.

CHAPTER 50

Moving on, not up

Being with Ted was like jumping out of a frying pan straight into an inferno. From that moment, my life took a nosedive. Ted was married—I knew him through our daughters' school friendship group. But I was told his wife, Candice, had gone AWOL. I met him during a rough patch with Chris and, like an idiot, leaned on him for advice.

Big mistake.

It all started in 2001 when my daughter, Nila, became besties with Ted's stepdaughter, Courtney. Playdates meant casual run-ins with Courtney's mother, Candice. We weren't tight, but friendly enough.

Candice was stunning—way too polished for my usual crowd. Long brown hair with perfect auburn highlights, make-up always on point and a wardrobe straight out of a fashion spread. The only thing we had in common was a love of lippy. Otherwise, she was in a whole different league.

She, already had her own clique—polished and perfect, the kind I usually avoided. But one day my life took a sharp turn. I showed up at Candice's place with my daughters, rattled after hearing some shocking news. The moment I saw her fragile state, I knew something was wrong. She looked drained, like life had been knocking her down one hit at a time and she had found rock bottom. She'd been in a car crash—during her grandmother's funeral procession, no less, and her spleen had ruptured. It had to be removed, and she was still recovering from the ordeal. As she rattled off her other health issues, which could've filled a small notebook, I felt an overwhelming need to introduce her to my Chinese doctor. He was a genius with his New Age treatments, and if anyone could give her some relief, it was him. A few needles and mysterious herbs might be the lifeline she needed.

On the appointed day, I met Candice at the doctor's office, her two-year-old son in tow. While she disappeared into the consultation room, I entertained the little one in the waiting room, with a mix of crayons, toy trucks, and a toddler-sized tantrum narrowly avoided. When she finally emerged I almost did a double take. Candice looked … lighter. Her tense shoulders had dropped and there was a spark of relief in her eyes, like she'd just stepped out of a spa instead of a doctor's office.

She grinned, telling me the doctor's plan to help her ditch some of the unnecessary prescription meds. It felt like hope was finally peeking through her storm clouds. We promised to catch up soon and headed off to our cars. Honestly, watching her slide behind the wheel after what she'd been through with the accident gave me chills. I thought it was fearless—or borderline crazy—that said, bravery came in all forms. Her newfound calm trailed behind her like a warm breeze, and I hoped it would stick.

Some time passed and during that stretch, our kids had the occasional playdate. Then, before I knew it, school break was over and the new year hit. I discovered a handwritten note in my home phone diary, one I'd clearly missed earlier. It was a reminder from one of my older daughters to contact Candice's husband, Ted, about the girls' school clothes for the upcoming term. Assuming Ted had already taken care of it, I brushed off the note, since school had already started.

At first, I didn't think twice when Candice's husband called instead of her. Blame it on the exhaustion from pulling night shifts at the brothels—I didn't have the energy to overanalyse.

Then Nila shared something that caught me off guard: Courtney had told her that her mother had run away. Initially, I dismissed it as silly kids' talk, not thinking much of Courtney's claim, until she came over for a playdate sometime later.

It was a Friday, and I had a day shift at the brothel. Chris, in a rare act of graciousness, picked up the kids from school, including Courtney. One of my older daughters and my husband held the fort with the younger ones until I got home. For all his usual selfishness, he managed to stay surprisingly chill when I was the one out there bringing home the bacon.

When I got home around six that evening, I found Ted lounging on the couch with Chris, sipping scotch like he owned the place. He was a striking contrast to Chris—tall, solidly built, with a voice that commanded attention. His hair, slicked back slightly, with a touch of mullet at the back (a classic Aussie cut), wasn't exactly my style, but it suited him. He was so well-spoken, too. In the excitement of the moment, my two youngest daughters and Courtney begged for a sleepover. Caught up in the commotion, I figured, what was one more kid in this already overflowing circus? So, I agreed.

That's when the puzzle pieces started to fall into place. Ted mentioned that Candice had gone to visit family in Cairns a few weeks ago. Suddenly, my daughter's comment about his wife running away made sense. Surely she wasn't missing—it was just an extended stay with family. Though why leave the kids behind? Why didn't she call? Oh well, maybe she needed a breather. We all did, right? And then there was that note in the diary—it all clicked. I didn't have the full picture, so I decided not to press Ted for details … yet.

The next morning, Ted showed up earlier than expected to pick up Courtney. I was making pancakes, and Courtney begged him to stay so she could enjoy pancakes with banana and ice cream. After breakfast, the girls went to play in their room. Ted and I stood by the sink, chatting while I washed the dishes.

Chris was off on some small electrical job and at that moment he called, fuming that I hadn't picked up the gear he needed from the local wholesaler. My hands dripping with dishwater, I listened to his tirade, cheeks burning with embarrassment. Without a word, I hung up, hiding my tears behind my fringe.

Then, out of nowhere, Ted stepped in close and asked if I was okay—a gesture that caught me off guard. No one had ever bothered to check in on me like that before.

I froze. Was this what it felt like to be noticed? Not just as the household workhorse or a human punching bag, but as an actual person? Weird. Unsettling. And, if I was being honest, nice. I forced a smile and assured him I was fine.

He gently pulled my fringe back and said I didn't deserve to be yelled at. He offered to help if I needed it.

Just then my teenage daughter rushed out, needing a ride to work. Flustered and mortified, I wiped my hands and apologised to Ted before telling my daughter I'd take her. But Ted offered instead, giving me time to drag the girls to the electrical wholesalers for Chris's precious cable. I was grateful for the help.

When Ted came back, something shifted. We sat and talked for ages, and that's when he admitted that Candice had left before, but never for this long. Three weeks had passed, and now the police suspected foul play.

I felt for him, sure, but I had my own mess to deal with—my marriage was circling the drain. Yet somehow, I got pulled into an entanglement of desire, and in the months that followed, Ted and I became closer. He was my escape, the one I could finally unburden myself to. By the latter half of the year, our friendship had turned into something more—something forbidden.

Lesson: Everything that glitters is not necessarily gold. Think deep and hard before you make a move.

CHAPTER 51

Divorce, it sucks!

My life was spiralling because I thought I was falling for Ted. Looking back, it was a disaster that exploded in my face at every turn. Maybe I wasn't in love—maybe Ted was just my escape from an abusive marriage.

After countless failed attempts, I pushed for a divorce. Ted's presence gave me the guts to go through with it this time. Maybe everything did happen for a reason, but being with Ted turned out to be a bigger horror show than life with Chris.

Instead of rushing into his arms, desperate for a rescue, I should've stepped back to figure out who I was and what I actually needed. Hindsight's a bitch, right? If I'd stayed single, reflecting and growing, I might've dodged a lot of drama. But fear had me convinced I couldn't go it alone.

It wasn't long before Ted became a suspect in his wife's disappearance. I wanted to believe Candice had left him and I never pressed him for details. I don't know why. Perhaps I was scared the truth would kill my shot at leaving my miserable marriage.

And then came the cherry on top: I, too, came under suspicion in connection with Candice's disappearance. There I was, cosying up to Ted so soon after his wife went missing. It didn't exactly paint me as the concerned friend. But for some reason, I didn't realise how bad it looked—or how much worse it was about to get.

I gave everyone all the ammunition they needed to attack my character. And I accepted it. The investigation into Ted's possible involvement made headlines, and with my name tied to his, hiding wasn't an option. Chris thought he'd won now that everyone knew about my connection to a man suspected in a disappearance.

By then my relationship with Chris had hit a whole new level of awful. Whenever Chris saw an opening, he pounced. He'd moved into the cabana out back, but that didn't stop him from barging into the house one afternoon, shouting like a lunatic. Before I knew it, he was charging after me down two flights of stairs, wielding an old-school orange Tupperware water jug—one of those tough-as-nails ones. In his rage, he raised it, ready to strike, but our fifteen-year-old daughter stepped between us. The jug's contents splashed everywhere, hitting him, which only angered him more. He struck her hard with his hand, leaving a raised red welt.

At first, I thought I could smooth things over, but my daughter had reached her breaking point. She screamed at me to call the police. I tried to lie, tried to reassure her, but even with that welt swelling on her face, I hesitated. Why? I still don't know. Trapped by fear and doubt, I guess. Then she looked me dead in the eyes and said, 'If you don't call the police, I'm running away and never coming back.' She marched up the driveway and onto the road, determination in every step. I chased after her, tears streaming, and finally realised there was no way I could risk losing her.

Chris went off, marching back inside, pissed off and rambling, 'Yeah, run away, take your fucking mother with you.'

That afternoon Chris got hauled off in a paddy wagon—an abuser's perfect accessory.

That wasn't just one night in a cell for Chris; it was the moment the last shred of compassion I had for him died. My stomach twisted all night, dreading what would come next. It hit me: I was done. Completely shattered, with no more pieces left to break.

I've replayed that moment a thousand times, asking myself why I didn't act sooner. Why didn't I call the police right away? I get it now, what holds so many women back: the twisted manipulation that messes with your mind, making you freeze, over and over again, fear slithering under every ounce of courage.

He was released the next day, spent a few weeks crashing at his brother's, and then came back with the suggestion of a trial separation. Don't ask me why I agreed—I just did. I figured he was pissed about me getting involved with Ted, but couldn't stomach the idea of losing control over me. So, he moved into the granny flat while I stayed in the front house with the girls. That was a decision I'd soon regret. Surprise, surprise—nothing changed.

Same old circus, same old acts.

Despite the cops advising me to file for an AVO, I didn't. Doubts crept in. What a total fuck-up. He kept making my life hell, doing everything he could to keep me locked in that misery. He taunted me, verbally and physically, whenever the coast was clear. I tried to ignore it until one day, in a fit of rage, he stormed through the back door, charged up the stairs, and threw me to the ground—in front of our daughters. I screamed at him to get the hell out, but he grabbed me by the shoulders and tossed me down like I weighed nothing.

The fear in my daughters' eyes? That was the final wake-up call. This shit had to stop.

Then came the sorry cards. He wrote one to each of them, apologising with his usual empty nonsense. *You saw me throw your mother across the floor last night, and that was wrong,* he wrote. As if that meant anything. That's when I finally decided to act and file for an AVO.

My neck was marked and I had zero support—if I didn't do something, next time I might end up in a body bag.

Keeping quiet about my mistreatment for decades had become a habit that only worked against me. I dreaded the judgement from people we knew, but I shouldn't have been surprised at how many jumped onto his side.

I saw it firsthand: the deep-rooted misogyny that lingered like an unwelcome house guest. Gender inequality and mistreatment of women was everywhere. No matter how many shiny speeches and progress charts we had, those outdated, harmful ideals were still alive and kicking. I lived it, I felt it, and the truth slapped me in the face repeatedly, making one thing crystal clear: the fight for equality was far from over. And there was no place it hit harder than in my own damn life.

Those letters and cards he kept leaving for me usually went straight into the trash, until one day I figured I'd better hold onto them, just in case. Well, guess what? They came in handy when Chris tried to paint himself as the abused husband and filed a case against me. Those sweet little notes of his became the proof I needed to expose his bullshit, and that case was tossed faster than his lies.

But even when I won, I still had to cough up thousands for an expert barrister. So much for winning—just another reminder that I couldn't catch a break.

Chris made it his mission to destroy me, aiming to take away the one thing that mattered—my kids. He dragged me back to court time and time again with ridiculous claims, hoping to break me down. He even accused me of stalking him and running him over with my car—because, apparently, I was the unhinged, unfit mother.

One day, after the parenting orders were made, Chris had the two youngest girls but was late returning them. I had organised a Christmas party for them, planned weeks in advance, and he knew it. So I called him. He said he was running late and getting petrol first. After some back and forth on the phone, I decided a little sting was in order. I raced to the petrol station he was at, parked my car opposite his while he was inside paying and ushered my daughters into my car. Sure, it might've seemed a little crazy, but I was so pissed about how blasé he was. It was a party for the kids, after all.

Then there was the time Chris stealthily waited for me to finish work. When I drove off he pulled in front of me, with a mate of his tailgating behind me. He went to the police, claiming I was stalking him and tried to run him off the road, with his mate as the so-called witness. But it didn't hold up in court—he messed up and lied. Plus, I'd been at work—the sign-in and sign-out records were solid proof, an official document with every staff member's signature. No faking that. Guess Chris wasn't as clever as he thought. What a total dumb-arse.

He also tried to accuse me of assault over some mysterious bite marks. Of course, that went nowhere—surprise, surprise, no evidence. And just when you thought it couldn't get crazier, he dragged me to court claiming I had attacked him with a bag of lollies. Yep, a bag of lollies. Honestly, it was laughable—the lengths he'd go to, wasting time and money just to keep me tangled up in legal bullshit.

The real story was that he came to the house to tell me he couldn't have the kids that weekend, bringing with him a bag of lollies worth a few dollars. So I threw them at him. Yeah, I threw them. He couldn't afford to give me money to help raise the kids, but he could buy bloody lollies. They grazed past his ear, causing zero damage.

He took a different angle—roping in friends and family, making up stories, stretching the truth—all to humiliate me. He pinned the whole marriage breakdown on me, swearing to anyone who'd listen about my infidelities. By twisting the truth, he handed his allies all the ammo they needed to turn against me. Some people even went out of their way to insult and question my morals, fabricating reasons for why I walked out based on his distorted version of things. I guess I gave them plenty of fuel for the fire. After all, I was the scarlet woman, and my husband was the innocent vestal virgin—at least in his story.

No matter how much I pleaded my case, they tore me down, denying me any recognition as a casualty in this mess. Just like that, I was blacklisted by so many friends and family—disappointing, sure, but there was nothing I could do about their opinions. I realised I was fighting a losing battle, so I cut them out and focused on finalising the divorce. The collateral damage was beyond anything I'd imagined—it sucked, big time.

I was left feeling degraded by the stories Chris spread about me, but walking around with a bag over my head was not an option. Eventually, I had to suck it up and make changes.

First thing: a new job. If I wanted to keep custody of my girls, I needed something respectable, knowing damn well Chris would use my brothel job against me. So back to childcare I went.

The timing couldn't have been worse. During the court battle, I was also caring for my mother, who had dementia and lived with me. It was a daily struggle. Despite my best efforts, she'd wander off in the middle of the night, adding to my anxiety.

I must've been on autopilot to survive it all—work, home, my mother's decline, and those pointless court battles. Then, as if I didn't have enough on my plate, Chris started a relationship with a nurse he met while recovering from a hernia operation. His siblings hated her, convinced she was after his money, and hated me for pushing him into her arms. Seriously, could I get a fucking break?

To stir me up, Chris would taunt me, telling me his new girlfriend was younger, more beautiful and more adored. It wore me down at first—he got under my skin. But looking back, I see it was all a game to make me jealous. And, shamefully, he succeeded. It wasn't until much later that I found out she was younger than me by less than a year, and I felt like a fool for letting it get to me. He was just punishing me for leaving him.

I also felt stupid for falling for his promises about taking care of the kids. Shocker: he never lifted a finger or helped financially. That was all on me.

And to make things worse, this mess became an obsession. I couldn't stop thinking about what he was up to, and the anger was constant. He was in my head twenty-four seven, and that led me straight into a supernatural experience that left me completely shaken.

One night, I was woken by the feeling of someone gripping my face on both sides. I opened my eyes, and there he was—Chris, standing over me, making eye contact like he had a right to be there. I could feel his hands on my head and his breath on my face. Oddly, my bedhead was up against the wall, so I couldn't figure out how the hell he was standing there. I tried to break free, but nope, I was paralysed, in a nightmare I didn't ask for. Then, the bristles of his stupid moustache brushed my forehead as he kissed me and said, 'I beat you to the altar.'

I was *livid*. With every ounce of anger I could muster, I thrashed my head and screamed, 'Go, go, go!'—and just like that, he disappeared. Poof. Gone.

I sat up, drenched in sweat, totally thrown by the whole thing. Naturally, I called my solicitor, which also gave me a chance to mention the small fortune Chris owed me from the house settlement. What he said next was jaw-dropping.

Turns out he was about to call me anyway. He'd spoken to Chris's solicitor earlier that morning—Chris was unreachable because he was off on a two-week honeymoon.

I was torn between wanting to scream and to vomit. There was no rational explanation for my dream vision, but it sure as hell felt like a warning.

And here's the gut punch: Chris could fork out for a wedding and honeymoon but couldn't be bothered to pay me back from the house sale. I was left picking up the pieces, struggling to rebuild my daughters' lives.

I also discovered that Chris owed money to his solicitor. While I needed the money, there was a small sense of satisfaction in knowing that his solicitor, who had been ruthless towards me during our divorce, was now facing his own karmic challenge.

Then Chris opted to permanently settle in Cyprus. Oh, that pissed me off—he'd made zero effort to contact his daughters. His absence showed his total disregard for them. He'd abandoned all responsibility—no emotional support, no financial help. It was like his new life replaced any love for our children.

That was when I turned to the supernatural for some much-needed help with my ex. Post split, a friend recommended psychic healing to clear out his bad energy. The plan was simple: write down everything I wanted to banish and then burn it. Easy, right? Well, in true me fashion, I managed to go slightly off-script …

Like a bloody idiot, I underestimated the whole spiritual energies thing. I half-followed the instructions, then impulsively tossed all of Chris's belongings into the flames. What was a small ritual burn turned into a full-on bonfire.

In a moment of madness, I decided to go full witch mode and cast a curse on him. I was done with his crap, and I wanted to make him pay. It felt oddly satisfying, yelling all the things I wished upon him into the flames—like a long-overdue dose of justice. And guess what? A year later, everything played out just like I'd predicted.

I've since learned the hard way that holding onto grudges is like inviting a boomerang to the face—those bad vibes come back in ways you'd never expect. Let's just say I had a gift for making waves, even when I didn't mean to. Hindsight's twenty–twenty, right?

I should've let go of the anger and let the universe handle it. But no, there I was, drowning in the wreckage of what Chris had left behind. All I wanted was for him to face the mess he made of my life—and our daughters'.

But his actions did teach me something valuable: how to be ready for anything. Getting dragged through court over and over didn't wear me down, it toughened me up. Sure, it was brutal, but those battles made me stronger.

As for Chris, karma came for him—and it hit like a tidal wave. An incredibly unfortunate event.

Lesson: Let justice run its course. Don't waste time stressing over what others did to you—keep moving and watch the universe sort it out.

CHAPTER 52

Missing person case

Candice, Ted's second wife, had vanished, and suddenly, she was everywhere—newspapers, magazines, TV. The woman I knew had become another statistic.

She was last seen on 14 January 2002 in Gladesville. Her dark green Holden later turned up in Merewether, a beachside suburb in Newcastle—because nothing screamed suspicious like your car relocating itself without you. Was she on the run? Had she skipped the country? Or was there something darker at play? No one had seen or heard from her since, and concerns for her safety were growing.

And now that it was official. The investigation began, and I needed to be dragged into another court case like I needed a hole in the head.

I remember attending court to give evidence, but honestly, the whole thing was a blur. My reputation didn't do me any favours when I took the stand. I stumbled through it, trying to make sense of all the big legal words they threw at me. It was hard enough to focus when my mind was already a runaway train.

Ted's elderly parents were also called to testify. His father was a towering man with an overbearing presence; his mother, a frail little thing with a heart of gold. She was a nervous wreck on the stand, poor woman. She floundered through it, her memory fogging up like a window on a cold day. I couldn't help but think that all the crap she'd endured with her husband and Ted during this investigation had taken its toll. Her husband had a nasty temper—I'd seen it up close. She was a good soul, though, just trying to hold it together.

It all came to a head at a coronial inquest at Westmead into Candice's disappearance. The coroner ruled her deceased—there had been no phone calls, no credit card swipes, not a single sighting.

I didn't want to believe it. My mind clung to the desperate hope that she was out there somewhere. I just couldn't accept that she was gone. I wanted Ted's story to be true—that she'd walked out, that this whole mess would eventually blow over. Maybe I'd been blind to it all, only seeing what I wanted to see.

Everywhere I looked, there she was—her face plastered across articles alongside Ted's. And before long, mine started showing up too, lurking in the background of some shots. The media, hungry for a glimpse of Ted in his element, caught me holding his hand, coming and going from court. It was like living in a real-life nightmare, watching my life unravel in the headlines like a TV drama.

But not all media coverage was a waste of time. One night, while watching the news at Ted's parents' place, there it was: a picture of Ted's old school buddy, Gene, now tangled up in a scandal with a Sydney stockbroker convicted of insider trading. And that's when it hit me—Xenia, the woman I knew from my days on the adult phone lines. It had nothing to do with the scandal, but I remembered how she once went with a guy to this stockbroker's house. How strange it was that the past kept creeping up in unexpected ways. Small world, right?

Ted explained that Gene owned a smaller company and had casually chatted with an entrepreneur about a potential sale. After the entrepreneur's tragic downfall, Gene was cleared of any wrongdoing. With the news finally out, Ted reached out to Gene, who offered him a job and invited us to his lavish holiday property in Merriwa—just the break we needed.

Gene didn't hold back. Before long, Ted, his parents and some of the kids were joyriding in a helicopter—talk about an unforgettable experience. The sprawling estate had massive wrought-iron gates imported from France, standing tall as we drove past vineyards and rows of lush green pencil pines. There was this stunning copper water feature, practically begging you to stop and admire it, sitting like a mini spa in the middle of the path between buildings. Cattle grazed nearby, like they were designed to be part of the luxurious landscape. And the estate itself? There were several buildings, including two homes, a helipad, and a landing strip for his private jet. It was like the place had been plucked straight out of a dream.

Inside the main house, art was everywhere, but one piece was impossible to ignore—an abstract painting of 9/11. Then there were the stables, the fully equipped cabin and the billiards room, which had a jukebox, fireplace, kitchen, and firepit by the heated pool. It was like stepping into a scene from a movie. And that was just the start. Gene didn't skimp on anything: a separate cinema, quads, tennis court, gym with indoor spa, sauna and sound system. I was half-waiting for someone to pinch me—this couldn't possibly be real, could it?

The evenings were magic. We'd sit outside, gazing at a sky full of stars, so clear you could almost reach up and touch them. So different from the city, where everything was a rush and the noise never let you breathe. The country was peaceful, calming and, best of all, had no media lurking around. I couldn't help but feel lucky. But there was also this weird push and pull inside me: on one hand, I was grateful to be here, experiencing this crazy luxury with Ted. On the other? I kinda wished I could run away from his mess and live a normal life.

Thanks to Gene, though, we got to experience something unforgettable, something I'll always be thankful for. Twice we flew in Gene's private helicopter, were treated to lunch, and got a case of his homegrown wine. So different from the years with Chris, who couldn't even muster the energy for a road trip to Queensland without it turning into a big, whiny ordeal.

Gene's circle included wealthy, high-profile people who often stayed at his property. While I didn't exactly share their status, I probably slept in the same beds and used the same toilet. I mean, we all shit, right? Maybe my path had crossed with these people for some reason; some lesson I wasn't yet meant to understand. All I knew was that I wanted a better life, but which direction to take? That was still a mystery.

I got used to living under a microscope. For more than a decade, I was in the media spotlight, detectives tapping my phone and home. All because I was tangled up with a man suspected of murder. Reporters and investigators were relentless, showing up uninvited wherever Ted went—on the street, at his parents' house, at our home, his workplace, even at the airport, trying to corner him like an animal. Even though he faced serious charges, it felt unfair in a way, like the media had tried him before the court ever got the chance. Trial by newspaper.

They were playing a game, and we were caught in the crossfire.

For me, it was an ongoing intrusion—at home and at my job at a childcare centre, where they'd camp out for hours, hoping to catch a glimpse of something they could print. I didn't know much about legal jargon at the time, but I quickly became acquainted with some— *investigation, charged, arraignment, coronial inquest, pre-trial hearings,* and *trial*. These weren't just words; they came at a heavy cost to Ted—more than money, they took a toll on his soul. It hit me too, not knowing where it would all lead.

Standing by his side wasn't just unpleasant; *living hell* didn't even scratch the surface. But it became my norm, life in this strange bubble of chaos. When Ted and I moved in together in 2005, I had a false sense of security, thinking we had each other's backs. That belief didn't last long.

Every time Ted went to court, the news dragged me right back to Candice. The missing wife story, now officially labelled deceased by the coroner, was everywhere. The question of what if she was really gone for good kept creeping in. What then? At least if she was still out there, I could handle the whole *so you and my husband are a thing just because I took off* scenario. But the idea that she could be dead? Unbelievable. And frankly, not something I was ready to accept.

The answer would come two years later.

In the meantime, I consulted several psychics, even putting one in touch with the police, hoping they'd somehow find Candice. Crazy, maybe, then again, psychics had been known to help, right? Every one of them told me the same thing: Candice was dead, surrounded by liquid, maybe even buried under concrete. My skin prickled.

Deep down, I wanted to believe she'd show up one day, out of the blue, like some dramatic plot twist. But as the years dragged on that hope faded. The question still gnawed at me—where the hell was she?

And Gene? Well, he was more than just a friend to Ted and our family—he had a pivotal role to play in all of this.

Lesson: Just remember, you're capable of surviving what's meant to destroy you, so don't let fear blind you to the truth.

CHAPTER 53

Karma's a bitch and then some

It was meant to be the year I found stability: 2005. Thanks to my new partner, Ted, I was feeling optimistic. I took out a mortgage and bought a house in my own name, using what was left from my divorce settlement, and thought, *This is it. We've made it*. Ted and I moved in together, and for the first time, I really believed we were building something solid.

Our new home was cosy. Simple. Three bedrooms for the six of us—Ted, his almost-six-year-old son, Miguel, three of my daughters (Luna, ten; Nila, twelve; and Katya, nineteen), and me. Courtney, Ted's stepdaughter, moved in with her biological father but would visit occasionally. We were making it work, and the tight squeeze didn't bother me too much. Except the one-bathroom situation. That made things interesting.

Even the cracks in the floorboards with the creeping vine growing through and the rain that seeped through the old aluminium windows into our bedroom gave the place an outdoorsy vibe—if I had to look at the positives. But it was a fresh start. I'd put down my deposit from selling my previous house, and Ted promised he'd help with the finances. Life was sweet—or so I thought.

Just when it seemed like we were finally in a good place, reconnecting with Gene felt like fate stepping in. It all clicked years later—when Ted seemed to be running out of options, Gene showed up. But I couldn't help feeling for Gene. Despite his wealth, his life wasn't exactly sunshine and rainbows. Eventually he had to sell his country estate and his Sydney home. That country estate had a dark cloud hovering over it—one of the caretakers was found dead on the grounds.

Gene's kindness gave us a much-needed break from the media frenzy. The investigation had been brutal: police statements, court hearings, the media camped at our door, articles and photos splashed across the papers, even our phones tapped. Gene offered us a slice of peace amid the wreckage of our reality.

That same year, I enrolled in a part-time fine arts course at the local college, set to begin in 2006. Within a month, my mother passed. It was bittersweet; a relief, really, as she had deteriorated and didn't recognise anyone anymore.

So having something else to focus on was a lifesaver. Between my part-time job, juggling studies and home duties, I found a sense of fulfillment—maybe even a bit of peace. We were a family now, and I was happy.

Being a step-parent was a whole new challenge. I thought treating Miguel like one of my own kids would do the trick, but I hadn't factored in Ted's parents, who spoiled him rotten.

My girls hadn't had grandparents to fuss over them, so they weren't used to that kind of pampering. And it was clear that Miguel was getting a bit too used to it. This led to plenty of fiery discussions with Ted about parenting. And where did it get us? Nowhere. Mostly, it left me frustrated—well, actually, downright pissed off. I felt Ted saw me as being capable of handling all the responsibilities of raising a family, but somehow not capable of guiding Miguel the way I thought best. I wondered, was it just me, or did all step-parents go through this?

Did biological parents worry that a stronger bond might grow between their child and the step-parent? Maybe they deliberately kept some distance—just enough to ensure they stayed top dog.

I knew parenting would throw some challenges our way, and I was holding onto the hope that we'd figure it out together. But step-parenting was a tricky dance, and I had no idea that our problems were just getting started.

By 2007 the shit hit the fan. On top of all our personal drama, bigger issues started creeping in, and then Ted walked out. I was left feeling like I was losing my mind—raging, isolated and spinning in circles.

Even though we weren't technically together, I still showed up at every damn case-related hearing I could. The coronial inquest at Westmead was a big one, and it took its toll. I was numb from the whole thing, and somewhere, driving home along Victoria Road, we got engaged.

It was like watching a train derail in slow motion. No formal proposal. No ring. Just Ted handing me a small platinum duck from his keychain as a promise—a keepsake I still have today.

A damn fucking duck.

It all happened so fast; I didn't even think about what I was agreeing to. The conversation began with us venting about the draining day we'd just survived, and ended with him asking, 'I suppose you don't want to marry me now?'

In my head, I screamed, *No fucking way!* But my mouth betrayed me and blurted out, 'Of course I do.' I almost wished he hadn't heard me, but he did.

It wasn't until later that I realised just how wrong I was to say yes. Classic me, speaking before thinking.

Things between us shifted after that. My gut was screaming that I'd ignored the red flags, and it was clear the relationship was missing the love and intimacy I craved. Maybe it was enough for him, but it sure as hell wasn't for me. We stayed living in separate homes, only seeing each other when it was time to deal with the kids. No sex, no real conversations, no special moments together, just a whole lot of distance growing between us.

I didn't blame Ted for it—I blamed myself for not being honest with myself or with him. My anger turned inward. I'd let my needs slide to the backseat while his took the wheel. I let myself down by not speaking up, too afraid, too ashamed to admit what I wanted.

And that damn question about Candice still lingered. Why the hell did I keep ending up in these situations?

The coronial inquest was devastating—not just for me, but for Candice's family and friends. Can you imagine a court declaring someone dead without a body? It felt like a sick joke. But there it was—the official word. A trial was on the horizon, preparations began, and we braced ourselves for the nightmare ahead.

But I kept pushing through; hanging on to what could only be described as a complicated, half-hearted relationship. Then it hit me—our engagement was a total sham. It was time to pull the plug. I broke it off, but kept that fucking platinum duck.

We welcomed the new year separately. Anger had been replaced with a new coping mechanism: friends. They were there for me to unburden my frustrations on.

By now, it had been four years since I or three of my daughters had heard from Chris. Our eldest, who was twenty-two, maintained contact, which strained her relationship with her sisters, but there was nothing I could do about it. I'd accepted that Chris was out of our lives for good. The chances of him ever facing consequences for how he treated us was next to zero. Still, I was relieved—not having to share my girls with him was a win in itself.

As for karma? It packed more of a punch than I'd expected. I used to think it was about revenge, especially on Chris, for the hell he put us through. But nope, I had it wrong. Karma didn't need a cheerleader, it worked on its own schedule and would always find a way to balance the scales.

Remember that little ritual I'd performed?

Well, after he and his second wife packed up for Cyprus, less than a year later she ditched him and hightailed it back to Australia. I didn't know it then, but Chris was tucked away, living the kind of reclusive life I'd secretly wished on him.

But the universe wasn't done with him yet.

In March 2008, Chris's cousin hadn't heard from him in a while, even though they lived close by in the same village of Nicosia, Cyprus. Concerned, the cousin forced his way into Chris's house and found him dead. His decomposing body, which had been rotting away for nearly three weeks, was sprawled in the hallway.

When the news reached me, it hit like a gut punch. Oh God—had my words actually worked their dark magic?

It stirred up a storm of emotions I wasn't ready for—anger, guilt, frustration—hell, it was like I'd invented a whole new cocktail. I couldn't shake the worry about how my daughters would handle the news. They'd already been through so much. Four years of silence, and yet they still needed to be told. It wasn't going to be easy. There was no soft way to deliver the news. It felt like I was failing them all over again.

For me, his death brought an end to the monsters in my head, but my emotions were still haunted by the bitter words I had unleashed into the world. I feared becoming like him, so I saw a shrink. I didn't want the anger to consume me the way it had consumed Chris. The 'head doctor' pointed out the obvious: I was dealing with depression. No surprise there, given the relationship disaster and Ted's grand exit. It was like hitting the emotional jackpot, just not the kind I wanted.

I decided to travel to Cyprus with one of my daughters for Chris's funeral—looking for closure, I guess. But as soon as I applied for the passport, his brothers made their stance clear: if we showed up, they'd make sure we'd be shunned by the townsfolk.

Oh, and they'd keep the burial site a secret, too.

I thought better of it. We'd end up stranded in Cyprus, unwanted and unsupported. I couldn't tell if their grudge was about their hatred for me or just their bloated pride. But deep down, I knew something else was at play. Karma had taken the wheel.

And, as fate would have it, karma delivered. A week after the funeral, I caught wind of some juicy details. First, the brothers' luggage went missing at the airport. Then their taxi got lost. And to top it off, one of them tripped while being a pallbearer.

Sure, minor mishaps, but to me it felt like poetic justice. It was as if the universe was giving them a little reminder of how they'd treated me and my daughters. As bad as it sounds, I couldn't help but secretly cheer and thank the universe for being on my side for a change.

No amount of revenge would fix what happened, so I decided to step up. I couldn't change the past, but I could shape the future. I focused on building a better life for my kids. I started furthering my education, working towards a career that would allow me to provide for them. It wasn't just about surviving; it was about showing them that women could achieve greatness without relying on anyone but themselves.

Lesson: Stop looking for justice. The universe has its own way of addressing matters in due time.

CHAPTER 54

Three's a crowd, four's chaos

A year had flown by since Ted moved out. To keep my mind from unravelling over the wreck my life had become, I threw myself into art school. That's when I met Carter.

He was thirty-two, I was forty-six, but somehow, the age gap didn't matter. His maturity drew me in. We became art buddies, frequently exploring exhibitions and attending night classes at the Arthouse Hotel. What started as a purely platonic connection blossomed into a solid friendship, giving me a comforting confidant I didn't know I needed.

One evening, we found ourselves at the Museum of Contemporary Art in Circular Quay, immersed in a dimly lit room where a film played on a loop against the wall. As an art student, I was supposed to decipher its meaning, but I just revelled in the experience of art for art's sake.

Carter leaned in behind me, his breath brushing my ear. 'So what are your thoughts on this piece?'

Startled, I spun around, almost knocking him over in the process. He reached out to steady himself, and before I knew it, we were face-to-face, our lips nearly touching. The heat of the moment was unbearable and naturally, I blurted out an excuse and made a hasty retreat.

I rushed to the restroom, splashed cold water on my face and tried to shake it off. But when I re-emerged, there he was—waiting outside, looking sheepish and apologising for startling me. I downplayed it, offering a weak smile, and he shot one right back at me, making the butterflies in my stomach do a little happy dance. Damn, he was handsome.

'So what did you think?' he asked, a playful glint in his eye.

'About the installation?' I shot back, raising an eyebrow.

'Yes, the installation,' he said, almost sarcastically. I hesitated to admit I hadn't understood a thing about it, despite my best efforts.

Before I could respond, Carter just nodded and flashed me a smile. 'You don't have to say a thing; I couldn't make sense of it, either.' We both burst into laughter, the tension evaporating like mist in the morning sun.

Hunger kicked in, so we decided to grab a bite at the cafe. While waiting in line, I spotted Henry, another art student. He was ahead of us, hands clasped together, head bowed over his tray of food like he was praying, but I wasn't sure what kind of prayer you said over a sandwich.

Carter nudged me just enough that I bumped into Henry. Startled, he turned around, dazed.

My face flushed as I quickly stammered, 'Sorry!'

'Oh, that's okay. I took a moment too long to give thanks for this food,' Henry replied, a hint of humour in his tone.

'Of course, no problem, Henry,' I said, though deep down, I felt humiliated to have been intentionally pushed into him.

I shot an annoyed glance at Carter; clearly, he wasn't as mature as I'd thought.

Henry explained that he chanted whenever he could to show gratitude for whatever nourished his body and brought him joy. It was a concept I hadn't encountered before. Years later, when I grasped the positive impact of gratitude, I started incorporating a similar practice into my life.

Despite my initial irritation at Carter's antics, the attraction between us was as obvious as a pair of balls on a bull—impossible to miss and a little ridiculous. Still, I couldn't help but relish the attention.

After that incident, Carter and I began sitting together during our meal breaks between classes. The more time we spent together, the stronger our friendship grew.

Preparing for an upcoming art exhibition, Carter and I placed our pieces on the display wall side by side. As I struggled to hold up a heavy canvas, Carter swooped in to rescue me, grabbing it before it could fall. Our hands brushed, sending a delightful shiver through my body. I needed to pull away before things got too intense.

The next day, Carter confessed he was developing feelings for me and wanted to take me out on a proper date. I suspected it might just be infatuation, so I started limiting our conversations. When we did talk, I nudged him to consider women closer to his age.

At that time, I couldn't fathom why a younger man would be drawn to me, but I've since learned that true connections go beyond appearances. The best relationships are built on shared values, emotional bonds and intellectual sparks.

Eventually, Carter began seeing someone, but we remained friends, even attending the Biennale art exhibition at Cockatoo Island together. It was a major event that drew thousands of visitors. Stepping into a cottage, I was confronted by a massive painting layered in shiny pastels, unmistakably depicting a vagina in all its splendid glory.

A woman and her young child strolled in, the boy rushing ahead to stand in front of the painting, his tiny fingers reaching out to touch it as he giggled.

'Look, Mummy, bumpy! Come feel, Mummy!' he yelled.

His mother must have realised what it was, because she leaped in front of me, blocking my view of the masterpiece, yanked her child by the arm, and whisked him right out the door.

I laughed, but I couldn't help but admire the beauty of the massive painting before me. It resembled one that had captivated me in Josie from the phone lines' portfolio years ago, and I was convinced it must have been her work. I couldn't recall seeing a signature on the painting, nor did I know Josie's last name—or even if Josie was her real name.

Throughout the years, I often thought about her, hoping her dream of gaining recognition for her art had come true. Her aspiration inspired me, convincing me that I, too, could create and sell art—and guess what? Years later, it became a reality!

But back then, I stayed faithful to a man who, by late 2009, was more like a roommate who lived miles apart—emotionally, geographically and possibly in different time zones—than a partner. Ted did the 'honourable' thing—still covering the mortgage—while I took care of Miguel. In other words, he got to keep his hands clean while I juggled everything else. But then, out of nowhere, he cut me off financially, blaming the impending murder trial.

With reconciliation officially off the table, I was left to pay the mortgage on my own. So what did I do? Took on two jobs, of course, because turning myself into a walking zombie was the obvious choice when trying to keep a roof over my daughters' heads without selling the house. Who wouldn't want to juggle mountains of stress on fumes?

Three days a week, I slogged it out in childcare, two days were for art class, and three nights plus occasional weekends I found myself back at the Chatswood brothels working for Leanna. Yeah, I know, I had returned to a boss who made tearing me down her full-time hobby. But she was happy to have me back, and I was desperate enough to accept.

As exhausted as I was, I found myself craving affection—or maybe I was just plain horny. Either way, I filled the void with a few short flings squeezed into the cracks of my limited free time. None of them lasted, but, at least they helped pass the time.

Enter Leo, a broker. He wasn't the typical heartthrob, but he had brains, attentiveness and a knack for hitting the spot, if you catch my drift. Our first time was insane. I walked into his office and the tension was palpable. We both knew exactly what was about to happen. He locked the door behind him, and with one swift motion, his muscular arm swept everything off his desk and onto the floor. It was like a scene straight out of an erotic movie. Then he leaned me against the desk—wide oak timber, gorgeous—and had sex with me. Twice.

At first meeting twice a week felt like a breeze, but soon I was literally bending over backwards to accommodate him, sacrificing my own time. So I called it quits—I wasn't about to live at the mercy of anyone's demands.

It was mid-2010 when Sebastian entered my life—a selfish lover who didn't leave much of an impression. But in that brief encounter, I learned that my worth wasn't measured by how well I kept others happy, it was about chasing my own spark and doing what lit me up.

Funnily enough, three decades earlier, Sebastian had played master of ceremonies at my wedding, fresh off the back of his flashy soccer career. Sure, the guy still had a trace of his former charm, but let's be real, good looks could only carry so much dead weight. He tried bringing his soccer techniques into the bedroom, but let's just say it didn't score. As he neared the finish line, he'd shout '*punto*', which meant 'goal' in Italian—honestly, it still makes me cringe. Our month-long fling was all I needed to realise I wanted more than a quick fix. That's when Alfie stepped in.

It so happened that the day we met was the last time Sebastian and I would see each other.

Sebastian's friend, Alfie, was loaning Sebastian the use of his home while he was out. We had arranged to meet there, and when I reached the front door and knocked, I was taken aback to find an unfamiliar man opening it.

My initial thought was that I had the wrong address. However, Alfie introduced himself and clarified that Sebastian had been delayed and had asked him to let me in. Naturally, I felt embarrassed, as Alfie would have been well aware that Sebastian and I planned to have a bonk in his home. I supposed one could say Alfie was simply being a good mate.

As it turned out, Alfie was considerate, making coffee and sitting with me while waiting for Sebastian's arrival. Rather than being awkward, our conversation flowed effortlessly. We shared similarities and circumstances, even with our upbringing. His name had been changed from Alfonso to Alfie while at the Catholic school he attended back in the 1960s, and he was also a divorcee.

His on-and-off relationship with a woman was officially off at that point. Mine with Sebastian was too. We were both single. The sexual chemistry sizzled between us, but more than that, Alfie did something I wasn't used to—he made eye contact when listening to me. What a novel concept! Most of my previous partners used eye contact like a weapon to wear me down, forcing me to withdraw mid-argument.

I made it clear to Alfie that I wasn't looking for a fling, but he seemed to be on the same page. Too bad when Sebastian arrived, our conversation was cut short. I didn't want it to end.

For the first time in a while, I was enjoying a face-to-face conversation with a man.

Alfie left Sebastian and me to get down to business. My head wasn't in it, but for some ridiculous reason, I felt like I owed Sebastian a pity fuck. I know, right? But you'd be surprised how many women I've talked to who've done the same, just to get out of a situation.

So I ended things officially with Sebastian. He kept chasing me for months, unaware that I had already moved on to his friend.

Something shifted when I was around Alfie. He made me feel comfortable being myself. He taught me the value of selflessness and boosted my confidence to ask for what I needed in bed. With Alfie, it was all about pleasing me. He never expected anything in return—his pleasure came from making me happy.

He used to say, 'Making love to you is like a mind fuck for me, and I don't expect anything back.' Those words floored me, just like our conversations and laughter. Being with him was easy—something I'd never experienced in a relationship before. *Easy.*

He believed in me, too. Every time I mentioned wanting to study or level up, he'd give me that *you've got this* pep talk, and I actually did! Alfie became my personal cheerleader—minus the pom-poms, thank God. I'll always be grateful for that. The love and kindness we shared created memories that still make me smile today.

By late 2010, life was in overdrive. I was knee-deep in chaos—selling my home, searching for a rental and barely keeping it together. Then Ted pitched the brilliant idea of finding a place big enough for all of us to share … as friends. What could possibly go wrong? Well, as it turned out, a lot.

At this point, I was still seeing Alfie, and the trial preparations were ramping up. I was torn between wanting a future with Alfie and feeling the pressure to do right by Ted's young son.

Ted and I had set up living arrangements in the same house, but separate—he was downstairs, I was upstairs. Seven bedrooms, two kitchens, two bathrooms. The place was a disaster inside, but it was affordable, thanks to the rent split. Somehow, amid the madness, Ted managed to win me back. If he went to jail, who the hell was going to raise Miguel? Not Ted's ageing parents, that's for sure. So I made the decision to let Alfie go. Worst decision ever.

I even went so far as to ask Ted to marry me and bought him a ring. What was I thinking? Was it some misplaced sense of obligation or concern for his son? I'd ended a relationship with a man who could've been perfect for me. Sticking with Ted through the trial was one of the biggest mistakes of my life—sacrificing something real for someone who made me feel like a pawn in their game.

Alfie and I stayed close friends, like one of those things a psychic predicted. I'd visit him regularly, hoping for a glimpse of a better future. But as far as romance between us? Not a chance. It was like some cosmic joke—we were always on opposite relationship tracks. When one of us was tangled up in drama, the other was flying solo. Despite all the back and forth, our friendship stuck around like an old pair of jeans—comfortably familiar, no matter how worn things got.

Lesson: Set your boundaries, trust your gut, and know when to bail. Tossing more people into the mix doesn't solve anything. It just turns the mess into a full-blown disaster.

CHAPTER 55

The murder trial

Ted's murder trial kicked off in November 2011, in front of Justice DP. Before that, the media had whipped up a frenzy, sensationalising the whole thing. News flashed across every platform—radio, TV, newspapers, magazines and even social media, with everyone chiming in with their oh-so-informed opinions.

At that point, I was playing the defensive card for anyone in my family—Ted included. Whether I liked it or not, he was still part of the circus, and I wasn't about to let them tear him apart without a fight.

Ted had to attend a bunch of things and I had to show up for others, but mostly, I was there for moral support. There was the case conference, where the prosecutor and Ted's lawyer hashed out the details; then the committal hearing, where the magistrate decided if there was enough to send the case to a higher court. There were also directions and administrative hearings to check the case's progress.

From memory—which isn't the best—the pre-trial review was the first court appearance, and it was supposed to settle the case. Of course it didn't, so the magistrate set the next steps. Then came the endless pre-trial hoops—like the bail application, where Ted was free-ish while awaiting trial. Free enough, anyway. I do remember he had to check in at the police station constantly at one point. Guess they wanted to make sure the bird didn't fly out of its cage. And then there was pre-trial disclosure, where the defence got all the information from the prosecution. It went over my head back then, but I got the hang of it eventually.

The court hearings were horrendous. The media was all up in our faces, day in and day out. Everywhere I looked, there were people—judging, whispering, wondering why the hell I was standing by him. Meanwhile, I felt I needed to look polished and upper-class—nothing like my usual casual self. After all, I was an educator, more used to comfy clothes than courtroom chic. So I gave high heels a shot, but after one day of blisters, I was back to flats. Guess I'll never be a shoe model, so why pretend?

The Crown's case was that Ted killed Candice because she knew about sexual abuse allegations made against his father. Ted's defence argued that the alleged abuse happened after Candice disappeared. Talk about a courtroom showdown.

During the trial, a secret came out that shattered me. My home and phone had been bugged—every conversation with past lovers recorded without my knowledge. And the prosecution planned to use those recordings to tear my testimony apart.

I was humiliated, terrified of being branded the town slut—judged and shamed by people who had no clue about my story or struggles. The thought of it cut deeper than I cared to admit.

I only found out because they had no choice but to tell me. But Ted and his team had known all along. I felt like an absolute fool—there I was, acting all prim and proper while they had every dirty detail of my life in their hands. Every fling, every moment of comfort I'd found, they'd recorded it all.

But the universe must have taken pity on me. In the end, I didn't take the stand. My reputation stayed intact, but my emotions … those were shredded. That moment broke me.

Here's the kicker: I wasn't even with Ted at the time. He'd left me. Abandoned me. I had to figure life out on my own, and I did. I found comfort where I could, in the arms of men who made me feel something. But of course, because I was a woman, I wasn't supposed to do that, right?

With me out of the way, they zeroed in on Ted, claiming his motive for murder stemmed from what his father had been accused of. But during closing submissions, Ted's barrister threw out a startling alternative theory: what if Ted's wife wasn't dead at all? Maybe she'd assumed a new identity overseas, been deported, or ended up in a psychiatric facility. Candice had never been found. Why stop looking? Why throw in the towel?

It was a bold move that left the jury reeling. They took their sweet time, weighing every detail before delivering their verdict in January 2012, nearly ten years after Candice vanished: not guilty. Ted was acquitted of her murder.

Hearing the verdict felt like a weight lifting off me, a fragile glimmer of normalcy piercing through the chaos. Maybe this was a chance to rebuild, to find a better life. Maybe, just maybe, I could learn to love Ted again.

That flicker of hope didn't last long.

That night, friends and family swarmed the house to celebrate the end of this nightmare. Laughter mingled with the clinking of glasses, a rare moment of relief in what had been a never-ending storm. By one in the morning, the last guest shuffled out, and for the first time in forever, Ted and I collapsed into bed, drained but strangely at ease.

At three a.m. the peace shattered—literally. Glass smashed somewhere in the house, jolting us from sleep. Ted's brother-in-law burst into our room and flicked on the lights.

Ted and I blinked awake, sprawled on top of the sheets in our underwear—it was a scorcher of a night.

'Get up. Get dressed. We've got to go to the hospital,' he barked, his voice edged with urgency. My stomach twisted—that tone never brought good news. 'Something's happened to your mama.'

The drive to the hospital was a blur, the road flashing by in fragments, but we already knew we were too late. Ted's mother, who'd been treated days earlier for a broken foot, was gone.

A broken foot, and she died? How did that even happen?

I'd heard whispers that the police found her death suspicious—some even hinted they were linking it to Ted. But it wasn't possible. He was right beside me, asleep in bed, when she passed. Maybe her heart just gave up. I never asked—I didn't want to know.

At the hospital, her husband caused a full-blown scene, yelling and carrying on like we were in the middle of a soap opera. And that's when her death hit us like a rogue wave—sharp, disorienting and impossible to outrun. It cast a strange shadow over what should've been a fresh start.

I held my breath, staring at Ted's father. *Is this what I have to deal with from now on?* Maybe it was selfish to think that, but we'd just been through life's grinder and now we had him to contend with. I knew he had a temper, but this was next level. He was shouting, tears streaming, and then—bam!—he hurled his walking stick across the room like he was aiming for a gold medal in the temper tantrum Olympics.

I wanted to yell, *Calm your farm, mate!* But I bit my tongue. He was grieving—we all were—but come on. It was too much.

We mourned a kind, beautiful soul—Ted's mama had a warmth that could brighten even the hardest days. Her loss felt like the final blow in a long, draining fight and soon after, things got rocky with his dad. He became more needy, demanding constant attention, and it was downright overwhelming at times. So we hatched a plan: scrape together funds and build a granny flat so he could live with us—close, but not too close. We figured it was the best way to save what was left of our sanity, and we began planning.

As life settled down, Ted slipped back into his usual routine of travelling for work, sometimes for weeks at a time. It felt like we'd finally found our rhythm, like maybe this was our new normal. That's when I decided it was time to solidify the family.

In early January 2013 we were in Patonga, a little slice of paradise where emerald-green bushland leaned into the salty kiss of the sea. In that quiet, beachside corner of the Central Coast, we had a no-fuss ceremony: just us, the kids and a handful of close friends. Standing there, I thought, *This is it. A clean slate.*

Except the wedding night didn't go as planned. We argued, and the next morning, I woke up realising I had jumped the gun, as only I could do.

Oh well, let's see where this goes.

Lesson: *Be bold. Keep going through betrayal, judgement and chaos. Stand tall, adapt and push forward—even when it feels impossible.*

CHAPTER 56

Never open the door to a killer

On a scorching summer morning in January 2014, a knock at my front door yanked me from a deep sleep. It was around five a.m. and I was home alone with the kids while Ted was off on one of his business trips. He seemed to be away more than ever, hardly home, only widening the gap between us.

I opened the door. There stood a man, probably in his forties, and even in my groggy state, I could tell he was handsome—clean-shaven, tall, with short brown hair and a solid build. I'd always had a thing for sizing up good-looking men. Sweat beaded on his forehead—not exactly sexy, but understandable in the heat. Still, something about him didn't sit right. Was that my gut instinct giving me the side-eye?

As he wiped the sweat off his brow, he introduced himself as Dean, claiming he'd once lived in the house with his family. His ramblings about missing paperwork and some potentially hidden belongings had me struggling to catch up, still half-asleep. According to him, his father had been swindled out of money by a relative, who was also his business partner. Dean was convinced the missing cash was rightfully his, and the misplaced paperwork could prove it.

But he'd driven eighty-five kilometres from Wentworth Falls to my house over paperwork.

That was at least an hour's drive. Meaning this guy was on the road at the crack of dawn. Now, looking back, it was clear he wasn't just out for a scenic drive. Something had him in a rush, because who the hell showed up at a stranger's house that early unless it was serious?

Dean was like a broken record, banging on about this small wooden box where his father stored business papers. He thought it might be somewhere here. His agitated tone and jerky movements weren't exactly calming.

I shut him down with a firm, 'No way.' His confused, almost offended look only made me more irritated—like I was the one being unreasonable here. The more he insisted on coming inside to rummage for that damn box, the more my gut screamed *Get rid of him already!*

So I did what any sensible person would do: I pointed him to the neighbours. Figured they might've known Dean and his family and could maybe help. At least, that's what I told him.

Truth was, I just wanted him gone so I could crawl back into bed.

Later it hit me that sending Dean next door might've been a risky move. In his half-baked state, he could've decided the sweet elderly neighbours were part of some grand conspiracy, hiding that stupid box. Then I remembered they were out of town enjoying their holiday home. Whoops. Guess my brain decided to take its own little vacation on that detail.

My moment of peace didn't last. I crawled back into bed for what felt like a few minutes, only to be jolted awake again by another knock at the door. With the kids still asleep, including my now-teenage stepson across the hall, I rushed to answer it, praying the banging wouldn't wake him. Then again, Miguel could sleep through an earthquake.

Expecting the crazy man to have returned, I was stunned to find two police officers at my doorstep. It was especially jarring given my husband had only recently been acquitted of murder charges. For a split second their words were just background noise. The male officer's mouth was moving, but my brain wasn't connected to the Wi-Fi yet.

Rubbing the sleep from my eyes with a big yawn, I waved at them, indicating for them to wait. I pulled the door closed behind me and stepped onto the verandah. 'Go back, go back,' I muttered as I ushered them away, nearly tripping the poor male officer on the concrete steps.

Not my finest moment, oh well, it was early and I wasn't all there.

Awoken twice from a deep sleep, I must have looked like a hot mess. Placing my fingers to my lips, I whispered, 'Shush, my kids are asleep. What's going on today, for God's sake?' *Wait—did I just shush the police? Yep, I sure did.*

They introduced themselves politely, even apologising for the early visit.

Still annoyed, I blurted out, 'My husband's not home, what the hell man?'

They stood there and gave each other a puzzled look. I confess, I was a little confused myself and assumed their visit had something to do with Ted. After all, a police knock on my door wasn't exactly a rare occurrence.

The male officer explained that they wanted to ask about Dean.

'Oh, Dean. Yeah, he's been missing for a while. Wow, word really gets around.'

They shot each other a look, like they'd just smelled something bad, and then the male officer pulled out a small notepad and began scribbling notes as I answered his questions about my connection with Dean.

'He's my daughter's boyfriend,' I explained.

That got me a raised eyebrow. Then came the follow-up: 'And how old is your daughter?'

'Luna's eighteen.' My voice was laced with confusion and irritation. Their faces only deepened the mystery. What on earth was so shocking? Before I could ask, they were politely —yet—firmly requesting to speak with her.

All I could think was *What does Dean have to do with this?* Dean and Luna had broken up barely a week ago, and now he was already neck-deep in some kind of stressful mess. His family had told us he'd up and left and a few days later, they were in full-blown panic mode. I figured the cops just wanted to see if Luna knew anything about his whereabouts, given his recent mental state.

Despite my messy appearance—no bra, mismatched pyjamas and my hair looking like it had just lost a fight with a tornado—I led them upstairs.

When the male officer asked, 'How long was Dean here speaking with you this morning?' that's when it hit me. I stopped halfway up the two flights of stairs, realisation halting me in my tracks. Something important had just clicked.

That abrupt halt caught the officer off guard. He was just one step behind me, perfectly positioned for an awkward encounter. As I spun around, my nipples came dangerously close to grazing his face. I swear, if he'd been a fraction taller, my twin peaks would've left their mark.

Panic took over, and I bumbled out, 'Oh, no, not that Dean! My daughter's boyfriend is named Dean, too.'

The officers shot each other a side glance, like I'd just started speaking in riddles. Now they were the ones looking lost. Throwing people off track? Yeah, I had a knack for that.

I pressed a finger to my lips, leaned in like we were plotting a heist, and whispered, 'Shhhh!

Quick, let's get back downstairs. Geez, I can't believe I mixed them up. Go, go, go!'

I waved them off, full Italian mode, and ushered them down the stairs. They followed, looking equal parts baffled and amused, which, honestly, was fair.

Once again, I'd jumped to all the wrong conclusions—classic me. The officers were probably questioning my sanity. And fair enough—Dean, the man at my door, was forty-six. My daughter's boyfriend was barely eighteen.

After a quick chat, they informed me they would be in touch to get a witness statement from me. I agreed, still completely clueless about what on earth had just happened.

It wasn't until I watched the nightly news that I finally understood what transpired the morning of Dean's visit. When Dean stood at my doorway, I missed the fact that he had a bleeding stab wound to his upper body. I saw no blood-stained clothes, nor did he appear to be in pain. Apart from his agitated movements and erratic speech, he seemed normal.

Apparently, after leaving my place, Dean went next door, but no one was home. He then drove himself two kilometres to the local police station at Ryde and disclosed what he had done. Within a very short time, police from surrounding areas, including Wentworth Falls, drove to the house Dean shared with his fifty-two-year-old sister and made the grim discovery of her deceased body.

It was only after hearing these details that I grasped the severity of the situation. There I was, chatting casually with a man who had just stabbed his sister to death. If anything, I'd given him an earful for waking me up so early. I mean, it was school break and we were in full hibernation!

I'm grateful he didn't flip out when I told him he couldn't come into the house. I could have been his second victim for the day. Then again, it wasn't the first time I'd been in the presence of an accused killer. Maybe my naive, trusting nature saved my life, making me feel like I had nine lives.

As for Dean's stab wound, I read that he'd tried to self-harm by fixing a knife to a wall and pushing himself against it. The car he drove to Ryde Police Station was apparently drenched in blood—no shock there, considering he'd been bleeding for over an hour. It's a wonder he didn't pass out on the way.

It soon came out that Dean had psychiatric issues and he was taken to Royal North Shore Hospital in a serious condition, under police guard. Crazy, right? This was the kind of stuff movies were made of, and it was happening right in front of me.

Now, I was no stranger to the media and police hovering around, but it still felt surreal when reporters started swarming our door, hounding us for info on Dean. Thank God they didn't drag Ted's case into it, especially since the acquittal had literally just happened. What really got under my skin, though, was watching them stomp all over our property like they owned the place. Same old story.

One journalist even made his way into my backyard, and I had to firmly tell him to get out. Another reporter wouldn't take no for an answer and knocked on my door repeatedly, even after I told her to get lost. Eventually, she left a note with her contact details. The only one who showed any decency was Charles Croucher—he apologised for the disruption.

On 6 February I gave my witness statement at the Ryde Police Station, which would later be used as evidence in a court hearing. Some time later, I found out Dean had been diagnosed with a mental illness and was being treated at Long Bay Prison Hospital. He was too unwell to appear in court, which meant he couldn't be prosecuted.

Dean's financial troubles eventually surfaced—he owed the Australian Taxation Office $40,000. Maybe that's what sent him off the deep end. But during my police interview, I blanked on some of the stuff Dean had told me. It was like my memory went on a coffee break and forgot to come back.

Here's where the story took a strange turn: one of my closest girlfriends, Sandy, had dated Dean in her teens. Sandy's a total knockout—long blonde hair, a smile that could light up a room and, yep, a great set of boobs to match. And she's not just a pretty face; the girl's got brains, too. I'd give anything to borrow a bit of that brainpower.

How's that for six degrees of separation? Man, talk about dodging a bullet.

Not long after that little incident, I stumbled upon a large homemade metal pipe safe hidden under the floor of a clothes cupboard. Locked, of course, but that didn't stop us—we cut right through it. And what did we find? Nothing. Empty.

Then, a few more years down the track during some house renovations, we discovered two more homemade vaults hidden in the brick walls. They were about fifteen centimetres wide and thirty long, identical to the first one. Empty again.

The most exciting find was a bong wedged between the inside and outside toilets. Given everything else that happened, I was honestly relieved it wasn't another dead body. We sure didn't need any more media attention.

With all the strange connections to murder and mystery, my life felt like a soap opera that never ended, always waiting for the next bizarre twist.

Which, of course, unfolded almost exactly a year later.

Lesson: Trust your gut, but don't jump to conclusions. Not everything is as it seems, and the truth is often stranger (and more complicated) than you think.

CHAPTER 57

Death at a cemetery

It was 28 December 2014 when life served another gut punch. Ted had taken his father to Rockwood Cemetery for their usual visit to his mother's grave. Same routine every time: dust off the cobwebs, pop a cheerful bunch of flowers into the marble vase and head home. Only this time, routine took the day off and disaster clocked in.

All I knew at first was there'd been an accident at the cemetery. No one could—or would—tell me exactly what. Hours later, I rushed to Auburn Hospital, where Ted had been carted. They'd taken blood and urine samples, but I'd have bet my last dollar the only things they'd find in his system were caffeine and the carcinogenic cloud from his cancer sticks. He relied on those like a car relied on gas—coffee to rev him up, smokes to keep him going.

Without them, the guy would've been about as useful as a broken shopping trolley.

Then came the questioning. I had no clue how Ted was even coherent. His face had that deer-in-the-headlights look, like his brain had just hit a wall and kept sliding. I'd have been surprised if he remembered his own name, let alone pieced together the calamity that landed him there.

And what a calamity it was. After their visit to his mother's grave, Ted climbed into the car to switch on the air-conditioning for his dad. The car was running, Ted's foot on the brake. His dad, shuffling towards the car, tripped on the uneven grass. In his panic, Ted rushed out of the car to help but didn't apply the handbrake. The car lurched forward. He jumped back in and somehow hit the accelerator instead of the brake. In the blink of an eye, the car slammed into his father, knocking him lifeless to the ground … right next to his wife's grave.

When the facts hit me, I froze, the words bouncing around in my brain like a pinball. Numbness turned into disbelief, which quickly morphed into a cocktail of anxiety and rage. I mean, honestly, how the hell had I been roped into yet another disaster? This marked the fourth case of a mysterious death in my life—surprisingly, it seemed the body count list had grown. My life wasn't just a movie plot, it was a full-blown TV series; a relentless loop of chaos I couldn't break free from.

Grief for my father-in-law or concern for Ted didn't even make a guest appearance that day. Instead, frustration and dread set up camp in my head. Selfish? Maybe. But all I could picture were more headlines, courtrooms and legal battles.

Once I got home I called my sister-in-law, who was holidaying somewhere far sunnier than this living hell. Her cheery tone turned to a guttural scream the second I told her. Through her sobs, she choked out, 'No, no, this can't be happening again.'

Her words echoed my own thoughts. But buried deep, was another emotion I couldn't admit out loud—quiet, guilty relief. The man I secretly held doubts about, the man who had been accused of sexual assault, the very thing that allegedly caused Ted's fight with Candice the night before she disappeared, was gone. He was the essence of more than a decade of misery, which dragged me through courtroom dramas and endless heartache. It was like the box that had held me captive cracked open, letting in the faintest breeze of freedom.

But that freedom carried its own weight. Was this my chance to finally walk away from it all? The thought terrified me. My future felt like a dark, endless tunnel and all I wanted was to run far, far away from this black hole of misery.

My body trembled uncontrollably and the pressure of it all exploded out of me in a bloodcurdling scream. Right after I hung up the phone, of course—because even in a breakdown, I somehow managed to keep my manners. Guess I mastered the fine art of the well-timed scream.

Days blurred together, each one dragging like a slow-motion train wreck. The funeral was unbearably tense, with mourners stealing sideways glances at Ted, as if they were waiting for him to crumble or confess. The air was thick with unspoken words and barely concealed judgement, a storm just waiting to unleash. I absorbed it all, like a thousand tiny swords piercing my skin.

The only way I survived after this was by sneaking away to the local park, where I'd sit by the water, watching ripples flow across its surface, pretending life hadn't turned into a shitshow. Water had always been my safe space, my escape when everything became too much.

Standing by Ted's side that day—and every day after—was torture. Forget about grief. That natural process had been ripped away, replaced by seeds of doubt planted by the police and media. They couldn't resist making their presence known, always looming, like a bad smell you couldn't scrub off.

For weeks reporters camped outside our house, knocking on the door or lurking near the driveway, hoping to catch a sliver of scandal. Leaving for work felt like plotting a jailbreak. I'd sneak out the back door, only to be spotted as I climbed into my car. The vultures rushed in, cameras flashing, only deflating when they realised it wasn't Ted.

The constant harassment was unbearable. In private, I broke down, sobbing into my hands as I asked myself over and over: Why the hell did this happen?

And then came Ted's sentencing at Burwood Local Court. Naturally, I decided I needed to dress for the cameras, buying a pair of high heels I had no business wearing. By the time I arrived my feet were blistered to kingdom come—fifty-cent-coin-sized monstrosities mocking my every step. What was I thinking? That I was some Hollywood starlet facing trial? Clearly, my brain had checked out by then, replaced by mush and bad decisions.

Fortunately, luck and good legal representation were on Ted's side. He was charged with negligent driving occasioning death, which landed him a twenty-four-month licence disqualification and one hundred fifty hours of community service at the Exodus Foundation in Ashfield.

After the sentencing, we waited an appropriate amount of time before embarking on our treacherous trek to the car. Dodging cameramen and microphones shoved in our faces required Olympic-level agility.

I played the role of the supportive wife like a pro, driving Ted to and from his community service every weekend. By the final Sunday, Ted slumped into the passenger seat, reeking of sweat and something that could only be described as compost gone wrong. Filthy from a day of food prep, he looked like he'd rolled around in a dumpster for fun.

Despite my gag reflex working overtime, I kept my mouth shut. Ted sighed dramatically, muttering about how glad he was to be done with 'hell', as he called it. He declared he'd never miss that place.

I, being the queen of timing, couldn't help myself. 'Oh, man, I'm really going to miss it a lot,' I said. Probably one of those thoughts better left unsaid.

Ted's head whipped around so fast I thought he might sprain his neck. His bloodshot eyes locked on me, shooting lasers of fury. If looks could kill, I'd have been ash. My spine tingled under his glare, a harsh reminder that sometimes my mouth worked faster than my brain.

What I meant to say was I'd miss the little things—like my sneaky coffee and treat runs on the way home. Playing chauffeur every weekend wasn't exactly a dream gig, so I figured I'd earned a little reward.

Besides, I always brought treats home for the kids. It was a nice little routine while it lasted.

Courtney, Candice's daughter, moved in with us, which seemed like a great chance for her to reconnect with her half-brother, Miguel, and for Ted to build a stronger bond with her too. I figured it'd be good for everyone. With seven bedrooms, we had the space.

But her arrival brought a new set of unknowns—our blended family had settled together nicely, and welcoming her in without fully knowing what she'd been through had the potential for disruption. Still, I was happy to have her with us and willing to figure it out as we went.

One way we all spent time together was at the park, just a short stroll from home. I often took the kids there—it was the perfect spot to hang out and let them burn off some energy. They would tear off ahead, leaving me trailing behind. Sometimes Courtney tagged along, but this one time, instead of racing ahead, she stuck by my side, matching my pace. This was some time after the court case had settled, and those quiet walks with her felt like a small step towards something better.

I couldn't shake the feeling that I shouldn't ask, but curiosity gnawed at me, relentless. Something in me needed to know, even if I wasn't ready for the answer. Maybe it was a need for closure, or maybe I was just fooling myself. I asked if everything the police said about the incident—and the allegations involving her step-grandfather—was true.

She confirmed it, and suddenly, I wished I hadn't asked at all.

I never told Ted what I'd learned. Not sure why. Maybe it was fear of hearing his reaction, or maybe my mind and heart were at war, struggling to accept the brutal truth of what had unfolded over a decade of heartache and drama. That night, I hid in the shower, letting my tears mix with the water. I was shattered, lost in confusion. I didn't want to believe her, but my gut wouldn't let me ignore it. Had I really been that blind? Was my entire reality built on lies?

From that moment, I became cautious, terrified of saying the wrong thing. The horrors of the last decade seemed to circle back, ready to pounce. My mind spiralled into a dark place, struggling to make sense of it all.

Less than a year later, Courtney moved out. I think she felt confined in the routine of a family household, or maybe she was just all grown up and needed her own space. Honestly, I didn't really know, and maybe it was for the best. Ted and I were arguing a lot, and that wasn't something she needed to be part of. By 2016 our relationship had crumbled. Ted and I were nothing but sparks and explosions. The gap between us wasn't just wide, it was a damn canyon, with no bridge left to cross.

With his community service behind him and his licence reinstated, Ted no longer needed me to drive him. Something about him had shifted. Then, one day, he walked out—again—taking Miguel with him. This time it felt different. In an instant, I was catapulted back to 2007, the first time he left. The same emotions roared through me. *Not again!*

That was the moment I started honestly questioning what was real and what wasn't in the tangled mess of his missing wife. Desperation had me grasping at straws, turning to friends, professionals and even psychics, all in a frantic search for answers.

Ted's departure left me drowning in uncertainty. Our communication had shrivelled to practically nothing and I was left feeling abandoned, helpless. My life felt like it was falling apart around me, along with whatever confidence I had left.

I carried on with the renovations we'd started on our house, playing the part of lackey for the builder while managing a childcare centre. It was exhausting, but I kept pushing through, hoping I could somehow show Ted that we could still be a family and create a comfortable home. But why? Why the hell were my emotions bouncing around like a ping-pong ball? My thoughts were a whirlwind. Some days,

I missed him like crazy. Other times, I hated him so much I wished he'd just disappear. Was I out of my mind for even considering it?

One day I walked into work to find a large yellow envelope sitting on my desk. The words 'Private and Confidential' practically shouted at me in bold red letters. The postmark showed it came from the Chatswood post office.

My heart pounded as I tore it open. Inside were transcripts from the Supreme Court of New South Wales, dated between 2009 and 2011. Someone wanted me to read these. Someone thought that after everything—especially now that Ted had decided I was no longer needed—I'd reconsider what I thought I knew about him. Maybe they believed my anger would be enough to make me spill whatever secrets I'd held onto.

The pages were filled with cross-examination questions, answers about my husband's murder trial in connection with his missing wife. But it was the handwritten letter on top of the 2011 hearing transcript that sent chills down my spine. It felt too personal, too deliberate—like someone knew exactly how to get to me.

Dear Lucia,
You will find enclosed the court transcripts taken from XXXXXX in relation to her XXXX disappearance following the revelation that XXXXX had been XXXXXXXX her.

After XXXXXX revealed that to XXX, they argued and subsequently XXXX disappeared.

XXXX defence objecting against what was being said and that it would go against him in court.

I think you can draw your own conclusions if you read the statements and choose to do with it what you will.

I think it is about time the truth came out and XXXXXXXX and her family can put this to rest and move on.

A FRIEND

Sitting alone in my office, I slammed my fist on the desk, frustration boiling over. I could still feel it, the day he left—sitting on my back porch, tears streaming down my face, clothes soaked. That god-awful conversation with Ted kept echoing in my head. I shook my head, half in disbelief, half in self-loathing. That was the past. It had to be. I needed to stop drowning in it. But damn was it hard to let go.

Ally-cat—my affectionate nickname for one of my work colleagues—walked into the office. She took one look at my face and knew exactly what I was going through. Everyone did. My life with Ted was public knowledge.

She pulled me into a hug and said, 'You're okay. Stay strong—and fuck him off out of your life for good.'

I laughed through my tears when she said that. And in that instant, it hit me—I'd betrayed my own maverick spirit. For too long, I'd handed my independence to a man who didn't deserve a single piece of it, instead of blazing my own damn trail. The way out was leaving his life for good. He'd done me a favour by walking away first. In that moment, I realised his absence wasn't a loss, it was my golden ticket to start over.

After wasting too much time wallowing in the past, I decided to stop feeling sorry for myself and move forward. Sure, I was scared of failing, but I trusted my instincts. Ally's words stuck with me, and I was forever grateful for that.

The next time I saw Ted, I told him it was time for a divorce. No more compromising my future. I'd made my mistakes, but they weren't going to define me. I'd spent far too long pleasing everyone else. Enough was enough. I was done lying to everyone, including myself. The truth was, I was a hot mess inside, even if I looked like I had it all together.

So I did what any self-respecting woman would do: I took an axe to Ted's stuff. Anything he left behind—his so-called 'handmade' treasures, like the bookcase, kitchen cabinet, or those frames with photos in them—I smashed. First, I shoved the big stuff down two flights of stairs, then I went to town and fucked shit up. It felt better than I cared to admit. I wasn't just breaking his things; I was breaking free. The rage, the satisfaction, was ridiculously satisfying.

Ted put me through the wringer with the divorce, but for some reason, I still felt guilty—don't ask me why, I couldn't explain it. It took a long time to realise the guilt and blame weren't mine. They belonged to the men who'd abandoned me.

My biggest regret? Watching my kids carry the emotional weight of everything—Ted's court cases, the media circus, all of it. They were just young girls and they had to deal with everyone knowing their connection to the mess we were caught in. It kills me now, knowing the impact it had on them. I'd give anything to have had a better head on my shoulders back then. To have had the brains to see what I was putting them through. Seeing them struggle because of the choices I made hurt more than anything.

When Ted left, I felt like a total failure. I couldn't undo the damage, but hell, I could build a better life from here. That, at least, was still mine to control. But how the hell was I supposed to get my girls to trust me again? How could I convince them I wouldn't screw it up this time?

I had to build a legacy—one they could look back on with pride. I'd own my own home, one that could never be taken from me, one I could leave to them someday. But more than that, I wanted to leave them something even more valuable: courage, wisdom, and the unshakable belief that they could take life's punches and still come out swinging. If nothing else, this book proves I did just that. Every mess, every misstep, every *oh, shit* moment—I put it all in here, not just to tell a story, but to show them that no matter how hard life hits, you stand your ground and be brave. That's the real inheritance. The house is just the bonus.

After the divorce, the media and cops stuck around for a while, but eventually they realised I wasn't the answer to the lingering questions surrounding the mystery of his missing wife or his father's death. When they finally gave up, I could breathe again. Normalcy started to settle in, and I thought, *Well, this isn't so bad.*

Lesson: Our failures aren't just screw-ups; they're the things that teach us the most. Every bump in the road makes us stronger. And trust me, I've got a few scars to prove it.

CHAPTER 58

Spooked: Tales from the other realm

I'll never understand whether supernatural energies were attached to me or just the environment I inhabited, but one thing was clear: they followed me to the house I shared with Ted.

Our house was a large, charming old two-storey property with a wraparound timber porch. The ground floor, made of sturdy brick and timber, exuded character. But the top storey was something else entirely, like a factory unit slapped on by someone with zero sense of architecture.

The so-called 'builder' who owned and lived in it had clearly cut corners. Maybe he got his builder's permit out of a cereal box. That original owner? Dean's father. Yep, Dean, the guy who showed up on my doorstep after killing his sister. It was hard not to wonder if the house absorbed all that unsettling energy—or worse, carried the energy of death itself.

That top storey had crooked walls, plumbing that sounded like a snake on caffeine whenever you turned on the taps, and absolutely no insulation. It was unbearable year-round. While the ground floor was solid and charming, the top was a slapdash nightmare of scavenged materials. It was miserable, but we made do.

It was in this house that Dean had grown up, surrounded by his parents, his grandmother Mabel on his father's side, his brother and his sister—the one he later killed.

The house seemed to hold its fair share of secrets, which might explain why the kids and I often saw ghostly apparitions. Sometimes we'd catch a ghostly female figure perched at the edge of a bed; other times, she'd stand silently in a room, as if sizing us up. She never scared me, though. If anything, she made me wonder what had brought her here.

About three years after we moved out, something strange happened. One of my daughters' partners—who didn't exactly strike me as a believer—casually mentioned he'd felt a presence in that house. He hadn't seen her, but he described the vibe—a dark aura, like an old woman lingering in the shadows.

Not long after that conversation, I decided to visit my old neighbours—you know, the ones who'd conveniently been on vacation when I sent Dean over to talk to them. They still lived next door to that house, and what they told me left me floored.

To my surprise, they unveiled a flourishing rosebush. At first, I didn't think anything of it besides how beautiful it was, but when I recounted the story to my daughter later, things started to click.

During my time in that house, one of my daughters had decided to do some weeding. She stumbled upon a rosebush buried beneath a jungle of overgrowth. Determined to tame it, she pruned it down to the ground, despite the thorns giving her a good fight.

Some time passed, and I eventually rolled up my sleeves to tackle the garden myself. That's when I discovered a single white rosebud, defiantly peeking out from beneath the weeds on a long, sturdy stem. I decided to let it be and see what came of it.

Fast-forward to when we were preparing to leave the house for good. I felt an inexplicable urge to dig up that rose, repot it, and gift it to my neighbour. Her reaction was pure shock.

She couldn't believe where it had come from.

That's when she dropped a bombshell. According to her, that rose shouldn't have even existed. She went on to explain how Mabel, Dean's grandmother, had a deep love for roses—a love that drove her daughter-in-law crazy. Mabel had planted one in the back of the home, only for her daughter-in-law to haphazardly prune it whenever it bore roses.

Predictably, Mabel and her daughter-in-law did not see eye-to-eye.

Now my daughter who had pruned the bush was consistently visited by a rather disgruntled spirit that would sit at the end of her bed. At the time, we couldn't figure out why the ghost seemed to favour her over the rest of us. But with this new information, the dots finally connected and the ghostly grudge started to make sense. It turned out the rosebush I'd gifted to my neighbour—the one that had miraculously resurfaced—was the very same one my daughter had ruthlessly pruned down years earlier.

But the mysteries didn't stop with the rosebush. That house was practically a magnet for the unexplainable. Objects moved when no one was around, and there were times I'd feel an undeniable presence—like being watched, but not in a fun way. My kitchen cupboard doors had a habit of flinging themselves open when nobody was looking. And those curtains I'd carefully tied somehow always drew shut by the time I came home. Even the timber windows, snug in the morning, were wide open by evening.

Every time I interrogated the kids, the response was the same: 'Nope, not us.' So what was left to conclude? Mabel wasn't just haunting us, she was putting on a show.

I couldn't prove it, but I wondered whether Mabel was protecting us from something way worse.

Then, in 2016 and 2017, two psychics wandered into my haunted life. Both picked up on two protective female spirits—one older, one younger. Naturally, I wondered what on earth I needed protection from. One psychic mentioned a creepy male entity—described him as a living corpse, stuck in darkness. His energy was so heavy it rattled her to the point she bailed early. Now, that's when you know it's serious.

Both psychics agreed the younger spirit was probably my ex-husband's missing wife, watching over me. That part made sense; I thought about her constantly, holding out hope she was alive. Her presence never felt threatening—more like a quiet companion, listening as I promised I'd figure out what happened to her.

But the real trouble came from a dark energy I suspected was from someone very much alive—and familiar. One night, while I was alone with my cat Faisal, his sudden unease set me on edge. His eyes darted to the balcony, and then—creaky footsteps.

I got up to check, and just like that, it stopped. My gut told me they were near the outdoor toilet room, where Ted kept legal documents tied to Candice's murder trial.

I panicked and called my daughter Nila. She rushed over with her boyfriend, but by the time they arrived, everything was quiet. Her eyeroll at my 'paranoia' stung more than I cared to admit. After that, I kept my fears to myself.

How could I doubt what I heard, especially when my cat was backing me up? Unsure of my sanity, I turned to yet another psychic, who warned, 'Spirit is telling you to get out before something bad happens.'

Making things even weirder, the police investigators seemed hellbent on freaking me out.

They told me Ted's sudden exit was suspicious, and even hinted that I could be next on his 'list'. What the hell did that mean?! Their words wormed their way into my thoughts, leaving me paranoid and terrified of staying in that house. For months they wouldn't let up, spinning their web of concern and suspicion. I couldn't tell if they were genuinely worried about my safety or testing to see if I'd crack under pressure. Maybe they were just fishing for dirt on Ted. Either way, I felt like a pawn in someone else's twisted chess game.

In the end, I trusted the psychics more than the investigators. Deep down, I had a hunch the cops were stirring up fear to get what they wanted.

Moving out became a no-brainer. With the divorce looming and the family home needing to be sold, staying wasn't an option. The unease in that house had become unbearable—thick enough to choke on.

Maybe this sounds stupid, but I was desperate to get that house sold, pocket the money I'd sunk into it, and make sure my kids and I had a future. The thought of not being around long enough to see that happen drove me nuts. Those cops really did a number on my mind. Yet somehow I had to pull myself together, prioritise my safety and move forward, no matter how chaotic it got.

Those words from the psychic haunted me daily. I clung to the hope that leaving would make the strange happenings stop. But let me tell you, it didn't.

By late 2017 I found myself in a red-brick rental that turned out to be my unexpected sanctuary. Sure, it was old, lacked air-conditioning and didn't have a cat door, but I handled that. My cat wasn't about to rough it, thank you very much. The house had its quirks, but it also had charm. Nestled in lush greenery and filled with the cheerful laughter of kookaburras, it felt like nature itself was trying to heal me, one chuckle at a time.

For the first time in what felt like forever, I exhaled; a real, deep, soul-cleansing exhale. I cried happy tears, laughed like a lunatic and savoured the silence. No more waking up to arguments about parenting my stepson. No more endless battles over property division. I was finally on my own.

That little house wasn't just a rental, it was my haven. Watering the garden, patching up the broken flyscreens and soaking up the sun on the balcony became my small but powerful joys. It gave me the space to unpack the emotional baggage I'd been hauling around for years.

Freedom felt incredible—cool in a way I'd almost forgotten existed.

Normal still seemed like a far-off dream, but this? This felt like the start of something better.

But no matter how much I tried to move forward, I couldn't stop thinking about Ted's missing wife. Fifteen years had passed since she vanished and her whereabouts were a shadow I couldn't shake.

One evening, while chopping vegetables in the kitchen, I blurted out my frustrations like I was hosting my own one-woman talk show. 'For crying out loud, Candice, just show up so I can stop worrying about you!'

Talking to the departed wasn't exactly a new hobby for me. They never answered—no shock there—but I liked to think they listened and maybe even pitched in a little. 'Please,' I begged the air, 'send me a sign that you'll be found. Show someone—anything! I need this nightmare to end.'

As I spoke, tears welled up, probably from all the crap I'd been holding in for so long. Then, out of nowhere, a cold breeze whooshed past me. Through blurry eyes, I could've sworn I saw my daughter in her grey hooded nightgown, darting into my bedroom.

'What the heck are you doing in there?' I called, but no response. 'Hey, you need help finding something?' I said, louder this time.

I paused, irritated, and headed towards my bedroom. It was around six in the evening, a cold winter night with just enough moonlight creeping in to make the room feel like a scene straight out of a spooky movie.

'For God's sake, turn on the light! How can you see what you're doing?' Still nothing. I flipped the light switch, to find no one there. I checked under the bed, opened cupboard doors. Not a single sign of life. And then I felt it: chills running down my neck and straight down my spine. I froze for a second, my heart pounding in my ears. Then, without thinking twice, I bolted the hell out of there.

I rushed out—through the kitchen, past the lounge and down the hallway so fast I swear I left tracks on the floorboards. I shoved open my daughter's door, took a few steps into the room, and shook my head in disbelief.

I was home alone.

The next day, I turned to my friend Sandy. She had psychic vibes, and I needed someone to explain what the hell had happened. She told me I'd unknowingly invited a spirit into my home and advised me to let it go.

Let it go. That struck a chord, making me realise how tightly I was still holding on to painful memories.

'Stop worrying about that situation,' she said. 'Let the universe take care of it.'

By taking her advice to heart, I felt a strange shift—a lighter energy surrounding me, making me believe everything unfolded the way it did for a reason.

The whole thing still keeps me guessing, but one thing was for sure: I might not control everything, but damn if I couldn't call the shots on how it all played out.

Lesson: Stop stressing over what you can't control and embrace the mysteries. Not everything's meant to be figured out—and that's okay.

CHAPTER 59

If it looks like a duck

Vito was seventy when we met and I was fifty-seven. Sure, a bit of a gap, but it never felt that way. The man had the energy of someone half his age and a charm that could talk a rattlesnake into handing over its rattle. I wasn't a newbie to life's bombshells, but meeting him was like thinking you'd wrapped up the book of your life, only to find there was a surprise chapter—and it was way juicier than the rest.

We crossed paths when most people were trading dreams for recliners, yet there we were, plotting adventures like a couple of kids. Vito had this old-school gentleman thing going on—the kind that made you laugh and feel seen all at once.

I met Vito at a birthday party in October 2018. My girlfriend, who was turning forty, had spent a year trying to convince me to meet him. At first, I refused to even attend the party knowing he'd be there. But when she told me what he said after seeing a photo of me, I was drawn in like a bull to a red flag. My ears pricked, horns ready to knock him over. 'She's too old for me—not my type at all,' he'd said.

Charming, right? I stewed over it for a while, then thought, *Why not?* But honestly, why the hell did she show him a photo of me after a run we'd done together, when I was sweaty and far from glamorous?

So I showed up at that party, ready to give him an earful and hypnotise him with my charm—and, of course, my well-exposed cleavage. With my wit cranked up to one hundred, I was about to give him a masterclass in what older women were really made of.

He wasn't just there for the cake. His plan? Swing by, say happy birthday, size me up, confirm his theory that older women weren't his thing, grab a drink, and head back to his farm in the Hunter district, where his cows greeted him like old pals and life stayed blissfully simple. He was already done with his younger girlfriend, Delaine—a small detail I wasn't privy to at the time, even though they were still living together. Perhaps their frostbitten relationship, once full of spark during his stuntman glory days, now as hollow as an old stunt car, was something he preferred to keep secret until he cemented a new one.

Then I showed up and suddenly his plan wasn't going so smoothly. Guess the joke was on him. That night, Vito was caught off guard by how well we clicked. It wasn't love at first sight, but the chemistry was undeniable. Once I decided to prove that older women were far from a passing fancy, the evening turned into something neither of us saw coming.

Vito, a businessman with a colourful past as a stuntman, had spent years living the high life—performing his world-renowned horse stunt show around the world, charming, beautiful young women, all while with Delaine (unbeknown to her, of course—typical, right?). By the time we met, those wild days were long behind him. He was stuck in a relationship with a woman younger than his own kids, miserable and craving something more, but clueless about what that *more* could be. That was, until he met me, a fiery, straight-shooting woman who didn't sugarcoat a damn thing.

He'd wanted out of his relationship for years and had voiced it loud and clear, but she wasn't having it. So he settled for flings on the side to scratch whatever itch was missing. Even before meeting me, Vito had scoffed to my friend, 'She'll never keep up with me.' But something clicked—maybe it was the whole Italian thing that pulled him in. What he didn't expect was that we'd have more than just a past in common; we had a connection that felt real.

But it wasn't smooth sailing. We broke it off twice because Vito was dragging his feet and too scared to move forward. So I walked away. Eventually, he realised he wasn't just looking for affection; he wanted real love—the kind where you got something back.

It took almost three years for Vito and Delaine to split completely, and a year later, I moved in temporarily for three months to care for him after he got his leg trapped in a rotary hoe on the farm. Of course, Vito made headlines—being airlifted to the hospital, snapping selfies with the ambos, cops and rescue teams while high on painkillers. You know, the kind that make you all happy when you've shattered a bone or two.

Finally he started seeing things differently. I took care of him, asking for nothing in return, while still juggling my work. And somewhere between the chaos and the healing, things began to change.

When I moved back into my place, we both realised we needed to be together. Of course, life had other plans. His middle-aged kids weren't exactly thrilled, and his choice for happiness was almost yanked away.

By then it had been four years since we started our relationship. Our plans to move in together were set and we were only a week away from the big move. I found myself sitting on the concrete steps of my apartment, waiting for the removal van to take me to Vito's place.

Unknowingly, I wasn't just nursing a broken foot, I was about to tend to a broken heart, too.

Something didn't feel right. Was it intuition? Maybe. Was I just being dramatic? Probably. But I'd ignored that feeling before—like the time I thought, *This is a bad idea*, and brushed it off. Spoiler: it was. And life was about to prove me right again.

The day before, I'd rolled my foot and felt a pain so sharp I thought a cold blade had cut through me. Still, with the move breathing down my neck, I powered through. I strapped an ice brick to my foot with the last of my packing tape—innovative, ridiculous and barely effective—but I had no time to be delicate.

By morning my foot had grown two goose-egg-sized lumps, but I was too busy herding movers to care. Then the lift broke. Because of course it did. The movers had to haul everything down seven flights of stairs.

To make matters worse, I had to keep hobbling up and down the stairs, reopening doors so the crew could get in and out. Other tenants—ever the inconsiderate jerks—kept shutting them, despite my notes begging them not to. Finally, I wedged a massive concrete pot plant against the door. Picture me, balancing like an injured trapeze artist, one foot in the air, swearing like a sailor. It was ridiculous, and I was barely holding it together.

The extra chaos was draining my wallet faster than I could drain a bottle of wine. Frustrated and worn thin, I called Vito. Tearfully, I ranted about my cursed move, convinced the universe was out to get me.

And then, clear as day, I had a vision. Vito's kids, all three of them, standing on his front lawn with pitchforks, blocking my path. My flashes of intuition had come true before, so when I told Vito about it, I half-expected him to panic. Instead, he calmly reassured me, 'Don't worry. I've told my kids you'll sign the financial agreement. They know you're not making any claims on my assets.'

Well, okay. His words gave me a little reassurance and I shook off my concerns, admitting to myself that I had been overly anxious. I told him we'd reach his house within half an hour. He asked if I wanted him there. I told him I'd be fine, that I'd unpack slowly, but I wanted to surprise him by having most things in place when he got home. Moving in was something he wanted, but change overwhelmed him.

Arriving at Vito's home, I felt a lingering sense of unease. I watched as the movers began moving things indoors. While standing out the front, I noticed two of Vito's daughters drive by the house. That was bizarre.

I shot Vito a message. He brushed it off, saying it was just a coincidence they happened to drive by. But my suspicions weren't entirely off.

By two-thirty, just an hour after the movers left—the doorbell rang. I hobbled into the kitchen, glanced down the hall and froze. There he was, my partner's forty-eight-year-old son, struggling with the newly installed screen door like it was some damn puzzle. My phone was about to die, so I shoved it into the charger. I limped down the hall, bracing myself for a visit I didn't ask for and sure as hell didn't want.

Apprehensively, I opened the wooden door while keeping the security screen door locked, informing him that his father wasn't home. He responded by saying he'd just spoken with his dad and had come to see me. In a lapse of judgement, believing he and his father had sorted this shit out, I allowed him to come inside. This was my first mistake.

Little did I know, when he'd talked to his father, he'd mentioned his failed attempt to open the door, prompting his dad to tell him to ring the doorbell. What really got under my skin was the fact that he knew the combination to the wooden door lock, giving him access. If I hadn't locked the screen door, his surprise visit would've been more than just unsettling—it would've been downright terrifying.

Though I appreciated the protection of the screen, I was disappointed in myself for letting him in. The first red flags popped up the moment he followed me inside.

Balancing on one foot in the kitchen, leaning against the bench, I pretended to check the plug on my phone while quietly activating the video camera. Perhaps my gut was warning me about the eighteen-minute verbal outburst that followed.

Every attempt I made to speak up was drowned out by him talking over me. He was like one of those men you heard about in the media—someone who used a fearsome tone to force his opinions on women. His ranting killed any hope of a logical conversation, leaving me feeling small and intimidated by his towering six-foot frame.

I wobbled a little on my good foot; standing for so long wasn't easy. He glanced at my bandaged foot and didn't say a word of concern—something that struck me as downright rude. *What a prick, seriously.*

Throughout his explosive anger, he raised his voice, hurled profanities and made disparaging remarks about his own father. Desperate to defend my partner, I tried to counter the venomous onslaught, insisting he was a good man, a kind man. But it was like trying to put out a wildfire with a teacup.

He wouldn't let go of this 'fucking financial agreement', treating it like some kind of golden ticket. The more I tried to justify moving in together, the angrier he got, until he demanded a copy of the signed agreement, right then and there.

'I'm not going to let this slide,' he snarled. 'I will make your life and my father's life hell every day until I get a copy.'

Was that a threat? Hell yes, it was. What the actual fuck was wrong with this guy? I was shaking, tears welling up, caught between fury and fear.

Without a hint of empathy, he callously remarked, 'Stop playing the victim.'

I managed to compose myself and told him I wasn't playing the victim, and that he couldn't go around threatening people.

'I didn't threaten you,' he shot back. 'You can take whatever I said however you want. I haven't threatened you. I'm just telling you I'm not going to accept this.'

I was overwhelmed and scared, but I tried to keep a level head, suggesting I'd talk to his father about speeding up the financial agreement. I found myself nervously smiling between my words—guess that's how I dealt with stress. It was my go-to coping mechanism to stop myself from completely breaking down. But of course, how would he know? I was certain he lacked any shred of compassion, especially when it came to speaking to a woman—one who should be shown respect.

Still fuming and ranting, with each outburst his demeanour grew nastier. Trying to reason with him was pointless—no matter what I said, I wasn't getting anywhere.

My heart pounded in my chest. I kept calm, trying to pacify him, agreeing each time he suggested, 'We could get past this and become friends.' But in my head all I wanted to do was kick him in the nuts and tell him to fuck off.

Finally, after exhausting all options, I promised to address it with his father. We made our way to the front door. He led, and I hobbled behind. He stopped short of the door and repeated, 'There's no reason we can't get past this.' Then, in a split second, his tone shifted, turning almost sinister. A demon must have entered his body at that point, perhaps through the darkest part of him—his arsehole—as he added, 'Just remember what I said.'

My thoughts were reeling. *Oh, I remember, all right. You dickwad.*

I promised, like a whipped dog, to do what he asked. I felt like a slave to a master. His finger wagging in the air, he turned and walked out.

I stumbled to the bedroom, collapsed on the bed and broke down in tears, feeling like I might puke in my own mouth. My mind spun out of control, ready to crash. I was in shock.

I couldn't shake the question: why the hell wasn't Vito here when his son came over? He should've been here to protect me, but instead I was left hanging. I wanted answers, but I was too upset to reach out. So I waited—just waited, lying there as if recovering from major surgery.

The whole outburst reminded me of the violence I'd endured under Chris's control, and it hit me harder than I expected. It was emotional torture, and I never thought I'd be forced to relive that nightmare.

After a while, I decided to shoot Vito a message, asking when he'd be home. His reply came a few minutes later: he'd be leaving work in about an hour. Perfect. That gave me just enough time to pull myself together before facing him and whatever excuses he had lined up.

I heard the front door creak open, followed by Vito's voice. 'Hey, how's it going? How'd everything go today?'

I stayed in the bedroom, telling him I was resting my foot.

Vito walked in, grinning like everything was normal. Rage bubbled up inside me. My smile was tight, forced. I patted the spot next to me on the bed, trying to appear calm, though I could feel myself teetering on the edge of blowing up.

When I asked him why he hadn't come home, knowing his son was here, he brushed it off like it was no big deal, saying his son just wanted to 'chat'. My blood boiled and I wanted to scream at him: *This was no friendly visit—it was an ambush!*

Vito and I had spent months hashing out the financial agreement. I knew we had time—it wasn't like I was about to drag him to court for his money. What I didn't know was that his three kids—well, his juvenile middle-aged kids—had been on his back, demanding he 'secure things' before I moved in. I wasn't that stupid or underhanded to take something that wasn't mine.

Looking back, the signs were there. A week before I moved in, we went to a family wedding. As Vito and I got out of the car, he thought it was the perfect time to tell me to 'tone down my comical self.' Apparently, joking around with his son Lucifer and calling him 'son' was a no-go. Never had been an issue before, but now it was!

This new information hit me like a brick square in the head. I was confused, puzzled, and yet we were just a few metres from the venue's entrance. With other people walking behind us, I kept going, but my legs were ready to turn right back around and hightail it out of there. I could feel it, the sense that I'd just stepped into a gunfight in Dodge City.

Out of the three, only one of his kids even bothered to acknowledge me. The rest acted like I was some invisible party crasher. In fact, I'm sure I would've been treated better if I was. I remember thinking, *Well, this is awkward*. Little did I know, their resentment ran deep—and they weren't about to let their father's decision go uncontested.

Honestly, I thought their concerns were ridiculous. Vito was in his seventies, and I in my sixties. We weren't impulsive twenty-somethings eloping in Vegas. But he never clued me in on how much they opposed me moving in. Not until it was too late. Still, that was no excuse for his son's appalling actions towards me. I should've realised then that things were about to go downhill, but nope, I was still convincing myself it would all pan out.

On moving day, when his son unleashed that tirade on me, it rattled me, dredging up memories I'd worked hard to bury. I let Vito listen to the entire eighteen-minute recording, hoping it would make him understand how serious it was. Instead, he made excuses, suggesting his son might be on steroids. Even after hearing his son call him 'a fucking spineless cunt', Vito shrugged it off. He acted like it was some schoolyard incident and that I was overreacting.

I was dumbfounded. I'd always believed that if you truly loved someone, you'd defend them. Yet, there I was, abandoned and humiliated. My partner couldn't even stand up for himself, let alone for me. Was he suffocated under his kids' thumbs? I wanted to dig deeper into the reasons, but honestly, I was drained.

That wasn't the only betrayal. Despite me advocating for the financial agreement, Vito dawdled, leaving me vulnerable. I knew it wasn't my job to push it, it was his. I'd already agreed to sign once it was finalised, but his procrastination left the door wide open for his kids to meddle.

This was the unravelling of everything I thought we'd built. I'd poured my heart into helping Vito after his accident, believing his family would see me for what I was: compassionate. Instead, they slapped a gold-digger label on me. Like I spent all that time plotting to claim assets I had zero interest in. The kicker? Even if I had wanted to, I wouldn't have had a leg to stand on legally. But none of that mattered to them. They sized up the situation and judged, cold and harsh, completely off base.

The whole thing spiralled fast. I knew I couldn't stay, especially with his son likely to return. But going back to my apartment wasn't an option, either. I'd promised it to one of my daughters and her partner, who'd already terminated their lease. Now either they or I needed to find a new place in a week.

Within hours I tried to handle it myself, quietly reaching out to friends for emergency housing. They offered short-term stays, but I couldn't keep couch-surfing, not at my age and definitely not with my pride already in pieces. The thought of telling my daughters made my stomach churn. What if they thought I was a fool for trusting Vito? Or worse, what if they never spoke to me again? What a mess I'd made, not just of my own life, but of my daughter's and her partner's, too. Geez, why could I never get it right?

Then, when Nila called to check in, I lost it. The dam burst and I spilled the whole messy story. To my surprise, she wasn't mad at me. Instead, she was furious at Vito for not standing up for me. 'Move back home,' she said firmly. 'We'll figure everything else out.' Her words were a lifeline, just enough to keep me from falling apart.

She nailed it. Moving back was the only option. I hated the thought of disrupting my youngest daughter and her partner's lives, but Nila had my back. 'How dare a man intimidate you?' she said. And damn right—no man had the right to make a woman feel unsafe.

As I packed, I couldn't stop thinking about how blind I'd been. I'd trusted Vito to protect me, but his failure to stand up to his kids showed me how little he deserved me. Love wasn't enough when respect and support were missing.

Hoping for a miracle, I spent the night with Vito. Despite everything, I still loved him and hoped he'd finally confront his family and fix things. But nothing changed. Disappointed, I gathered a few belongings the next morning and headed back to my apartment—empty except for an outdoor lounge.

Now I faced the daunting task of organising the move back home. I mustered the courage to call the same removalist company. Thankfully, they were understanding and reassured me that these situations happened more often than you'd think. Glad I wasn't the only dumb-arse who could get things so wrong!

It was like a record-breaking Hollywood split—in and out in less than twenty-four hours. Despite the embarrassment, I walked away with a hard-earned lesson: you're never too old to learn new tricks, even if they came wrapped in heartbreak and regret.

A day after I moved out, Nila and her husband, Brayden, drove me back to Vito's house while he was at his farm. They helped me grab a few more boxes of my things, since the movers weren't scheduled for another three days. After Brayden placed the last of the boxes in the car, he wrapped his arm around me and offered words I desperately needed to hear: 'Don't worry. You took a chance on love; it just sucks it didn't work out.'

His words wrapped around me like a cosy hug, then hit me like a ton of bricks. Tears blended with laughter, so much that I almost peed my pants.

In that moment, I felt a rush of gratitude for my family's unwavering support, a stark contrast to the coldness I'd gotten from some of Vito's. I shouldn't have expected anything less, but it still stung—they never even apologised, as if me uprooting my whole life was no big deal.

Even Luna and her partner, Nico, who I had inconvenienced, accepted the situation and found a place to stay without making me the target of their disappointment. That was a big thing.

A few days later, my things were back in my apartment and I was surrounded by family, food and helping hands. Empathy had become my healing balm after the wounds inflicted by others.

As for Vito, I gave him the chance to figure things out on his own.

Unfortunately, he either couldn't, or he was just too scared to upset his kids, the same ones who resented him for wanting to be happy with me. When he asked if we could repair the damage and still be a couple, living separately, I thought long and hard.

But his let's live apart idea—straight from his son's rant—was a dealbreaker. At some point, he needed to grow a set of balls and stop letting his adult kids run his life.

To top it off, Vito later dropped more negative things his family had said about me months earlier. Stuff he never bothered to mention at the time. This revelation made me wonder if their words not only planted doubt in his mind about me but also led me to suspect that he might've subconsciously never wanted me to move in, too afraid to say it out loud.

That realisation didn't sit well with me. I didn't want to be some convenience for him. I wanted to be part of a loving couple, especially given our ages. I was sixty-two and he was seventy-five—it should've made sense.

We ended things, and I held onto the hope that one day he might understand and fight for his freedom from his kids—and for our love.

After that, I moved on and forgave him—but not his family. Forgiveness isn't automatic; it's earned, and only when your emotions have had time to heal. I was learning to deal with our relationship piece by piece, instead of shoving it all under the rug.

Vito stopped worrying about his family's expectations and embraced his love for me. That was when he finally found the courage to fight for us.

Loving someone that deeply doesn't come with an off switch. Even when they've cut through your heart, the bond doesn't just disappear. Love isn't simple; it's messy, complicated and sometimes hits you like a storm you never saw coming.

My life's been a challenging road, but a damn interesting one, full of lessons. I truly get the saying 'Trust your gut'. If something doesn't feel right, don't do it. Sit on it until you're clear on your decision, or walk away, trust your instincts and don't let yourself be misled by false appearances or hopes.

Lesson: If it looks like a duck, quacks like a duck and waddles like a duck, then it is a fucking duck.

CHAPTER 60

Call me brave

Finally, my screwed-up life didn't feel like I was trapped in the hole I'd dug for myself. I was fighting my way out, holding on to whatever control I could like it was my lifeline.

I had my moments, sure. Times I barely held it together—teetering on the edge of a breakdown no one saw coming until it was nearly too late. Thank God for my girlfriends.

Why didn't I speak up sooner? Probably because I'd been taught to smile through it, tough it out and keep quiet. So I did, and that nearly gutted me.

Funny how the wake-up call doesn't always come from your bestie or some therapist. Sometimes, it's a stranger. Or a job you never imagined would teach you anything.

When I first picked up the phone at the call centre, I had no clue I was about to face myself. Real change doesn't show up wrapped in confidence. It shows up messy—with shaky hands and a pounding heart. It's not about having all the answers. It's about showing up anyway and being brave enough to face it.

If the roles had been reversed back then—me on the other end of the line, hearing someone say, 'Face your fears. Call me when you're brave'—maybe I wouldn't have stumbled through so much crap to find peace. Maybe I could've dodged some of the drama, skipped the character-building detours and lived a quieter, less complicated life.

But where's the fun in that?

I guess that's what being brave looks like.

Truth is, we're not supposed to have everything sorted. Sometimes, we need the chaos, the heartbreak, the what-the-hell-was-I-thinking?' detours to shake us awake. Looking back, every misstep was a breadcrumb leading me home, to a version of myself that didn't shrink, didn't apologise, and finally stopped faking 'fine'.

I didn't wake up fearless. I just got tired of living scared. And bit by bit, I faced it—not with some big movie moment, but with small, awkward steps that somehow kept me going.

What once felt like chaos—the men, the mess, the noise—started to feel like something else entirely. It didn't break me. It cracked me open. I didn't need to have it all figured out. I just needed to keep going. And that counts.

It's wild to think how I went from hiding my sex industry job to making it a pivotal part of my journey. The women I met along the way were extraordinary—fierce, unapologetic and real. We shared secrets, embraced our flaws and built bonds that carried us through anything.

They weren't just colleagues; they were my survival squad. When the world fell apart, they didn't flinch. They taught me to trust my gut, own my choices and stop apologising for existing.

I never held a grudge against my parents for the madness of my upbringing.

They were just surviving their own mess, doing the best they could. As for me? I could've written a whole damn book on my disasters. Wait, scratch that—I did. Every misstep and facepalm moment became part of my messy, beautifully flawed story.

Was my upbringing dysfunctional? You bet. It shaped how I saw relationships, choices and what I thought was 'normal'. Chaos had been my normal. But survival wasn't just about the past; it was about what I chose to do with it.

Years of pretending I was fine made me a survival pro. But faking it got old fast. I wanted better—for me and my daughters. That meant stepping into the unknown, even when it scared the hell out of me. Learning from my mistakes was my biggest win. Cutting toxic people loose unlocked doors I didn't know existed. I stopped worrying about what others thought. If they didn't get me, too bad. I quit apologising for being me—and so should you.

In 2018, I sat on a bus and watched the old call centre building where I'd worked eighteen years earlier get demolished. It felt like a metaphor for my life. Watching it crumble was the universe's way of saying: *It's time to rewrite your story*. Those chaotic years weren't for nothing. They gave me a voice strong enough to share my truth.

Divorce? It was brutal, but staying in a suffocating marriage was far worse. To any woman thinking about it, here's my advice: don't skip the details. Cross every t, dot every i, and question everything. Protect yourself. Stash documents. Get advice. Trust your gut—it's never wrong. Divorce might break you, but it could also rebuild you. When it felt impossible I paused, reassessed and pushed forward. No way in hell was I letting anyone who tried to tear me down have the satisfaction of seeing me stay there.

Leaving what was familiar—even when it was toxic—was terrifying. That fear could easily keep women stuck. But here's the truth: it's not the situation holding you back, it's the comfort of the familiar. I never knew my true strength until I stepped into the uncertainty and faced it on my own.

Looking back, I didn't just survive—I reclaimed myself. Piece by piece, I built the woman I was meant to be. I took back my dignity, my choices and my life. No one else had the right to define me, and I refused to let my past—or the men who underestimated me—hold me back.

The women I met along the way proved that strength comes in all forms. We weren't just survivors; we were warriors. We carried our scars like battle wounds, not shame. Together, we lifted each other up, proving that when women stand together we are unstoppable.

I once believed my worth was tied to what others thought of me. Not anymore. I learned to stop waiting for permission to live on my own terms. To any woman still questioning her strength—you already have it. Now it's time to own it.

If I could do it, then hell yes, you can too.

You don't have to call me perfect, or fearless, or anything I'm not.

But after everything—I dare you to call me brave.

www.ingramcontent.com/pod-product-compliance
Lightning Source LLC
Chambersburg PA
CBHW020350080526
44584CB00014B/972